The Committed Observer

RAYMOND ARON
The Committed Observer
Le Spectateur Engagé

Interviews with
Jean-Louis Missika
and
Dominique Wolton

Translated from the French
by
James and Marie McIntosh

Regnery Gateway
Chicago

Published by Regnery Gateway, Inc., 360 West Superior Street, Chicago, Illinois 60610-0890 by arrangement with Editions Julliard.

Manufactured in the United States of America.

ISBN: 0-89526-624-5

Library of Congress Cataloging in Publication Data

Aron, Raymond, 1905-
  The committed observer.

  Translation of: Le spectateur engagé.
    1. Aron, Raymond, 1905-   . 2. France—History—20th century. 3. World politics—1945-   . 4. Journalists—France—Interviews. 5. Intellectuals—France—Interviews. I. Missika, Jean Louis. II. Wolton, Dominique. III. Title. IV. Title: Spectateur engagé.
CT1018.A69A3713   1983   944.08′092′4   82-42902
ISBN 0-89526-624-5

CONTENTS

INTRODUCTION

Raymond Aron holds a special place among French intellectuals. His philosophical and political education should normally have led him to a commitment similar to that of the other intellectuals of his generation, particularly Jean-Paul Sartre, his friend from student days, and Maurice Merleau-Ponty.

Why, then, did he gradually identify himself with the broad stream of liberal thought, today in the minority in France (though it has roots here with people like Alexis de Tocqueville and Benjamin Constant) and that has more widely flourished in the contemporary period in the Anglo-Saxon countries?

At the end of the war, why did he counter the dominant trend of the French intelligentsia—whose values and perceptions he shared to an extent—thus accepting a break with his friends and an insulation that must certainly have been difficult?

Why, when most intellectuals rejected the division engendered by the cold war, did he speak out firmly in favor of the Atlantic Alliance and against neutralism, consolidating these positions by becoming *Le Figaro's* editorialist and advocating a return to power by de Gaulle?

These were probably the principal questions that led us to meet with Raymond Aron and propose these interviews. Rather than pursue with him a theoretical discussion on interpretations of history, morality, and government, or on the contradictions between different political philosophies, it seemed preferable to try to understand the positions he took in the maze of contemporary history. And what history! France in the 1930s, Nazism, the war, the cold war, decolonization, peaceful coexistence, European unity.... So, we wanted to examine the thought and the analysis of an anti-conformist intellectual, labeled in France as a rightist since the cold war, who had swum against the current of prevailing ideas of the Left, who had perceived the truth, before others, about the nature of the Soviet regime, about Stalinism and about other questions and who had had the courage to stand by his opinions, at the risk of being ostracized by the intelligentsia—all the while creating a body of scientific work whose value is undisputed. It is rare that over such a long period, marked by so many events and crises—and in roles as different as those of journalist, historian, philosopher, sociologist—an intellectual has tried to analyze history-in-the-making, and in which he is a participant, while nonetheless retaining a critical distance.

It is these three roles of analyst, interpreter, and actor that, with their constraints, their contradictions, and their greatness, fascinated and intrigued us.

For our generation, which had its political birth in 1968, Raymond Aron's thought has represented a kind of "negative pole." Intellectual education developed mostly around Marxism during the 1960s. One had the feeling that it was indispensable to position oneself with reference to this philosophy, with its several variants, its deviations, its negations, and its rebirths. We were not all Marxists in the sense of political or of philosophical choice and we realized that, before us, a goodly number of intellectuals had changed since the mid-1950s; some had, in fact, performed their "autocriticism," but in the final analysis, almost all of them continued to reflect with reference to this system of thought which, after its "rebirth" in the mid-1960s, permeated the atmosphere of the period. It seemed to furnish the theoretical tools necessary to judge world events. Moreover, the multitude of philosophical controversies, the diversity of interpretations, and of the political regimes inspired by it seemed to prove its richness and justify Sartre's formula: the unsurpassable horizon of our time. Is this, perhaps, a dominant ideology?

In any case, this generation was saturated with Marxism, it was hardened in May 1968, and it was warmed by the sun of the Left. Why did it accept this deterministic explanation of history? It is difficult to answer. Probably the horrors of the wars and revolutions of the first half of the twentieth century could be endured only with the help of a coherent explanations. Could history be so absurd? Surely, beyond the absurdity there must have been a sense somewhere. In a way, we had little historical consciousness or geopolitical discernment, the tragic events of the century seemed to have so broken something in the continuity of time. And when our own vision of history was nonetheless shaped during the mid-1960s, it found a target in American imperialism, because the war in Vietnam was going on at the time. Since then, a portion of this generation experienced in the mid-1970s the jarring revelation of the limits of Marxism, of the crimes of the Soviet Union, and of redemption through the human rights theme. This all-out approbation of that which had yesterday been detested troubles us because we find in it similar thought mechanisms: self-complacency, intolerance, dogmatism. The manner of expression that some have chosen is not consistent with the ideas they are discovering after a long detour, for there is less often the awareness of the complexity of the facts than the transition from one Manicheanism to another.

For those of us who during the 1970s gradually detached ourselves from Marxist claims of monopoly on the idea of progress and of arrogating to themselves the privilege of deciding who is on the Right and who on the Left, the discovery of Raymond Aron's thought was a distinct pleasure. Obviously, it was not unknown to us, for we had studied it at the university, but it had been catalogued as "reactionary." It was less understood as such than so perceived through an ideological filter and the Right-Left cleavage. In short, it was intelligent, but rightist? This attitude permitted one to recognize the quality of his analyses and at the same time to be wary of them.

Nevertheless, Raymond Aron's rigorous knowledge of Marxism and his ability to challenge it were rather troubling. The more so, since his books analyzing the changes in our societies used some Marxist concepts and patterns, less as dogma or systems of reference than as simple analytical tools among others. But on the whole, his moderate positions, his *Figaro* editorials, his anti-Sovietism, and his closeness to the relativist philosophers of history and to the nineteenth century liberal thinkers sufficed during the decade 1968-1978 to convince us that, as it was so succinctly noted in a leftist weekly to which he had given an interview: "Raymond Aron is not one of ours...."

Briefly, we discovered the thought of Raymond Aron in three stages. First, by reading with ideological glasses, particularly his *Dix-huit leçons sur la sociètè industrielle* and *Peace and War Among Nations*.[1] Then, the recognition of the man who had been right before the others on Stalinism, with *The Opium of the Intellectuals*.[2] Finally, after the discovery of his *Introduction to the Philosophy of History*,[3] access to a process of thought that was not merely critical, but also positive, and that has its place in one of the great movements of philosophic and political thought that was for a long time caricatured in France.

In reading his books, we perceived the basic choice that oriented those positions, that is, a particular philosophy of history.

For Aron, history is neither determined nor oriented in advance by a purpose or sense. It remains open, dependent in the long run on men's actions, on their freedom or on their arbitrariness. That explains his refusal of messianism, in whose name the twentieth century perpetrated so many crimes, and his distrust of ideology as a global interpretation of the world and as a guide to action.

This relativist conception of history is enhanced on the philosophical level with reference to the idea of reason. In fact, from Kantian philosophy he singles out the idea of reason as the sole means available to men to give order to their view of the world and to guide their desire to transform it.

Finally, he found in liberal philosophy the system of values that could provide the structure for an action model. For him, liberal philosophy, by respecting the pluralism of ideas and by favoring empiricism in analysis and action, is the least bad system to inspire governance.

On that basis, one views twentieth century events in a wholly different way: Nuclear strategy, the East-West confrontation, growth and change in industrial societies, the decline of the American empire—all are viewed differently than through the environment of Marxism that, by laziness or in good conscience, arranged in pat order this helter-skelter of events and the relationship of forces. Marxism can no longer be considered as a tool of knowledge, ignoring the fact that it is also, and perhaps above all, the model of reference and of action of one of the two economic and political systems that have been in a state of confrontation since the beginning of the century. The problem is no longer only that of American imperialism, but also of the West's ability to preserve a model of civilization, quite apart from whether one favors that model partially or totally. There is in that, of course, a turnabout in the "sense" of history, but above all a new awareness of the hazards and fragilities of our value system. During the course of these interviews, what we found in the thought of Raymond Aron is the materialization of a change that had occurred in our world view. In a way, we already knew what he thought and on a number of points we agreed with him; what was new, essentially, did not stem so much from the analyses as from the consequences that flowed from them in terms of choices and responsibilities for us and our generation. That is: to act in a way that would have been unthinkable ten years ago. We have gradually accepted the absence of a different "model," because the one we thought of as such is much worse than the one we are judging here. As a consequence, it is necessary to act within the western system, the single precaution being that we must make sure that the acts of western countries match the values to which they claim allegiance.

The consequence we draw is less banal than it might appear when one recalls the lack of courage and determination displayed by twentieth century Europeans who on so many historical occasions forgot their ideals.

When Raymond Aron speaks of events that he has lived through, one understands better the difference between a generation swept along by the turbulence of history and another generation—our own—that in France, presently at least, has had the feeling of being outside of history. For us, "history" was before or elsewhere, but not here. This fact, by the way, explains why certain people have searched for it in Peking, Hanoi, or Cuba. Raymond Aron and his generation experienced the savagery of which political regimes are capable in the name of ideals. They saw the despotism and violence, so well summed up in the phrase he is so fond of: "History as usual." He knows that our society is mortal, something that our generation has difficulty in sensing, though it understands it in the abstract. Having lived through the collapse of societies, he understands their fragility. He realizes that once fundamental instability sets in, nothing can stop it. This is the source of his constant preoccupation, even obsession, with social cohesion, and his concern with avoiding confrontations that risk dividing and weakening society. One appreciates the difference from our generation that, born and matured in stable societies, almost without histories, has never had the sensation of fragility and risk of collapse. For us, history was first of all the result of internal social contradictions. Conflicts and changes relating to labor conditions, urban development, education, social customs, seemed the principal source of renovation, with little danger that local instability would threaten general cohesion. Even May 1968, despite the disorder that it meant, had no destabilizing effect upon society. It was our impression that conflicts in these areas were at once a means of going beyond the class struggle in the strict sense of the term, and of changing the structure of society.

Moreover, there had been no alternation of power since 1958 and, with the Left excluded, political stability was a given, society seemed immobile despite the many conflicts that buffeted it, and certainly was in no way menaced in its basic equilibrium. What is known as "Aronian scepticism" is probably rooted to some degree in his awareness of the fragility of society. His experience of history and his perception of the thin margin of maneuver enjoyed by those who have governed in France and in the United States is doubtless responsible to some extent for his lack of illusions about the possibilities for political change. And from this stems our difficulty in understanding his conception of order and change. For us, the first symbolizes roughly, the Right, and the second, the Left, while Aron never ceases to repeat that the France governed by the Right has changed considerably. It is true that it has become modernized, that the standard of living has broadly improved, that some social inequalities have been reduced, and that the school system has become partially democratized. But because our generation has directly experienced these transformations without having known the earlier circumstances, we have found them, in a certain way, natural, and, instead of being satisfied with the growth and enrichment of life that has taken place, we have tended, rather, to focus our energies on the fight to eliminate the stubborn social and cultural inequalities that remain. With a different historical experience, Raymond Aron compares—and is not certain that the Left would have followed the same policy of modernization. He believes that the Left-Right opposition is a confrontation between two concepts of change. The Right prefers to mobilize individual initiative, competition; the Left favors redistribution, planning. While we did not always share his distrust of the Left, we nevertheless quickly understood that this distrust is something quite different from conservatism. It is the fruit of experience and of reflection on the contradiction between liberty and equality—a contradiction that is without doubt more difficult to overcome than some people (and not merely members of our generation) imagine. But, conversely, we also know that the new social conflicts, the changes in cultural behavior, and the rapport between the individual and his society that have shaped our way of living and thinking since the 1960s—and to which Raymond Aron and others have not been very sensitive—amount to truly structural, if invisible, changes in our societies. These cultural transformations have been accompanied by a change of ideas toward linguistic or psychoanalytical approaches, for example, that will quite possibly be useful to the understanding of social mechanisms. Without rejecting these new ideas, Raymond Aron tends to consider them in relation to the major themes and philosophies of history. Thus viewed, they suddenly appear unsubstantial or secondary.

Obviously, these cultural transformations are not about to change the world's equilibrium, but it is possible that they forge intellectual tools, open up new ways of perceiving reality and diversify the range of knowledge. We will see whether these cultural modifications that have so marked our generation will affect our social and political life, or whether they are merely changes of a secondary nature in comparison with more fundamental movements of history, during an exceptional period of strong economic growth and political stability.

The thing that fascinated us most about Raymond Aron is the anti-conformist nature, compared to the habitual scenarios of the Right and Left, of his analyses of significant contemporary events. It was of little interest to us whether he was right or wrong on one question or another; what we wanted to understand was how his philosophical and political positions challenged leftist thought. The two ends of the circle finally meet, in the sense that, while being violently rejected by the intellectual Left, Aron was often its bad conscience, saying out loud what a number of its members did not dare to think or say.

Three aspects of his thought particularly impressed us.

The first concerns the difference between morality and government. Aron claims that Sartre was above all a moralist. Whence his difficulty not to condemn from a moral point of view those who failed to take positions similar to his own. This attitudinal difference goes well beyond the two men and could apply to many intellectuals; it virtually characterized that which separates Aron from the Left. For him, all social systems are imperfect, and government is not the battle between good and evil, but the choice between the preferable and the desirable. This does not signify a desire to exclude ethics entirely from government, but rather the recognition of the specificity of governance and the necessity to avoid applying moral attributes to it in the same manner that they are applied to other human activities. To govern is not solely to perform good acts. No one can say what the general welfare is; for the gravest errors have often resulted from the inability to admit that facts are stubborn and that morality does not suffice to master them. With the accession of the Left to power, this problem has again become a topic of current concern. To accept in practice the fact that there is a gap between government and morality requires more courage than one might think. It leads less to cynicism or to Machiavellianism than to the need to think of political activity in relation to the qualities peculiar to it. The wish to make morality coincide with government or to think of government as a kind of morality easily salves the conscience, satisfies virtuous indignation, provides a view of the world in black and white and leads to a refusal to accept political action with its violence, its turnabouts, its force relationships—briefly, its amoralism. From this stems Raymond Aron's point about morality as a

way *not* to think about governing. Or, to state things more po-
lemically, it is a matter of conflict between the "noble souls"
and those who accept the sometimes unsavory struggles that
are a part of political activity.

It is this that explains Aron's reluctance to grant, for example, that action in favor of human rights is an adequate platform on which to base a political program. The struggle for
human rights constitutes an evident and admirable political
commitment, but in itself it does not constitute a program of
government.

This notion of government implies the rejection of Manicheanism in history. The adversary's opinion is not necessarily an absolute evil, unless one is dealing with totalitarianism.
This attitude explains Aron's nuanced judgments, sometimes
surprising, on the Popular Front, Vichy France, Algeria, Vietnam, Gaullism. Regarding each, the pro and the con are
weighed; the arguments opposing the choices made are developed at length.

The second aspect that impressed us concerns the moral responsibility of the individual citizen that Raymond Aron sup-
plicates. For our generation, the idea of fatherland has always
seemed rather "retro." Not that we are supranational or even
European, for our education and values root us in our country. But so many wars have been fought in the name of the nation that democracy for us is incarnated rather more in
society than in the fatherland. We find it difficult today to
think of democracy without society, while it is on the other
hand more rare for us to associate the idea of democracy with
the defense of a geographical area, even though we realize in
the abstract that a society incapable of defending itself is condemned to disappear sooner or later. For Aron, civic consciousness is a prerequisite for the protection of democracy.
Or, to be more precise, if a democracy is to survive, it needs
citizens ready to assume certain duties. Finally, the concept of
democracy connotes two elements: a society and a nation.
We tended to idealize the first and forget the second because
it was too closely linked to the tragic events of contemporary
history, but also because it implies constraints, of which our
generation has never been very fond. . . .

Finally, Raymond Aron is not simply an intellectual who has
dabbled in journalism. An intellectual dabbling in journalism
generally chooses the subjects and the occasions on which he

wishes to comment and take a position. Aron, however, has imposed upon himself the discipline of commenting regularly upon events, without choosing the causes to defend or the moments in which to defend them. This resolve to pursue two careers at once over the last thirty-five years forces upon him something much more than discipline and a rigorous organization of his time. It makes it necessary to live with two different processes of thought, generally mutually exclusive, and thus pursued in a permanent state of tension. This alternating between two logical processes, two ways of looking at things (commenting upon an event and overall interpretation), leads to a world view more sensitive to the uncertainty and fragility of events than to the search for final causes. Perhaps we should perceive in this choice both the will toward personal transcendence and the mark of historic relativism. In any case, this constraint of regular confrontation with economic and political events has probably helped preserve Raymond Aron from the intoxication of ideology. Such confrontation makes it impossible to choose only the facts that support a theory—he must treat everything.

On the whole, these interviews come out as an interrogation of Raymond Aron's generation by our own, with all that implies in terms of a comparison between two different ways of thinking.

Someone closer to his orientations would probably have conceived these interviews differently. It is in this regard, indeed, that one must pay homage to Raymond Aron's liberalism. Because when we proposed the project to him, we did not know him personally and we told him immediately that we were not "Aronians."

In view of the fact that these interviews were designed as three television programs for the "Antenne-2" network on the theme, "Raymond Aron, a committed observer," the risk of confrontation was clearly increased. The project was more time-consuming than we had anticipated and was designed for a mass audience. We wanted to offer the television audience an opportunity to understand the analysis of fifty years of history by one of the most eminent witnesses of intellectual and political life. The programs were divided into three chronological periods (1930-1947; 1947-1967; 1967-1980),

each section constructed around three main themes:
—The trends in ideas and attitudes of intellectuals;
—The evolution of French society and the ability of its rul-
   ing class;
—The most significant international events.

Raymond Aron never wanted to discuss the overall plan or
the choice of themes on which we wanted to focus our dialogue. When we mentioned them to him, he would listen dis-
tractedly and respond, "Yes, that's good, do as you think
best." Once he was sure that we were well acquainted with
the events of this era, as well as with his works and with the
intellectual debates of the period, he gave us his trust.

It seemed to us that these interviews originally conceived
for television, could, in view of their significance, be revised
and published in book form, while conserving their dialogue
format. The reader will thus find here the dialogue in its integral form. Beyond his confidence in us, we were deeply impressed by Raymond Aron's human warmth, particularly in
view of his reputation for being cold and distant. Obviously,
this kindness did not exclude sharpness in the discussion, but
it is very real and we have treasured it since that day in April
1980 when we first visited him to propose the project.

In the exchange of views that follows, we dealt with a
finely-honed, exigent mind and a man who is sensitive, motivated by the search for truth, imbued with the awareness of
history-in-the-making. In a word: an intellect in action.

Since these interviews took place, a change in the political
majority occurred in France in December 1980. But the essence of the dialogue stands up well against the reversal represented by the accession to power of the Left in May and
June 1981. Certain passages will even assume a special flavor
for the reader, particularly that part of the dialogue devoted to
the failure of the Popular Front, since the present government
intends to find example and inspiration in Lèon Blum's government experience. The same holds true for May 1968,
which, until the spring of 1981 had been the Left's most recent great event, and which has been pushed back a little further into history at the very moment when a goodly number
of the themes and attitudes of the new government find their
source in it. Raymond Aron has written a conclusion on the

subject of the Left's accession to power. In doing so, he has chosen to pursue the dialogue with us, but this time, to be sure of the right answers, he has also posed the questions. . . .

Here, then, is Raymond Aron, an intellectual of the opposition—a paradox for one who has so often been criticized because his ideas put him on "the government's side"! For, his liberal conception of society irritated less than the political consequences that he drew from it, ever faithful to his philosophy. Some readers, as a matter of fact, will not see any difference between his present and earlier writings, so consistently did he refuse to be tied to the party in power even when he supported it. In fact, despite the affinity of his ideas with those of certain leaders, he always kept his distance. Rightly or wrongly, he drew a clear line of demarcation between his position as an intellectual and journalist, and that of a political practitioner. Is not it possible that leftist intellectuals, who will now be confronted with the problem of their rapport with the government, will find in the line of conduct Aron imposed upon himself an example to reflect upon? As a matter of fact, he never evinced the kind of reverence and reserve necessary to be a "counselor to the prince." And as he recalls with humor, he quarrelled with all the heads of state of the Fourth and Fifth Republics, with the exception of Valèry Giscard d'Estaing, whom he nonetheless did not coddle.

His principles are, to be sure, easier to articulate than to practice. The reader will judge throughout these interviews how well he held to this position, what is due to circumstances, and what is attributable to personal morality. Over such a long period, this ethic of commitment certainly required considerable discipline, for it prevented him from personifying one of the two figures that for him symbolize the choice of the intellectual: to be the confidant of providence or the counselor to the prince. A confidant of providence is one who is on the side of the oppressed, who speaks out in the name of universal morality, of which he is — or believes himself to be — the spokesman, and who appeals to the sense of history and to the "good society" that must be constructed. A counselor to the prince is one who takes into account the constraints of reality and who recognizes that political activity obliges whoever supports it to accept its constraints.

At this point we must return to the intellectuals of the Left. For a long time, and in good conscience, they were the confidants of providence. Then a number of them were seized by doubts—with the crisis of Marxism, the impossibility of disguising any longer the "achievements" of true socialism, the redefinition of the role and place of intellectuals in our society. . . . And it is precisely at this time that, thanks to the effects of universal suffrage, they find themselves in a situation in which it would be logical for them to become counselors to the prince. Will they assume that role? And in what manner? Will they impose upon themselves Raymond Aron's moral, that is, to continue to say what they think? At what point will some of them realize that there is a problem of incompatibility and therefore a need to choose between being an analyst and a counselor to the prince? Especially since political honeymoons last only as long as roses bloom, it will be necessary to write, comment upon events, analyze, criticize.

The period now beginning will be rich in lessons about the ability of the French intelligentsia to position itself in relation to a government it had called for by a large majority. Will the blindness that for such a long time rendered it powerless to denounce Stalinism and its innumerable variants because one shouldn't "make Billancourt unhappy"[4] recur, through one of history's tricks, because with the Left in power one must not "make the Elysée unhappy"?

Jean-Louis Missika
Dominique Wolton

Section One

France in the Tempest

I
A YOUNG INTELLECTUAL OF THE 1930S

a) Rue d'Ulm, 1928 – Berlin, 1933

D. Wolton. – Between 1924 and 1928, you were at the Ecole Normale Supérieure.[5] Your friends were Jean-Paul Sartre and Paul Nizan. What kind of education did you receive at the school?

Raymond Aron. – It was of two kinds. It was first of all the education acquired through one's friends and in an intellectual atmosphere that was to my thinking of exceptional quality; then I studied philosophy, or at least what was called philosophy. Two professors had a degree of influence upon men. One was Alain, who was not a professor at the Ecole Normale, but was a famous teacher of khagne[6] at the lycée[7] Henri IV. From time to time to time, I would go to see him at Henri IV and would accompany him home, on rue de Rennes. The other was Brunschvicg. They were about the same age and had a certain amount of respect for each other. Alain betrayed some irritation with regard to the "Sorbonnites" and to those teachers of philosophy who had, during the war, advocated total victory. What impressed us was that Alain had fought the war while hating it.

You cited Sartre and Nizan, the most famous student friends. But I had many others at the Ecole Normale: Lagache, Canguilhem, Marrou! I never met such a remarkable group of people, so much so that in all other milieux I have known since then, I've retained a kind of nostalgia for the Ecole Normale. Too, I've always thought that young adolescents are more intelligent and open than when they reach twenty or twenty-five. At twenty, Sartre detested "important" people. But he, and I, too, probably, have become at least half-important!

J.–L. Missika. – What were the important intellectual currents at the Ecole Normale?

R.A. – There were the "Tala,"[8] that is, those who went to the mass, the Catholics, and then the larger number: the Left, the Socialist. I was vaguely Socialist. Our strongest feeling was probably one of revolt against the war, thus, pacifist. I was passionately pacifist, both because of my revulsion against the war and the way one child, I, had lived through the war. I was nine years old when the war broke out, thirteen by the time it ended. Afterward, it occurred to me that I hadn't suffered from the war for a single instant, that I never once really felt compassion for the misfortunes of peoples. So I had the feeling that the egoism of children is something horrible, and I detested the war with a degree of fervor that matched my patriotism. During the war, I was ten or eleven years old; I wanted to be a captain, the little captain! I wrote long essays on the bravery of the little captain. Some years later, when I began to think, when I began to take philosophy, everything changed suddenly; everything was different. At the end of three months, I had decided to make philosophy my life's work! I was—how should I put it?—transformed by the philosophy class more than by all the others. What were the others? Literature, Latin, Greek, arithmetic, or mathematics! I was interested in them, more or less, but basically I was more taken by bicycling or tennis. . . .

D.W. – You were a good tennis player, weren't you?

R.A. – Yes, but above all, if I was a good student, up to then it was essentially out of pride, a motivation I judged rather contemptible. I wanted to be at the top of the class. But from the moment there was philosophy, I no longer wanted to be first—I wanted to be a philosopher; it was an entirely different thing. At the Ecole Normale, naturally I continued to study philosophy, but not enough. Then I devoted a whole year to Kant, for my degree. At that time, Brunschvicg came into the picture, a man who simultaneously instilled in you the meaning of the great philosophers and discouraged you from becoming one of them.

D.W. – Do you have the feeling that the education you received prepared you to understand the outside world?

R.A. – . . . *not* to understand it! What does one learn under the heading, "philosophy"? Plato, Aristotle, Descartes and the others. Almost no Marx, except for a bit in sociology. No post-Kantians, or practically none. No Hegel. There was epistemology, discussions about mathematics or physics, but no courses on political philosophy. I never heard the name de Tocqueville when I was at the Sorbonne or the Ecole Normale!

J.–L.M. – And Max Weber?

R.A. – Obviously not. Max Weber came later, that was my real education. The education I received during my four years at the Ecole Normale prepared me to become a professor of philosophy in a lycée, but nothing else. In 1928, after I passed the *agrégation*[9] of philosophy, brilliantly, as the saying goes, because I was at the top of the list—Sartre felt it necessary to flunk that year—I immediately experienced a kind of inner crisis. I was almost desperate at the thought of having lost years in learning almost nothing. I exaggerated, of course, because an education gained through reading the great philosophers is not a sterile experience. Nevertheless, I knew very little about the world, about social reality, about modern science. What to do? Do philosophy? On what? On nothing? Or do another thesis on Kant? So I fled, in a way. I left France, my surroundings, and I found something else.

D.W. – In your inaugural lecture at the *Collège de France,* in 1970, there is a phrase about your education: "The rise of national socialism, the revelation of politics, inspired in me a kind of revolt against the teaching I had received at the university."

R.A. – I think that people who have spent their whole lives in a university, first as students, then as professors, miss something. The university world is too soft. One becomes insufficiently acquainted with the sordidness, and hardness of human existence. However, I don't mean to belittle the study of Kant, to whose work I devoted myself for a year. The difficult study of a great philosopher was one of my most fertile experiences during those years. When I left for Germany, after my military duty, my rebelliousness was more general. I felt a revulsion against the war, against the policies of Poincaré, against a French foreign policy that I found completely devoid of generosity, and I dreamt of reconciliation between France and Germany.

D.W. – Why did you choose Germany instead of Great Britain or the United States?

R.A. – It was a tradition. When philosophers wanted to complete their education, they went to Germany. Durkheim, two generations before me, had gone to Germany and wrote there a little book on the social sciences in Germany. My faculty advisor, Bouglé, had done the same thing, and so did I, with a short book called *La Sociologie Allemande Contemporaine*. Sartre went there, too, but more by accident, and later, with my intervention.

J.–L.M. – What were your first impressions of Germany?

R.A. – An initial intuition, rather than an impression; a feeling I can only convey with Toynbee's, "History is again on the move." What struck me, what shocked me, what overwhelmed me, arriving in Germany in the spring of 1930, was the nationalistic violence of the Germans and, three months later in September 1930, the first great victory of the national socialists, the election of 107 Nazi deputies. From that moment, between 1930 and 1933, I lived in a psychological state entirely different from that of the Ecole Normale. The problem no longer was the madness of the earlier war; my problem—my obsession—became: How to avoid the coming war?

From my first contact with Germany, I had the feeling that this people refused to accept the destiny that had been imposed upon it, that there was a kind of deep-seated, fundamental revolt, aggravated by the economic crises. Suddenly, I hesitated between my earlier pacifism and the decisive political question: What should one do? All the articles I wrote when I was in Germany were awful. They were awful, first, because I didn't yet know how to observe political reality; moreover, I didn't know how to distinguish in clear-cut fashion the desirable from the possible. I was not capable of analyzing the situation without revealing my passions and my emotions, and my emotions were divided between my educational background (what I call "university idealism") and the sudden awareness of politics in its ruthless brutality. But though I hate to say it, my teachers, whether you take Alain or Brunschvicg, just didn't measure up when it came to dealing with Hitler. Or to say the least, they were in a different world from the one I found myself in when I was watching or listening to Hitler at mass meetings.

J.–L.M. – Nonetheless, this sudden awareness of the phenomenon of Nazism didn't discourage you from continuing to study German philosophy?

R.A. – Oh, no! You know, members of my generation detested, really detested and despised the intellectuals who had condemned German culture because of the 1914-18 war against Germany. One of our most violent reproaches against some of the preceding generation was the brainwashing that had taken place. As this brainwashing would have it, one should no longer listen to Wagner because he was German, or, as one would put it today, because he was an anti-Semite. For me, the clear-cut separation between German culture on the one hand, and German politics, on the other, was evident. Despite the 1939-1945 war, despite national socialism, I never allowed myself to condemn a people and a culture because of political conflicts.

J.–L.M. – And yet the German intellectuals you associated with were taken with national socialism?

R.A. – No, that's not true. Among the professors, I knew few who were. Among the students, yes, but it is necessary to tell the truth: when I was a lecturer at the University of Cologne, I knew a lot of students; relations were always excellent; there was never the slightest sign of anti-Semitism toward me, nor toward the professor, Leo Spitzer, also a Jew, at whose home I lived. You must not think that the German universities in 1931 were absolutely dominated by the national socialists. There were some, certainly. But it is important not to distort overly the picture of Germany of that period by the knowledge of what it became later. The Germany I knew in 1931 was not the Germany of 1942 or 1943.

D.W. – How did you react to the rise of Nazism in the Germany of 1931 and what did you talk about with your students? Politics, or mainly philosophy?

R.A. – There are two things to keep in mind: First, the elections that I mentioned earlier; second, the extraordinarily nationalistic passion that possessed these intelligent and friendly people with whom I was in contact. We came from France, from a more or less leftist milieu, in which nationalism had, one might say, gone out of fashion. And suddenly, we were meeting professors, students, people for whom German claims were vital; these claims were at once national and personal. What did I see when I was a professor, or assistant, at the University of Cologne? Young men and women who liked me, to whom I explained Mauriac, Claudel, and to whom I succeeded in communicating my enthusiasm, my affection for a Mauriac novel like *Le Désert de l'Amour* or for a Claudel play like *L'Annonce Faite à Marie*. When we were together, speaking French, living in a culture that was simultaneously theirs and our own, we could forget politics. But perhaps because I had a certain propensity for thinking about politics, for reading the newspapers, for studying events, let us say, I nevertheless sensed the rise of national socialism as early as 1930-31. Soon, everyone was aware of it!

J.–L.M. – And national socialism's acts of violence, the book burnings, the persecutions, did you see any of them?

R.A. – Oh, but much later. We are talking about 1931. French writers were coming to give university lectures: Duhamel, Chamson, and also Malraux. It was there that I met Malraux for the first time.

D.W. – You remained in Germany until when?

R.A. – Until August 1933, but I stayed in Cologne as an assistant for only a year and a half. Between 1931 and 1933, I was in Berlin. There, the German crisis was much more apparent. One saw a lot more unemployed. It was the center of political life and I used to go to political meetings. Of course, I heard Goebbels, who, by the way, was an orator of talent and spoke a very polished German. I listened to Hitler, whose German was frightful, and who immediately inspired in me a kind of fear and horror. One saw some brown uniforms, but for the most part *after* Hitler took power. Three weeks later, the number of Germans dressed in brown had increased remarkably. Even at the university house which I frequented— Humboldt Haus—several students I had known for two years and who were not Hitler sympathizers began to wear the uniform. That was the beginning of the tidal wave. Before 1933, one felt it coming at election time. And there were frequent elections. At the Französisches Akademikerhaus, where I boarded, we listened to the results and were appalled. The election returns foreshadowed in our minds the figure of Hitler gradually advancing toward the chancellery. But for most Berliners, Hitler's coming to power was not very perceptible. They didn't really "see" him until he appeared on the chancellery balcony. As for me, I was still a rather abstract and philosophic observer. I understood what was happening but I still didn't perceive the reality very well. I believe, however, that as far as Hitler as a person was concerned, I had the luck, or the bad luck, to sense his diabolic nature immediately. That was not evident to everyone at the beginning.

D.W. – You had the feeling of a march toward barbarism?

R.A. – Of a march toward war. I thought the only thing Hitler could do after having put the Germans back to work would be to go to war. The Germans wanted to challenge the results of the preceding war, and it seemed to me that he was delegated by a part of Germany to carry out this task. The tragic irony of it all, if you will, is that those who helped him gain power would have been satisfied with what he obtained in 1938 and would not have later started this unpardonable war. . . .

D.W. – What about anti-Semitism, did you see any of it in 1930?

R.A. – Yes, and the anti-Semitism of Hitler's group was violent. It is certain that it played a role in my becoming aware of the real significance of national socialism. When I arrived in Germany, I was a Jew and I knew it—but only slightly. My consciousness of my Judaism, as people call it these days, was extraordinarily weak. I had almost never been in a synagogue. I remember that, on the first day of school once at the Lycée Hoche—I was ten or eleven years old at the time—when the students were escorted to church, I went along with them. Then, in Germany, came the shock, not only of German national socialism, but of anti-Semitism. It would be a bit of an exaggeration to say it was only that. But nonetheless, national socialism, apart from the nationalistic aspect that was shared by other parties, was made conspicuous by an extreme of anti-Semitism; to such an extent that from that year on, I have always introduced myself first as a Jew. In 1934, for the first time in my life, on the occasion of a lecture on national socialism at the Ecole Normale, I underscored the fact that I was a Jew and that, being Jewish, I could be suspected of not being objective.

D.W. – The fact of being Jewish could, you feel, hinder you from being objective?

R.A. – No, certainly not. But with Hitler's coming to power, all French Jews were suspect. They were suspected of being anti-German, anti-Hitler, not so much as Frenchmen, but as Jews. In good part, the propaganda against "warmongers" stemmed from the very simple fact that, obviously, French Jews had stronger emotions about national socialism, not only as Frenchmen, but as Jews. I must add, however, that, the depth of my Judaism being rather shallow, my reaction to national socialism and to the German danger was essentially that of a Frenchman, as far as I am able to evaluate it. But it was precisely this French reaction that, to a large degree, paralyzed me. Except among friends, it was difficult for me to say what I thought about national socialism without being suspected of having been carried away by my Jewish emotions.

D.W. – It put you in an awkward position?

R.A. – No, it was the era of suspicion. I used this expression forty years later concerning one of General de Gaulle's press conferences. But, between 1933 and 1939, I really lived through an era of suspicion.

J.–L.M. – It's a paradoxical line of reasoning! Just because you are Jewish, you didn't have the right to criticize national socialism?

R.A. – No, no. I'm not saying I didn't have the right, but look . . . I had a close friend whose name was Henri Moysset. He edited Proudhon's works, and was a remarkable man, of whom I was very fond. He had been the *chef de cabinet* of the Navy Minister, Leygues, and had contributed significantly to the rebuilding of the French Navy between the two wars. He had close ties to the admirals and eventually became one of Marshal Pétain's ministers in 1943, perhaps even in 1944. He was not an anti-Semite by any means. Talking about the war one day in 1938, he said to me, "And you, my poor friend, what is going to become of you?" Another day, when I was telling him what I thought of French foreign policy, he said to me, "My dear friend, be careful: Don't speak too loudly, being what you are!"

D.W. – And you say he wasn't at all an anti-Semite?

R.A. – No, but he knew that if I said certain things, I would become suspect immediately, suspected of being motivated, not by an analysis of the real situation, not by French patriotism, but by my hatred of Nazi anti-Semitism. Since then, people have occasionally asked me, "Why didn't you write anything?" First of all, I did write occasional articles, one in 1934, another in 1938 or 1939. But I lacked a platform. At that time, I was not a journalist and was essentially dedicated to my reading and to writing my books; even if I had had the opportunity to write, I would have hesitated.

D.W. – Because of this "era of suspicion"?

R.A. – Exactly. Let me add the fact that Léon Blum, the head of the Socialist party who became Prime Minister, was a Jew, tended to exacerbate anti-Semitic feelings in the struggle between the "warmongers" and the "pacifists". . . .

D.W. – Did this "era of suspicion" last for you until the war?

R.A. – No. We can say that between 1931 and 1933, all Frenchmen, Jews or not, feared the coming to power of Hitler. But, once he became Chancellor, the French feared war, and rightly so! From that moment on, an intellectual and political struggle began: How to avoid war? Anyone who suggested resisting, at any given moment, was obviously suspected of wanting to drag France into war!

In this period, between 1933 and 1939, there were three dates fundamental in changing the course of history. The first was March 1936: German troops entered the Rhineland. This was the opportunity, the last opportunity, to stop Hitler without war. It was lost through the fault of everyone, and I mean everyone, because even those who would be ready to resist in 1938 did not favor in March 1936 a military response to the invasion of the Rhineland by German troops. At that time, Léon Blum wrote an astonishing article in *Le Populaire*. He recalled that France had the right by treaty to use military force against Germany. But he added, "No one has dreamed of using military force, and that is a sign of humanity's progress; the Socialist party is proud to have made a contribution to this progress." This "moral progress" meant the end of the French system of alliances and the near certainty of war. . . .

J.–L.M. – And the second date?

R.A. – That was Munich, in 1938. I think, to be truthful, sincere, I would say that I was emotionally against Munich, but intellectually, I was to an extent, uncertain. First of all, I was very irritated by those who favored resistance in the case of Czechoslovakia, using as their principal argument, "Resistance is the best way to avoid war." At the time, I said, "Perhaps! But we're not at all sure!"

D.W. – And the third date?

R.A. – Obviously, 1939, the year of the guarantee to Poland. It was an extraordinary diplomatic decision. No one had risked war for the Rhineland, nor for Czechoslovakia. But it was decided, following Great Britain's lead, to risk war for Poland even though it was impossible to do anything for that country. To guarantee the security of Poland in fact meant to accept the destruction of that country in a few weeks at most, and to fight a great war in order to try to destroy Germany in the aftermath. We still could have avoided honoring our commitment. But, at that moment, Great Britain had changed its policy and its psychology. We were linked to Great Britain. So we entered the war, a war that was declared but not fought, a war that we did not want to fight. . . .

D.W. – Let's return to your formative years. Between 1925 and 1930, who were the opinion setters for young people in France?

R.A. – During that period, I'm not sure there were any so-called opinion setters. I think Barrès was one for a time. Sartre was one during a twenty-year period, without any doubt. But when I think back to those years between 1924 and 1928, while I was at the Ecole Normale, well. . .there was Alain and his disciples. In him, his followers had a great man whom they admired profoundly; they called him "the man"; he was a man *par excellence,* at once a philosopher, a pacifist, and a warrior. It is possible that this combination was not a very rational one, but it was impressive. On the other hand, the literature of the period was certainly brilliant. Proust was no longer alive, but nonetheless his overpowering shadow loomed over us all. There was Valéry, and many others, but it seems to me that none were opinion setters. Among the philosophers, there was Brunschvicg. Historically, he was a neo-Kantian among many others. He impressed us to a certain extent, because he had studied the development of mathematical thought and the development of physics. He evinced a kind of asceticism in thought. For him, philosophical thought should be a reflection on science and should achieve the same rigor, precisely by taking scientific thought as its model. He concerned himself incessantly with the great philosophers and he helped us enter their temple—one from which he excluded himself, or so he said.

J.–L.M. – And the political thinkers in France in the interwar period?

R.A. – Two men inspired passion and devotion; one was Maurras; the other, Alain. Maurras represented a positivist theory of the monarchy, making an ideology of the French sense of order. I read little of what he wrote; he bored me. I found him exaggeratedly chauvinist. Even at the time when I was not an initiate of worldly society, I found his political philosophy, exclusively French, very "Provençal". . . . I did read a bit of him, but with total indifference. The other one who inspired admiration and devotion was Alain. He classified himself as a citizen challenging the state and as a pacifist. But for a citizen to define himself by his hostility to the state is fine, on the condition that the power of the state exists. But when the state is weak, to be against it is not much of a risk. Alain realized that. When I told him, around 1934 or 1935, or a little later, that I wanted to devote myself to political philosophy, and when I mentioned some of his ideas, he said to me—and this is genuine—"Don't take my political ideas seriously; all I really wanted to do was to say what I thought of a number of people I detested." In other words, he was very conscious of the limits of his political thought. He admitted that he neglected history, which, as far as politics is concerned, is essential.

D.W. – And France, was it open to ideas from the outside world at the time?

R.A. – Only slightly, it seems to me. The politicians who governed France knew very little about the United States; they didn't have a very clear picture of American economic power. They understood little about the Soviet Union. I remember that the journalist Pertinax, well respected at the time, said more or less the following after the war: "I know and understand European international politics very well, but when you go beyond Germany, you arrive in the Soviet Union, and it is all very blurred; and when you go west, you run into the United States, and that. . . well, that's another world." I would say that the Pertinax article is an accurate representation, if somewhat caricatured, of the French between the two wars.

D.W. – From an intellectual point of view, what did your stay in Germany do for you? What did you discover there, beyond the political events?

R.A. – I was about to say, "everything," which would be an exaggeration. But at the least I found everything that I had not found in France, principally the philosophy of history and political thought. Germany also gave me phenomenology, that is, a certain way to approach the humanities. Afterwards, I rediscovered part of that in France, but nevertheless I owe a great deal to German culture and when—a few years later—I wrote the big book on Clausewitz, I felt once again the same kind of enthusiasm I had known in my youth, when I left France and discovered another culture, with a philosophic language. When I arrived in Germany, I was dazzled at first. You know, the German language is exceptionally supple for philosophy, so we always tend to think that the German philosophers are more profound than they really are. There are two languages for philosophy, German and Greek. Thus, when you plunge into the German language, you feel enriched, to the point of being overwhelmed. At the beginning, I assumed all German philosophers were great ones. That didn't last, but I did find some from whom I learned a lot. First of all, I read Husserl's phenomenology; that was hardly known. I read the first of Heidegger, then I read the philosophers of history, Max Weber in particular.

It was in Max Weber that I found what I was looking for; a man who possessed at once the experience of history, an understanding of politics, the will to know the truth and, finally, the ability to decide and to act. Now, the determination to see, to seize upon the truth and reality, on the one hand, and, on the other hand, to act: these are, I believe, the two imperatives I have tried to follow all my life. I found this duality of imperatives in Weber. In my little volume on German sociology, I wrote a very long chapter on Max Weber that takes up nearly half the book. In France, the followers of Durkheim hardly knew Weber. I think I was the first to offer a portrait of Max Weber, today recognized throughout the world as one of the very great sociologists, of whom there are at most a half-dozen in history.

D.W. – Who were the intellectuals you associated with in Berlin? Were they philosophers of the Frankfurt School?

R.A. – Marcuse was not in Berlin. As for the philosophers of Frankfurt School, I did not know them until after 1933, that is, after they went into exile in France and the United States. On the other hand, I knew Karl Mannheim while I was in Germany; he was a professor at Frankfurt but did not belong to the School of Frankfurt group. He was considered to be a member of the Hungarian School of Marxism. Like Lukacs, he was Hungarian, but not really Marxist. However, he borrowed something from Marxism that he called "the sociology of knowledge," that is to say, the partial determination at the least, of men's way of thinking by the conditions in which they live. At one time, I was much influenced by Mannheim. I met him in Frankfurt; I had sent him an article that I had written on him and that, happily, he lost, because it was surely very bad. For six months, to a year, I was a Mannheimian. When I wrote a long study on Léon Brunschvicg, in order to get out from under his influence, there were even some passages in which I interpreted certain aspects of his thought in terms of his being bourgeois, Jewish, and the rest! He didn't like that at all, not at all. It wasn't written in an aggressive manner, but French Sorbonne professors did not imagine that one could "sociologize" them. I don't say that one would be right to do it, but after all, it was at least conceivable.

J.–L.M. – And psychoanalysis?

R.A. – Psychoanalysis was part of the normal education of philosophers of the time. I read Freud a bit, like everyone. But Freudianism was not yet accepted by everyone at the Sorbonne. Bouglé, my faculty advisor at the Ecole Normale, blew up when anyone spoke of psychoanalysis. "It's trash," he would say. The French were among the last to accept psychoanalysis. Even today, they accept it only with reticence. But, since the war, there has been the Lacan phenomenon. I knew Lacan well. He *is* a phenomenon. He was at the Kojève seminar between 1936 and 1938. It was there that he learned a little of his philosophy.

D.W. – Who else came to this seminar?

R.A. – There was Queneau. It was he who published the last Kojève course, which became his *Introduction à la Lecture de Hegel.* Koyré, Marjolin were there. Merleau-Ponty was often there. These were very distinguished people who made names for themselves later.

To come back to psychoanalysis, Freudianism constituted one of my most constant and impassioned discussion themes with Jean-Paul Sartre. He had decreed once and for all that Freudianism was unacceptable because it employed the concept of the unconscious. Sartre rejected any distinction between psychism and the conscious and, consequently, for him there could be no unconscious psychism. We had I don't know how many arguments on that subject. Generally, my conclusion, always the same, was, "My friend, you can refuse the unconscious if you wish to, but you have to accept the essential aspects of the content of psychoanalysis." And found the trick to get himself out of the difficulty.

D.W. – How?

R.A. – He found the trick: the deceit that gave him the opportunity to dispense with the unconscious while conserving the basics of psychoanalysis; that permitted him, that is, to translate into the conscious everything that is unconscious in Freudianism. In *Being and Nothingness*,[1] he develops a beautiful theme of existential psychoanalysis, really one of the most beautiful passages. I don't at all claim that it is because of our arguments, but from a certain moment on, he who had obstinately rejected psychoanalysis, reintroduced it into his philosophy through a dissemblance.

J.–L.M. – And with you, what role does psychoanalysis play?

R.A. – I'm tempted to answer, "And with you?" For all of us, psychoanalysis is an interrogation, an evaluation of the self, a necessary examination of the conscience. But in order to live, one must forget it to the extent possible. Each time that one forgets something, one must not tell oneself, as Koestler does, that one *wanted* to forget it. Only from time to time should one say that to oneself. But, really, I'm not a psychoanalyst and I don't have anything interesting to say about it, except that it is a part of my self-interrogation, of my inner life.

J.–L.M. – I meant the analysis of political and social events. You haven't tried—like some others—to use psychoanalysis?

R.A. – Oh, of course. The interiorization of the values and imperatives of a society in the unconscious can be explained, interpreted, through psychoanalysis. There is psychoanalysis in Talcot Parsons. In one way or another, one uses it. That much said, I am not very excited, for example, by the psychoanalytic interpretation of German anti-Semitism. Everything considered, I have not used psychoanalysis much; I should have used it more; I recognize its existence but, you know, I always tend to rationalize both my own arguments and the way others think. I have the feeling that it is not fair to demolish others' way of thinking, whether by sociologizing them, or by psychoanalyzing them. Mannheim, whom I mentioned earlier, sociologizes all ways of thinking. That is to say, he explains them according to social position and by the influence of the social milieu. Among the young scholars (young, that is, in comparison to me), Bourdieu, for example, tends to sociologize everything. He analyzes the aesthetic theory of Kant from a sociological base. He has written an article on Heidegger in which he "sociologizes" him; I mean that he tries to elucidate the social sense of his philosophy.

D.W. – You say: I prefer not to sociologize someone too much, or psychoanalyze him too much, to explain his thought.

R.A. – Yes. For my part, I prefer to keep the discussion on the intellectual level. Let's take Sartre. I have never sought the profound motivations of one or another of his assertions; I considered only his motivations that were so visible, so close to the surface, that taking them into account could not be considered as a kind of psychoanalysis.

D.W. – Let's return to Germany. What was most important for you there? Your intellectual education? Becoming aware of your Judaism? Or the political events?

R.A. – Oh, all three! All three. Concerning the contact with anti-Semitic Germany, a sudden awareness and a decision. The awareness that I accept my destiny as a Jew, with one affirmation always repeated: it is neither a title of pride, nor one of shame; I am a Jew just as someone else is not. From the moment one is in danger of being persecuted as a Jew or insulted as a Jew, one must always say that one is Jewish, as far as possible without aggressiveness, without ostentation, especially when one is not religious—like myself. Second, my contact with politics, that is, Hitler's coming to power. He was a man I had already judged to be a barbarian, one who rose to power with the support of the masses. This event could not but make me understand the fundamental irrationality of mass movements, the irrationality of politics and the necessity, for those who practice politics, to play on the irrational emotions of men. To reflect upon politics, one must be as rational as possible, but to be active in them, one must inevitably play upon the emotions of other men. Political activity is therefore impure and that is why I prefer to study it. And then, the third discovery: that was German thought and, I insist upon this point, the apprenticeship in the German language. I have always had the feeling that the ability to speak easily two different languages brings one a kind of freedom with respect to oneself that no other quality offers. When I speak English or German, I think a little bit differently than I do in French. Because of this, I am not a prisoner of my words. One of the qualities I attribute to myself, to be very vain, is the ability to understand others; this ability to understand the way others think I owe in part to the detachment that is possible in my own thought, in my words and in my ability to change words. When I shift from French into German or English, I am a little bit freer than others who are truly prisoners of their own system of thought as well as of their words.

But there is a negative aspect. The true creative thinkers are very much prisoners of their system of thought, but for the critical thinker the capacity to be detached from oneself is rather an advantage.

b) The Popular Front: The Left Enjoys Celebrating Its Defeats

D.W. – You left Germany in 1933. When you returned to France, in what way were you most changed?

R.A. – I had become conscious of the world. In other words, I had accomplished my political education. Not my sentimental education. In the spring of 1930, arriving in Germany, I was very naive. In 1933, I returned to France as an adult. I had become aware of what political life can be when it manifests its horrible side. But it was not Germany as such that changed me. It was Hitler in a Germany that had become Hitlerian. It isn't a big thing. I could have learned all that reading books, but I learned it in real life.

D.W. – Do you really believe that in reading books. . .?

R.A. – Yes, Aristotle and Machiavelli. All that was necessary was to understand them well! I finally stopped asking myself which ideology was the most appropriate; instead, I asked myself constantly: What should one do?

J.–L.M. – So, between 1934 and 1938, in France, what did you do?

R.A. – Well, I acted like a good boy. Married, with a daughter, I did my doctoral thesis. First, for a year, I was a professor at a lycée in Le Havre, replacing Sartre who was at the Berlin Academic House. And then, the time to start writing had come. I had not yet written anything, anything at all, except some articles on Germany that were not good. I had read and reflected a great deal, but I was tortured by the idea of not being able to write. You will say that I made up for it in the meantime! Well enough! But at the time, that was the case.

D.W. – Nevertheless, between 1934 and 1938, you wrote two books and your thesis, didn't you?

R.A. – Three, including the thesis. I wrote *La Sociologie Allemande Contemporaine* that appeared in 1935. Also in 1935, I finished the *Essai sur la Théorie de l'Histoire dans l'Allemagne Contemporaine* and in 1937 my *Introduction to the Philosophy of History* that had been my thesis. I defended it in March 1938, about three days before the German troops entered Vienna.

D.W. – You wrote these three books, but you didn't take a public stand. Why? On your return from Germany, why didn't you alert public opinion?

R.A. – Yes, others also, at one time or another, have reproached me for not having alerted public opinion. But even today, a half-century later, and though I enjoy a significantly wider reputation, I do not have much ability to sensitize French opinion. In 1934 or 1935, no one knew me, outside of a score of philosophers, and two-score students. And then, write where? Write what? Between 1934 and 1939, politics concerned Germany essentially. In 1936, at the moment when German troops entered the Rhineland, I thought—it was clear enough—that it was necessary to respond in a military way, and that if there were no military riposte, then the whole system of French alliances was lost. The decision had to be taken within forty-eight hours. At the end of forty-eight hours, it was taken—and it was the wrong decision. What could I have done?

D.W. – But you could have commented upon it!

R.A. – I tried. Look! I met Léon Brunschvicg on Boulevard Saint-Germain. He said to me, "The English are trying to calm us, thank goodness." I replied, "But you are completely mistaken," and I gave him the same argument I just gave you. To that, he replied, "You are probably right. Thankfully, I don't have any political responsibilities."

As for me, I had no means of political action. Moreover, I couldn't demonstrate what I affirmed. At the same time, I thought Hitler would make war, but that it depended on the French and the English to stop him from doing so; the proof: in 1936, one could have still stopped Hitler. But, taking into account what France was like at the time, I was convinced that France and Great Britain would not do what was necessary to prevent a war. Even in 1938, it was impossible to demonstrate that Hitler would make war. Because, essentially, in 1938, he was about to be given the domination of the whole of central Europe, something that would have fully satisfied the ambitions of the Germany of Wilhelm II. It was therefore not easy to prove that he would want more. My conviction was based on Hitler's psychology, but it was necessary to have a feeling for what Hitler was; it was necessary to feel what national socialism was. It could not be demonstrated.

D.W. – But there were other events. What about February 6, 1934?[10]

R.A. – I was a professor at Le Havre.

D.W. – I know, but at least you must have heard about it! And the Nuremberg Laws of September 1935, the first official anti-Jewish laws . . . ?

R.A. – Yes.

D.W. – And the Popular Front in France? And the Spanish war?

R.A. – Yes, yes.

D.W. – And the economic crisis?

R.A. – All right.

J.–L.M. – The intellectuals took a political position. Take the Committee of Vigilance of Anti-Fascist Intellectuals, for example. Why not you?

R.A. – All right, all right! I see the indictment: Raymond Aron, the inactive, the indifferent observer. Well, no, no, no! Let me go back. February sixth: I discussed it with my students at the lycée in Le Havre. I wasn't enthusiastic about all that. I even found it perfectly idiotic. As early as 1934, I believed a single question existed: it was Germany. Everything that divided or weakened the French people in the face of Germany was dangerous.

Right after February 6, 1934, there was an anti-fascist movement. Well! As usual, I didn't agree. So I remained alone.

D.W. – Why?

R.A. – I was obviously against fascism, but as I saw it, there was no fascist movement in France at the time. On the other hand, since the first imperative was to maintain French unity *vis-à-vis* Germany, it was my opinion that all partisan, emotional movements weakened the country and, in consequence, increased the danger in the face of Germany. To top it all, the group of anti-fascist intellectuals was composed of Alain's disciples and Communists. The first were pacifists at almost any cost; the others were for alliance with the Soviet Union at any cost. They were thus in contradiction on the basic issue. Now, I had already a certain taste for clarity and truth. I noted that this group of anti-fascists were divided among themselves, that their work was not effective. . . .

D.W. – But couldn't you have taken some action within the Committee? What was Malraux doing at the time?

R.A. – Malraux at that time was a para-Soviet. He was my friend, but I was not a para-Soviet.

D.W. – And Nizan?

R.A. – Nizan was thoroughly Communist. When he wrote for *Ce Soir,* the Communist newspaper, he explicated the theses and analyses of the Communist party. These were my friends, but at that time one could still be friends without agreeing on everything. It should be said nevertheless that while I was very close to Nizan at the Ecole Normale, I rarely saw him after he became an active Communist. Between 1934 and 1939, I saw him half a dozen times. What we had in common was being anti-fascist, but in very, very different ways. On the other hand, this same Nizan who had written his terrible book against the Sorbonne professors, wrote a letter or a book with a very friendly or respectful dedication to Brunschvicg in 1937 or 1938. Brunschvicg told me about it.

D.W. – At the time, you were leftist?

R.A. – Yes. I was vaguely socialist, but became less and less so as I studied political economy. I was a socialist as long as I had not studied political economy.

J.–L.M. – You were thirty-one years old at the time. We come to the Popular Front. You were not carried away with enthusiasm. Why?

R.A. – Oh! That's quite simple. All my friends were more or less for the Popular Front. Naturally, I voted for the Popular Front also. However, I had one decisive objection: the Popular Front's economic program was perfectly inane. It was senseless from the very beginning and had no chance to succeed. At the time, I was very friendly with Robert Marjolin, with whom I have remained close. He was a Socialist, a member of the Socialist party, but he sent notes incessantly to the Popular Front government explaining why the economic program was impossible. For example, the forty-hour workweek law. It would have been acceptable if it had been the limit beyond which overtime would begin. The moment it imposed the (absolute) limitation of forty hours as the duration of the workweek, it became absurd. The average workweek at the time was between forty-five and forty-six hours. The reduction to forty hours could only reduce available resources and, as a consequence, the standard of living.

When the judge at the Riom trial said that to Léon Blum, the latter declared, "It's the first time I have heard that." In other words, the economic ignorance of the governments of the period was unbelievable, totally inconceivable today. A certain number of people, a small group—there was Sauvy, Marjolin—we were all in favor of the Popular Front, but we were dismayed by the economic measures taken whose consequences were predictable. In the bargain, the Popular Front refused to devalue the franc, though a devaluation was clearly necessary.

J.–L.M. – What was the reason for this blindness?

R.A. – Ignorance. One shouldn't underestimate ignorance and always assume bad intentions. No, it was sheer ignorance. The economic ignorance of the men who governed France at the time was extraordinary. This includes Léon Blum, though Léon Blum was in his way a great man.

J.–L.M. – Do you think the Popular Front could have had a similar social policy with more positive economic measures?

R.A. – Absolutely! I wrote—it was my first political article— a think piece on the Popular Front's economic experiment. In order not to make it easy for rightist propaganda, I published

this article in the *Revue de Métaphysique et de Morale* to reduce the number of readers to the minimum. Since then, as
you know, I have lost the scruples of a university professor.
This article had some impact, because I explained why the experiment had failed. In fact, today, except for a few details,
everyone agrees with me!

D.W. – You couldn't have, like Marjolin, tried to act from
the inside?

R.A. – And obtain the same results he did!

D.W. – Ah! No, wait! Only history could have told that.
Since you were sympathetic to the Popular Front, but didn't
like the unrealistic nature of its economic program, why
didn't you, like other intellectuals, join the Popular Front and
make them listen to reason from the inside?

R.A. – All right. To tell you the truth, at that time I was not a
political person; I was not a political news writer or an editorialist. It was my books that interested me most. It might seem
a bit ridiculous, but I was in a hurry to reach my goal: to finish
them before the war broke out. As I have told you, I foresaw
the war. It was impossible to say who would survive or not
survive. In any case, I said to myself: If I don't finish my thesis
before the war, I know that I will never finish it.

D.W. – Why?

R.A. – Because I was persuaded that I would not be able to
resume the task. . . . Finally, in the 1934-1938 period, I considered that I had no way to exercise any influence on anyone. I
think I wrote a letter to Léon Blum, who naturally did not reply. He didn't know who Raymond Aron was, why should he
have replied? On top of everything else—as I've told you—I
was Jewish, I was suspect. . . . To come back to the Popular
Front program, it was drafted just like that, by some nonde-
script group, and the Popular Front government considered
itself bound to respect the commitments it had assumed. Today, however, we know that at the moment the decision was
taken to apply the forty-hour-week law (envisaged by the
Communist party, but not by the Popular Front program) in
the most rigorous manner, there were nonetheless some hesi-
tations within the government. Some said, "Perhaps we are
going too far." But finally they went along. So, once again, as
has been usual in my life, I found myself isolated in a small
group, between two large groups—that is, between those

who were furiously against the Popular Front and those who believed it represented the dawn of a new society. . . .

D.W. – Was the role of the intellectuals important in the Popular Front?

R.A. – Yes, indeed. It was considerable, but I don't like to take advantage of hindsight to accuse any group. The Popular Front was in part a political response to the February events—February 1934. Daladier had been largely discredited by his role in the 1934 events and in order to return to power, he dragged the Radical party into the Popular Front, that is, into an alliance of the Communist, Socialist, and Radical parties. The anti-fascist intellectuals encouraged the Popular Front movement and they contributed to the writing of the Popular Front's program. Who did draw up this program? Why did those in power accept it as it was? Once again, the basic reason was ignorance. Just think that the big industrialists, the *grands patrons,* were all against the devaluation of the franc between 1934 and 1936, although such a devaluation would have been in their interest! This is why I have often tended to think that ignorance and stupidity are factors of considerable importance in history. And I often say that, toward the end, the last book I should like to write would be on the role of stupidity in history.

J.–L.M. – A big book, certainly. . . . You speak of the economic ignorance of the Popular Front. But how did you acquire your own competence in economic matters?

R.A. – It was very limited. I had never studied political economy at the university, but I had read some books. You know, it's not too difficult to learn by oneself. Later, I gave a course on political economy at the Ecole Normale, along with Marjolin, in 1936 or 1937. We had a lot of students at the beginning; many fewer at the end. The subject seemed to them to be outside their universe. Today, it would be altogether different. I recall having given about that time a lecture at the Ecole Normale on the world crisis, in which I used such terms as international liquidities, floating capital, world prices, and some others of the same kind. They didn't understand the sense of these words. Their difficulty was understandable, but when speaking about economics these words were useful.

D.W. – You were never very attracted to Marxism, at least not in that period.

R.A. – It's much more complicated. To tell the truth, I was very attracted to it. When I chose my intellectual itinerary, when I decided to be both an observer of, and an actor in, history, I began by studying Marx, in particular *Das Kapital*. I hoped to find a true philosophy of history that would provide the incomparable advantage of teaching us simultaneously that which is and that which ought to be. Now, Marxism, in the way it is commonly understood, is a global interpretation of history, followed by this conclusion: One must be on the side of the proletariat; one must arrive at socialism, which represents the end of prehistory. But after having studied Marxism for almost an entire year, I concluded with regret that, in this form, it was not acceptable. The analysis of history does not permit one to determine the policy to follow and to foresee, as an end result, a society from which contradictions among men would be eliminated. It is in this sense that I have defined my ideas *vis-à-vis* Marxism. Even today, I am interested in the Marxism of Marx, but not in that of Breshnev, which is very boring. But Marx's Marxism is very, very interesting.

J.–L.M. – And Communism, that is, the Bolshevik revolution and the Soviet experience? What were your reactions? Did this attract you? You did not make the trip to Moscow.

R.A. – I made it, but very late, when my opinions were already formed. Why? Because the 1920s were really very different from the years of your youth. To go to Moscow if one were not a Communist was not so easy. Then, to go there the way Duhamel and Fabre-Luce did, one went from one hotel to another. One didn't learn much about the reality of the Soviet Union. I was ignorant of this reality, rather neutral, though interested, but not attracted to it because I do not like violence and because, then already, I was a liberal by temperament. I didn't believe in messianism or in millenialism. So, during the 1920s bolshevism was not a principal object of speculation for me. But in the 1930s, we were more and more obsessed by totalitarianism. And totalitarianism meant Hitler, but also Stalin.

D.W. – Nonetheless, Hitler more than Stalin?

R.A. – Yes. Malraux and I, like the others, we were all anti-Hitler. I was antifascist, with simply some reservations about the way the term antifascist was used to include as fascist everything that one didn't like. But when I reflect upon it, I believe that in the 1930s Hitler represented for me such a menace to France that I refused to recognize part of the Soviet reality.

D.W. – You didn't put Hitler and Stalin on the same level at the time?

R.A. – I always have reservations about comparisons, while admitting the similarity of certain phenomena. National socialism governed Germany in peacetime for only six years; it didn't become fully totalitarian until the war and it appears today as the adventure of a pathological personality, marked also by genius. Communism continues, a great historic movement that has in the meantime passed beyond the frontiers of the Soviet Union. That much said, we know today that Stalin brought about the deaths of a still greater number of innocent people than Hitler.

D.W. – Were there people in those years who denounced the Soviet camps?

R.A. – Yes, of course: Souvarine, for example. There was the book on Stalin by Souvarine that I read at the time. It was, I think, published in 1937, with much difficulty. Gallimard refused it. It was republished two or three years ago. One should read it. It remains a book that sparkles with lucidity. Souvarine had been a Communist and for a few years he was the representative of the Comintern in Paris. He was a Trotskyite, then he broke with Trotsky. He was one of the first Frenchmen to know what the Soviet regime really was.

But I became free, really free, in my vision and judgment of the Soviet Union only with the Hitler-Stalin pact. As long as we had counted on an alliance with the Soviet Union to win the war against Hitler, we were half-paralyzed. We shouldn't have been. Perhaps we should have been! It's difficult to say, even today. For example, my friend Manès Sperber, who thought the worst about the Soviet Union, felt that one shouldn't tell everything because the number one danger, the more immediate one, was Hitler. Today, I have some doubts about the attitude we adopted, but that's the way it was. The truth of the matter is that it is difficult to admit that one is confronting two diabolic menaces at the same time and that it is necessary to be allied to one of the two. It was not pleasant, but it was the historic situation that we found extremely difficult to accept.

J.–L.M. – You tended to think that Souvarine must have been exaggerating?

R.A. – No, not necessarily. The fact is that I thought about it as seldom as possible. Like all the others, I was probably a little cowardly facing up to a reality about which I had a presentiment. There was always the thought in the background: we need the Soviet alliance.

D.W. – And then there was the idea that the Soviet Union nevertheless represented the struggle of the Left, the proletariat, the trend of history.

R.A. – Yes. In addition, we felt more attracted to the people who were for the Soviet Union than to the others. We detested those who were pro-Hitler, while those in favor of Stalin were often closer to us. So much so that the affective and intellectual kinship of the antifascist coalition is understandable even today. Politically, it was an absurdity. But it took the war, and the post-war period, for this bizarre alliance to break up definitely.

J.–L.M. – Were you suprised by the German-Soviet pact of August 1939?

R.A. – My wife has reminded me that when I heard the news, I repeated for five minutes, "It can't be possible." And then I thought about it and realized that, everything considered, it was rational. I have recently come upon two of my comments to that effect. In a talk to the French Philosophy Society in June 1939, I said that Hitler might, if he needed to, make an alliance with Stalin. I was wrong to add, "for the moment, that seems to me improbable." And then, a friend of mine, Jean Duval, told me that I had once spoken to him of an alliance between Hitler and Stalin as one of the possible, even probable, eventualities. The fact is that, on learning the news, I was dumbfounded and almost refused to believe it, for it was clear that it spelled war. I recall a conversation I had at the Ecole Normale in July, a month before the event, with Marcel Mauss, an eminent sociologist, and with Marc Bloch, the great historian of the preceding generation. Marc Bloch demonstrated to us in the most convincing way with a very simple argument that war would have to break out that summer. "The West," he said, "is committed to defend Poland. At the same time, Hitler is determined to settle the Polish problem once and for all. The belligerents have gone so far, it is improbable that either can back away. . . . So, war seems to me almost inevitable." Using hindsight, let me note that it was the guarantee given Poland by Great Britain and France that was in large measure responsible for the Hitler-Stalin pact. From the moment the Soviets were guaranteed that the West would fight for Poland, they felt sure they would not be isolated in the face of Nazi Germany. We hadn't anything more to give the Soviet Union. Like children, we jumped with joy when Poland was given the guarantees. We said to ourselves, "At last, we are standing firm." We hoped that it would permit a halt in the march toward war. It was foolish. The will to be firm had come too late. In providing an opportunity for the Hitler-Stalin pact, firmness meant war.

D.W. – Let us return to your work. It was a year before these events, in 1938, that you published your first important book, *Introduction to the Philosophy of History.* This book treats the relationship between events, their explanation and historic truth. You refuse both the idea of a direction of history with, on the horizon, the creation of an ideal society, as well as the idea of history without meaning. For you, there is no deterministic explanation of history, but an aggregate of constraints with which man tries to deal. And it is in this action that he finds freedom. Can you outline for us the principal ideas of the book?

R.A. – Let us say that there were three key ideas that continue to be guiding principles for me. The first is the plurality of the possible interpretations of men and of men's works. That is what is called historic relativism in the interpretation of the past. Then, there is a second key idea that is found in the next part of the book, on determinism. I try to demonstrate with logical reasons that there can be no global determinism of history like Marxist determinism. And then there is a third idea, which is at the origin of my approach to political life. It concerns the conditions of political action. I don't very often use the Sartrian word, "commitment," but, rather, two words that are nearly its equivalent. The first is the word "choice"; the second is the word "decision." What I try to analyze, to point out, is that to think politically in a society, one must first make a fundamental choice. This fundamental choice is either the acceptance of the kind of society in which we live, or its rejection. One is either revolutionary, or one is not. If one is revolutionary—if one rejects the society in which one lives—one chooses violence and adventure. From this fundamental choice flow decisions, timely decisions, by which the individual defines himself. After 1945, I have tried to explain why I do not favor the society that represents the alternative to the existing society.

D.W. – What was the alternative?

R.A. – I am not in favor of the kind of society one finds in the Soviet world. I am for our kind of society, whether it be American, French, English, or German, that is to say, a liberal-democratic society. However, within this society, there are at each instant decisions to make by which one defines oneself. The decision, for example, to be for Algerian independence or for a French Algeria; or, to take another example, the decision to be for or against this or that political administration.

The point I stressed in this analysis of political action that I am summarizing is that political action in our century is not a game, not a secondary matter. It is something more than just deciding that the Radical-Socialists or the Moderates will govern France. I pointed out that the act of decision, in this century, concerns not only our society but ourselves. To live in a totalitarian or in a liberal country, to choose one or the other, is something fundamental through which each person asserts what he is and what he wants to become. I tried to show that one could think of politics in a philosophical way and that, through politics, one molded one's self. In that sense, perhaps, everything that I wrote afterward has been inspired by this point of view concerning politics and history.

D.W. – It has sometimes been said that your *Introduction to the Philosophy of History* was the first existentialist book in France.

R.A. – Oh, I don't know. After the war, people liked to say that it was the existentialist philosophy of history. But I do not know very well just what existentialism is! Let us say that the questions that Sartre and I asked ourselves were largely the same ones. After the war, when we came together again, he gave me a copy of his *Being and Nothingness* with the following dedication: "For my old schoolmate, the ontological introduction to the ontic philosophy of history," or something of the kind, meaning that it was an ontological introduction, while, in the vocabulary of phenomenology, my analysis of history was ontic; it was the essence of a particular area of human reality, that is, the historic area. We often discussed the same problems and there are a certain number of examples that are to be found in both the *Introduction to the Philosophy of History* and *Being and Nothingness.*

D.W. – At the time, you used a triple formula: "Man is in history; man is historic; man is history." Is that correct?

R.A. – Yes, but should we plunge into technical philosophy? We are, in fact, in history: in the Fifth Republic, which emerged from the Fourth, which emerged from the Third. We are French. There has been a France for a thousand years, and so on. As for the second formula, "Man is historic," it means that man is modeled by the historic milieu into which he is born. He exists *in* and through the evolution of institutions and societies. Finally, "Man is history" signifies that the whole of humanity is a story, an adventure that began with a carnivorous animal and that will have its culmination I do not know where—perhaps at the point when men will have really become men, or when they will no longer be mainly carnivorous animals. Since I do not know the outcome, I say that "man is a story unfinished."

D.W. – At the end of your thesis, you write that history is free because it is not written in advance nor determined like nature or fatality; that it is unpredictable, as man is for himself. Forty years later, after all the events that you have lived through, do you still subscribe to this philosophy of history?

R.A. – Certainly. But we should be a little more subtle. There are great movements in history that are by and large predictable; they are those called "ponderous movements." One can, obviously, predict approximately the size of the French population twenty or thirty years from now, excluding the accident of a war. But there is no global determination of historic events. Consequently, what concerns us most—the quality of our institutions, the nature of the state, the quality of men—all that is for the most part unpredictable. Yes, I would stay with the formula I like rather well: "History is unpredictable, as man is himself." In every man, we can expect the best and the worst; personally, I would like never to despair of any man, in any case never despair of men, even though our century has given us many reasons to despair.

c) The Decadence of France

J.–L.M. – Alas, it was the worst that appeared in 1938, the year your book was published. War seemed inevitable and yet in France, in this period, pacificism was dominant in all the social classes. Why?

R.A. – Because the French felt, rightly, that war, whatever its issue, would be a catastrophe for France. Drained of its life-blood in World War I, France could not stand a second such experience even if it ended in victory. A little bit like men acting under the stress of emotion, the French did their best from 1933 to 1939 to bring about war, because they were afraid of it, and the fear was a justified one. In 1936, the intellectuals drafted one resolution after another. "Thankfully," said everyone, "we didn't have to use military force." Everyone. In 1938, they all said, "We avoided war, and the mere fact of having avoided it is good." We had to be pushed to the wall for there to be a kind of acceptance of misfortune.

J.–L.M. – However, one of the significant events of the time was the war in Spain and some people were favorable to intervention there.

R.A. – Most of them were Communists and a small number of other people close to the Communists. For France, intervention wasn't the same thing as war. The Spanish problem was different. The revolution there came from the Right; it was a fascist-type revolution, if you will. It was supported by Mussolini and Hitler; by the Italians and the Germans. The question that confronted the Popular Front government was: Should we support officially, openly, the Spanish Republican party? Or should we keep foreign interventions to a minimum? Léon Blum made the decision not to intervene in Spain because the British government told him that if, following an intervention in Spain, there was a war, Great Britain would not follow or support him.

D.W. – Were you, personally, favorable to intervention in Spain or were you neutralist?

R.A. – I thought Léon Blum was right. The government did not have the right to intervene in Spain in a cause that profoundly divided the French.

D.W. – Yes, but all the same, the cause was democracy! And the Nazis and Fascists were helping Franco.

R.A. – Half of the French people were against intervention there. It was difficult to risk a diplomatic crisis with half the country against the government. Diplomatic accords somewhat reduced the German and Italian interventions. But it should be added that the Franco government did not intervene in World War II. That proves that for once we were not mistaken.

J.–L.M. – Did the ruling class understand international problems? Better than they understood economic questions?

R.A. – Look, I think that on the whole, neither the conservatives nor the socialists, for the most part, understood anything about national socialism or Russian communism. In the final years before the war, I often met Hermann Rauschning, who is still known today because his books have recently been republished, particularly *Germany's Revolution of Nihilism*. His searching analysis of naziism was understood by only a very few of the French. Twentieth-century events are difficult to understand for men whose formative years were in the nineteenth-century. Léon Blum was a superior figure, but his intellectual formation antedated 1914. He never understood the economy of the 1930s, the depression years. He did not have a deep understanding of national socialism. On communism, yes, he was extremely prescient. It was he who wanted to save the Socialist party from Communist domination. But whether it was a question of naziism or communism, even he did not fully understand, it seems to me, what we now have come to comprehend: the nature of the totalitarian phenomenon. Just think that in the nineteenth century—at the end of the nineteenth century—the deportation of seventy-five thousand Russians to Siberia was the scandal of Europe. The fact that one needed a passport or a visa to enter Russia was considered proof that it was not a truly modern country. In 1914, the world entered a period of violence and super-violence that nineteenth-century men have found difficult to understand. We of the succeeding generation were not superior to them. We simply understood more quickly than the older generation that something new was happening as a result of World War I. The democratic and liberal Europe of the end of the nineteenth century— democratic and liberal for itself, not for Africa or Asia—this bourgeois Europe was dead. The regimes that we were fated

to confront were radically different from our own. Even today, many of the deeds of national socialism remain difficult
to understand because of their diabolic excess. The same is
true of the Soviet Union. It is difficult to understand that a regime invoking Marxism and prosperity, is today essentially a
military power, with a standard of living much lower than
that of Spain. There is something about that quite grotesque
for logical processes of thought. To create an empire through
military power, in the name of Marxism . . . well, it took some
time to understand.

J.–L.M. – You are severe with Blum. To listen to you, he
failed in everything.

R.A. – No, if I mention him it is because he was the best of
them all. He was by far, morally and intellectually, the superior personality of the governing class. I am not trying to heap
blame upon him at all, quite the contrary. I respect him profoundly. But it would be fatuous to try to paint Léon Blum as a
man who was always right. No, he was always a courageous, a
respectable man, but he didn't understand economics. He
didn't understand the Popular Front program. He was often
mistaken, like everyone else. But compared to many others,
he had an intellectual and moral style that set him apart.

J.–L.M. – Who were the other outstanding men of the governing class of the period?

R.A. – There was one intelligent man, Paul Reynaud, and
he was the only one. I knew him rather well after the war; I
think he liked me, and I liked him. He understood before all
the others the need to devalue the franc, and he had argued
for necessary economic measures two years earlier. He understood what national socialism and Hitler's doctrine meant and
he tried to convince his Moderate party friends. He understood what tank divisions were. And he understood General
de Gaulle, or, rather, Colonel de Gaulle, at the time. All of
which signifies that on the fundamental questions of the
1930s, Reynaud, and he alone, was right. But there exists a
phenomenon that I will call "the tragedy of history." This
man who had for such a long time been right before the
others, arrived in power at a moment when he could only
preside over the disaster, and what a disaster! He turned
power over to the Marshal, to a faction that detested him. Let
me say simply that Reynaud represents the tragedy of a man

destined to be the guiding light of his generation, but who finally got the opportunity to accede to power only on the eve of the catastrophe that swept him away. It reminds me a bit of Cailloux in the preceding generation, during the 1914-18 war.

J.–L.M. – And Daladier?

R.A. – I didn't know him before the war, because I was not a political figure, not even a journalist. I saw him once or twice. My most precise recollection is at The Hague in 1947. There was a meeting on European union. I can still see him. He was alone. He was walking in a square of the city, as if in the past. No one went over to him. I had the feeling it was a kind of injustice. I went to him—I hardly knew him—and I talked with him at some length before I could bring him back to the present. After that, I saw him two or three times again. He was much more lucid about things than people say. I don't think he had the necessary moral strength to face up to events. But I think that the responsibility of individuals is to a very large extent surpassed by the collective responsibility of the nation. That is, from 1936 on, Hitler could not be stopped except by war, by a war that the French did not want!

D.W. – Is that the moral of the story?

R.A. – That's the moral of the story. And that war—the French were right not to want it.

D.W. – But it would have been possible to stop Hitler without risking war when he occupied the Rhineland in 1936?

R.A. – Without any risk. That's certain. Without risk. Hitler had given the order to the Bundeswehr to enter the Rhineland, with one reservation imposed upon the high command. If French troops advanced, the German troops were to withdraw. We know that today. We know that in March of 1936 the course of history could have been changed. That is part of my philosophy of history. That is a date, a fundamental one, when lucidity and a bit of courage would have sufficed to alter the future. But, unfortunately, Hitler was right. There was no chance of finding a government in France capable of taking that decision.

J.–L.M. – There was no government in France at that moment, was there?

R.A. – You are mistaken. It was when German troops entered Vienna, in 1938, that France was without a government. As early as March 1936, it was Albert Sarraut who defined the meaning of the term "unacceptable." He said that it was unacceptable to have Strasbourg under the fire of German cannon, but to say that it is unacceptable is to say that one accepts it.

D.W. – The last important event before the war was Munich, the Munich pact of 1938. In the final analysis, Munich meant dishonor, abandonment?

R.A. – It is difficult to say. At that time, I was teaching at the Ecole Normale at Saint-Cloud. Right after Munich, I opened my course by explaining for half-an-hour that what we had done, what France had done, was not very honorable. But I added that those who favored holding the line in order to avoid war were making things look too easy: There was absolutely no way of knowing, I told them, whether Hitler would have gone to war or not if we had resisted. Today, we know that Hitler had taken the decision to go to war if France and England opposed his aims. But we also knew that there was a military plot, about which my friend Rauschning had spoken to me, so there remains an incertitude even today. My present judgment is much more shaded than today's conventional opinion, according to which Munich signified both dishonor and war. In point of fact, showing firmness in 1938 would have been tantamount to accepting the risk of war. Would the war have been preferable in 1938, rather than in 1939? We're not at all sure. What is certain is that the Munich accords were not honorable. But in terms of *realpolitik*, the matter is still open to discussion. In any case, it seems to me unjust and egregious to make a clear-cut distinction between "good" people and "bad" people, according to whether they were for or against Munich. I'll give you a striking example. In 1938, after Munich, I had lunch with Sartre and Simone de Beauvoir. Both were in favor of Munich, for pacifist reasons, because—they said—one does not have the right to dispose of the life of others. Later, Sartre wrote a novel in which all those who were for Munich were depicted as bastards, which proves that one can, on the question of Munich, hold contradictory opinions without being, once and for all, either condemned or praised.

J.–L.M. – At the time, IFOP[11] conducted, on the subject of Munich, France's first public opinion poll. There were two questions. The first: "Do you approve the Munich accords?" Yes: 57%; No: 37%. The second question: "Do you think that

France and England should from now on resist any further exigencies on the part of Hitler?" Yes: 70%; No: 17%. Isn't that contradictory?

R.A. – No. It is understandable. As long as Ted Kennedy was not formally a candidate for the presidency, he had a very high rating in the polls. From one day to the next, when he became a candidate, his rating dropped by half. That poll on Munich reflects a similar phenomenon. When 70% of the French favored firmness "the next time," it concerned a situation that did not yet exist. After Munich, there was a majority of perfectly sincere Frenchmen ready to say, "No, things cannot go on like that! There must be a limit!" But just what does this will to be firm mean when one is not yet faced with the need actually to resist? And what is the real value of the poll that expresses such a readiness?

J.–L.M. – Were those in favor of Munich and those against acting as individuals? Or were they not, rather, the incarnation of social and political forces?

R.A. – It is difficult to say. On the side of those who were against Munich, there were the Communists, and a certain number of nationalists like Kérillis or Reynaud. There were those who were half-against Munich, like Léon Blum. You know the phrase, "cowardly relief." On the other hand, there were some Frenchmen who detested the Popular Front. I wouldn't say they were Nazi sympathizers, but their attitude (toward the Popular Front) inclined them to be more for Munich than against it. In so far as individuals are concerned, there were some favorable to Munich who became Resistance heroes. And some of those who were against Munich were not Resistance heroes. Well. I would say that overall, probably, those who were against Munich were later on the side of the Resistance, but I am not sure, and no one can confirm it with certainty.

To come back to the point. In a question of this gravity, one that put the very existence of France into the balance, I think it was necessary to calculate the available forces and, above all, the military forces. At the time, the English did not have the Spitfires. Those Spitfires that won the Battle of Britain— they wouldn't have had them in 1938. They did have them in 1940. There was another difficulty: The German claims to the Sudetenland were not entirely unjustified. The Germans of the Sudetenland were Germans. To start a world war in order to maintain Germans inside Czechoslovakia was at least a debatable question, even for men with a sense of moral responsibility. Now, what happened in Munich was not honorable in the light of French commitments, but on the other hand, Bénès could have refused to accept the Munich accords.

D.W. – But how could he have done that, since the accords were signed by Great Britain, France, and Hitler? And he wasn't present, or even invited?

R.A. – He could have refused. Do you know what Bénès said after the war? In 1946, he had the visit of a person whose name I will not cite; he opened the window and said, "Look, Prague is there, intact, and it is thanks to me, after all."

D.W. – All right. He could perhaps have refused the accords. But, then, that would have meant war a year earlier, as you have said. In delaying the outbreak of war until September 1939 did we at least gain the time to prepare ourselves militarily?

R.A. – No, at least an additional year would have been necessary.

J.–L.M. – Would it have been possible to prepare ourselves for war in two years?

R.A. – Yes, modern assault tanks would have been more numerous, airplanes also. That said, you understand, the 1940 defeat was not due solely to the lack of equipment; it was essentially a strategic military defeat. So it is very difficult to know what would have happened if the war had broken out in 1938.

J.–L.M. – Did the Popular Front's social legislation bear any responsibility in the lack of military preparation?

R.A. – Very, very little. Léon Blum made an exception to the forty-hour workweek law in the armament industries. The disorders that followed the Popular Front certainly slowed down industrial production for some months. But I do not at all believe that the Popular Front's decisions were directly responsible for the defeat. That would be ridiculous. I would even add that the Popular Front voted sizable appropriations for armament. On this point, it must be declared innocent.

J.–L.M. – And the military's responsibility in the defeat?

R.A. – I have written a good deal on the subject. I would have a great many things to say, but I don't think this is the occasion. I believe the 1940 defeat was essentially a military one. It was determined by a successful maneuver by the adversary against a French army that was incapable of reacting to the situation it faced. Don't force me to go back over the question of responsibility for the 1940 defeat. I am in no position to do that, especially in a few words here. A debate would be necessary.

To limit myself to the years preceding the war, to this long march toward war, I think that only the threat of war could have stopped Hitler and that, after 1936, the threat became progressively less credible as Hitler became militarily stronger than those who threatened him. It was he who wanted this war; the others did not want it. The role of chance in the course of events is this: after 1936, one could have stopped Hitler only by the threat of a general war; the threat was made in 1938; he didn't believe us and he was right, since we capitulated! He didn't believe in the threat in 1939, either. But that time, with the war breaking out unexpectedly, he accepted it because he wanted it. But he launched into it by improvising, without having really prepared for it. The most astonishing thing is that we believed at the time that he had accumulated enormous, powerful armaments. This was not true. When he began the French campaign, he had fewer than two thousand planes. Germany began the war in 1939 without being mobilized. It became fully mobilized only after the defeat at Stalingrad. What all that signifies is that it was a story, an adventure in which the principal actor was Hitler, and in which the others were the victims.

D.W. – When did you cease to be a pacifist?

R.A. – In a sense, I have remained one all my life. I detest war, that is why I have written so much about it. But it was in 1932 or 1933 that I stopped being a pacifist in Alain's sense of the term; that is, refusing once and for all to conceive the eventuality of a war. Alain liked to repeat Bertrand Russell's formula: "All the evils that we try to avoid by war are less grave than war itself." Beginning in 1932 or 1933, I believed this formula was wrong; I came to believe, that is, that the results of the enemy's victory can be worse than the misfortunes of war.

D.W. – War is not necessarily worse than all other evils?

R.A. – What do you think about that today? One can always argue indefinitely. One can say that if Hitler's Germany had been accepted, it would have become viable or livable after three generations! . . .

J.–L.M. – Was France still pacifist at the time it entered the war?

R.A. – Half-pacifist. It was resigned to the war. But, was it determined to fight the war? That is another question.

J.–L.M. – At what point did you begin to think that the war was inevitable?

R.A. – Listen, from 1936 on, I believed the war was very probable, but I nevertheless clung to the hope that it could be avoided. After 1938, for example, the most intelligent man I ever knew, A. Kojève, did not believe there would be a war. He felt that Great Britain, that British capitalism, had already put Europe in Hitler's hands. He didn't see any reason why Hitler should make war since, after 1938, he was already victorious. He was mistaken because he tried to interpret history in terms of concepts, of great fundamental forces, while national socialism was essentially Hitler, the personality of Hitler. You know what he said one day to the Ambassador of, I think, Great Britain. "I prefer to wage war while I am at the peak of my strength," he said, "at fifty years of age, not later." To say that is to give an almost extravagant personal quality to political action. He said often, "Only I am capable of leading this war." So, this war had to break out while he was there and in his prime, as he put it.

J.–L.M. – Did you sense this dimension of personal adventure at the time?

R.A. – Yes, to a certain degree. Nazism seemed to me, in fact, the adventure of an individual more than a historical movement like communism. I realize one might answer that if Hitler had destroyed the Soviet Union and communism, Nazism would have perhaps become a historical movement, and that possibly, the spread of communism that we have witnessed would not have occurred. I think that there was nevertheless more intellectual substance and ideology in communism. Because, if one wishes to create an empire, it is necessary to act like the Soviets: Proclaim the equality of all peoples and hypocritically pretend that they are self-governing. By doing so, one can create an empire, in the dissembling style of the twentieth century; but to begin by proclaiming, as Hitler did, the superiority of a master race and declaring other peoples inferior is not an effective means of domination. It is an absurdity.

J.–L.M. – Isn't it pushing the role of individuals in history a bit far to make a world war dependent on the will of a single man?

R.A. – That is not what I mean. After World War I, all the conditions for a second one were present. The Europe created at Versailles was not stable. As Bainville said, "The Versailles Treaty was too harsh in its mild features, too mild in its harsh aspects." Germany could not accept the statute of Versailles. The French alliances were fragile. The countries of eastern Europe between the Soviet Union and Germany were a prey offered to one or the other, or both. So, all the conditions necessary for the repetition of the first World War existed. I have spoken of a "chain of wars," meaning that it was the first war that triggered the second. But the particular form that this second war assumed: the date, the modalities, all that, owes much to Hitler, just as the French wars of the Revolution and the Empire owe something to Napoleon. That French troops went as far as Lisbon in one direction, and as far as Moscow in the other, is just as wild, when one thinks about it, as what Hitler did. Since Napoleon was French and a national hero, everyone assumed it was normal, but it wasn't at all!

D.W. – Did you return to Germany between 1934 and 1938?

R.A. – Never. I went back for the first time only in 1945 or 1946, amid the ruins.

J.–L.M. – Let's return to the situation in France just before the war. The Popular Front was the great event of the time. You have spoken to us about it mostly from an economic point of view. But the Popular Front was also a state of mind, an atmosphere, mass demonstrations. You seemed not to share this fervor. Why?

R.A. – So you're going back to it! For men of the Left, the Popular Front was an important moment in social history and in social reform in France. They obviously think back to the mass demonstrations, the general enthusiasm, paid vacations; and they recall the reduction of the workweek, the increase in salaries. For a few weeks, there was certainly for many a lyrical illusion of peaceful semi-revolution. But there is a half of France, a small half of France, that remembers another side of the Popular Front, a kind of anarchy, the occupation of factories, the threat to their conception of order. Those who belong neither to the Right nor to the Left, or who at least try to be above both, are torn, like myself, between two strong feelings. On the one hand, to be sure, it represented a great movement of social reform, and on the other, it represented the conduct of an absurd economic policy, whose consequences were deplorable. So when the Left extols the Popular Front, it reflects to some extent its propensity for celebrating its defeats, because at the end of the six months or a year, the Left had lost and its failure was due to an unworkable economic policy.

D.W. – Yes, but you have to admit that the international situation was particularly tense!

R.A. – Certainly, but that was part of the circumstances that had to be taken into account.

D.W. – You say there were strikes and factory sit-ins, but there is nothing extraordinary about that in a democratic system.

R.A. – Of course. I'm not arguing about the strikes. I am simply trying to explain the state of mind of a part of the French people who felt the country menaced by the rise in Nazi power. If we had been an island, it would have been different; but we were in a historical situation that was politically dangerous, perhaps already dramatic.

J.–L.M. – You are saying, in short, "It was unreasonable." But, isn't an emancipation from social domination always unreasonable?

R.A. – No! It was unreasonable to reduce the workweek to forty hours during a period when the average worktime was forty-five hours. I do not see the necessity, when one intends to improve the condition of men, to reduce available resources—and that's what the Popular Front did. I do not see the necessity, when one is on the Left and favors the well-being of the population, to apply perfectly unreasonable economic measures whose consequences were evident. You want to press me? All right! You belong to another generation; you did not live through those years. I lived through them precisely as I am describing them today, that is, in a state of exasperation against glaring economic errors; in despair that a reform movement—that could have been glorious—had to end up in a more or less disastrous defeat. These contradictory sentiments have always defined my person and, in this case, my attitude toward events.

D.W. – But isn't what happened earlier responsible for that failure?

R.A. – To say that I didn't agree with the Popular Front's policy doesn't mean that I agreed with the previous policy; I found it wholly unreasonable, also, in the opposite sense. A good part of the Right, for example the weeklies like *Je Suis partout, Candide, Gringoire,* were horrible, represented the extreme Right, and made me not only leftist but absolutely furious. Well. To top it all, the economic policy followed between 1933 and 1936 resulted not only in prolonging the crisis, but in assuring the Popular Front victory. The disorder of 1936 was provoked and justified to a large degree by the foolishness of the earlier measures taken by the Right. So you're not going to succeed in classifying me on one side or the other! You absolutely want to end up by doing so, but no, you don't stand a chance.

D.W. – We are only trying to understand why, in the face of one of the great moments of social and political emancipation in the history of France or in the history of the Left, in fact, you hesitate. . . .

R.A. – I repeat that necessary social reforms were accomplished and they should have been legislated long before, but that at the same time, these reforms were accompanied by an economic policy not very well conceived, to say the least, so that today the social reforms can be acclaimed only if one forgets the negative aspects of the Popular Front. But some people like myself have a certain difficulty in forgetting that, only two weeks after the Popular Front assumed power, we said, "The economic experiment has failed."

J.–L.M. – You have said, "The Left adores celebrating its defeats." What do you mean by that?

R.A. – Let's take the Commune, an atrocious episode, detestable from every point of view, even though there were some admirable men in the Commune. It was a people's revolt that was once again smothered and with terrible means: The French army, itself defeated by the Prussians and Germans, triumphed over the people of Paris before the eyes of the Germans. I do not know any episode in French history so heartrending for a Frenchman. Now, one always celebrates this period—one that makes me want to weep because there is nothing more terrible than a defeated army winning a victory over its own people! Nonetheless, every year people recall the glory of the Commune. There were admirable men in the Commune, that is certain! But as an episode in French history it is appalling. No? Don't you think so?

D.W. – If it is heartbreaking, it is because it was experienced as a repression of the people, and not as a victory for the Left.

R.A. – I don't like to praise civil wars. I detest civil wars and that of the Commune was one of the most detestable in French history, because nothing came of it, except deaths.

J.–L.M. – Something came of 1936, nonetheless?

R.A. – Yes. First, it wasn't horrible. Then, some reforms did emerge. But most of all it has remained a great memory. It is normal for people to live with a certain number of memories, even though the economist remembers something else, like failures and measures poorly conceived. A recollection of liberation: Certainly, I realize workers can find sustenance in that. But I don't want to be hypocritical. I have never been a worker. I was born in a bourgeois family, so I am a bourgeois, which didn't prevent me, by the way, from having desired, before 1936, the social reforms that were carried out in 1937. I wanted the Popular Front government to succeed. And I was not in despair, that would be perhaps exaggerated, but disappointed by a failure that was predictable and that could have been avoided if those who held responsibility had been more aware of economic reality.

J.–L.M. – You said, "The press of the Right and of the extreme Right was horrible." What was horrible about it?

R.A. – Everything. It lived on hate, it fed hate, it created a climate of permanent civil war in France. The way it spoke of Léon Blum, the Jews, the Left, the unions, the workers, was enough to drive one berserk. You didn't know the pre-war Right. It was inconceivable for a man like me to be its partisan. All that one could do was to write in the *Revue de Métaphysique et de Morale* that there were errors committed by the Popular Front. But to be on the side of those who are today labeled the Right—let's say Guy Mollet or Giscard d'Estaing—that is possible. Perhaps not for you, but for me it's possible.

The pre-war Right was both poorly informed about economic reality and ferocious in the defense of its privileges and power. It failed to understand the very essence of modern economics, growth. Of the Right of Charles Maurras there remains practically nothing. As for the so-called "New Right," that is something else again.

D.W. – You say that the Right was horrible. And yet, when you returned from Germany, you believed there was no fascist danger in France.

R.A. – For the following reason: In the elections, those elected from the Right were moderates and not extremists. Members of the *Croix-de-Feu*[12] were by no means fascist. They were war veterans. Colonel de la Rocque was not a charismatic leader capable of becoming a fascist dictator. There were elections in which the Right received a majority. But it was not a fascist Right. Well. One found among them a type of business leader who, to express myself with moderation, had little intelligence, who wasn't even aware of his interests and who clung to his positions. On the other hand, there were some intellectuals who were occasionally of the extreme Right or tending toward fascism. There were some fascist sects. But there was no big fascist party. There was never the equivalent of the German elections that produced a large number of deputies from the National Socialist party. It is in this sense that I meant that, at the time, there was not a fascist peril in the way there was a national socialist peril in Germany.

J.–L.M. – Your description of pre-war France gives the impression of a country in an impasse, of a country without awareness of itself.

R.A. – No, of a country in decadence. I lived through the 1930s in despondency about French decadence, with the feeling that France was sinking into nothingness. One should have had a presentiment of the catastrophe that the war would be. Basically, France didn't exist any longer. It existed only in the hatred of the French for each other.

J.–L.M. – But why this decadence?

R.A. – I really don't know! I cannot answer in a few words. I lived through it intensely, with profound sadness and with a single obsession: to avoid civil war. I would have wanted to explain to the men of the Left that if there was a war to fight, it wasn't against other Frenchmen, but one to fight all together against the real enemy—at that time, Nazi Germany. I would have wanted to explain the same thing to those on the Right who understood nothing of the situation. As often happened in my life, I was between two groups, without much opportunity to express myself or to be listened to. Many other Frenchmen around me recognized this decadence. The extenuating circumstance for those who became Fascists or even collaborators during the war lay in their revolt against the French decadence of the 1930s. For a man like Drieu La Rochelle, for example, who had been deeply affected by it, fascism was a means of ending French decadence, a dream in which France would find itself in a national socialist Europe. An idiotic idea, of course.

J.–L.M. – Were despair and sadness the dominant emotions of your youth?

R.A. – During the 1930s, yes. But I was young then and happy as a person. One can be happy with one's family, with one's friends, in one's work, and at the same time feel despair at the nation's decadence. When I try to evoke the 1930s, I recall feeling both emotions, despair and happiness, together and with exceptional intensity. My comrades, my friends, were people of exceptional intelligence: Eric Weil, Kojève, Alexandre Koyré, Robert Marjolin, Malraux, Sartre—in short, all people who had earned a reputation, and who had accomplished something in life. We discussed world history with Kojève, economic reconstruction with Marjolin. Koyré and Weil were philosophers of the highest order. They, too, viewed with despondency the decadence of France and the approach of War. What more is there to say? I have never again lived in a milieu so sparkling with intelligence and so warm in friendship as during the 1930s, and I have never again known historic despair to the same degree. Because, after 1945, France was transformed, but that's another story!

II
THE DARK YEARS, 1940-1945

a) Departure for London

J.–L. Missika. – The war broke out in September 1939; you were drafted.

Raymond Aron. – Yes. I did my military service in meteorology—not particularly glorious—as did Sartre after me. I was sent to a meteorological station that was called the OMI, near Charleville. After a few weeks, the captain and then the lieutenant, who were technicians, were sent elsewhere. I then became the head of this detachment of a dozen or so soldiers. We remained near Charleville during the "phony war." There wasn't much to do except to send up little balloons. I was able to work. In particular, I helped update Elie Halévy's *Histoire du Socialisme*. I also worked on Machiavelli. It was a study that I had begun before the war. And then, the attack came, exactly in the region where I was stationed. Those were the weeks of battle and disaster that were morally intolerable. One had the feeling of being totally useless, unable to do anything. Later, we were taken over by the army in full retreat, then swept up in the exodus of civilians. You cannot imagine what those weeks were for those who lived through them.

J.–L.M. – Did you receive orders?

R.A. – Oh, not always. When we sensed the Germans coming, we went away. It was just sheer luck that we were not taken prisoners. We crossed the Loire River at Gien. There was some bombing and we had one or two wounded. We watched the bombs falling, but did nothing—like the others. Those in meteorology units had been furnished rifles of 1885 or 1888 vintage. That was all. We never saw the Germans. Well, we did see the airplanes that flew overhead, but there was little chance of hitting them by firing 1885 rifles.

I had a feeling of shame, of unworthiness. It was unbearable to live through such a period in those conditions. Toward June 20th or 22nd, we found ourselves near Bordeaux. We heard Marshal Pétain's speech. I remembered something, inaccurately, as it turned out. I thought that he had said, "We are going to try to put an end to the struggle." But I don't think he could have said "to try"; that must have been in my imagination. Then I took a motorcycle and went to Toulouse, where my wife was staying. There, my wife and I decided that I should leave for Great Britain, where, in fact, I arrived on June 26th.

D. Wolton. – When you heard Marshal Pétain on the radio, what was your reaction?

R.A. – The same as that of all the Frenchmen around me; I felt rather relieved. It was very difficult, in the midst of all those defeated soldiers and displaced civilians, to say, "It's outrageous to sign the armistice!" One felt indignation, but also compassion. It was almost impossible not to share cowardly relief, in a way. But for me, the armistice did not mean the end of the war, even though it marked a temporary end of the war for France. I had no illusions about the Pétain government that had assumed power. It represented those Frenchmen who had been against what they called "warmongering" and who had sought accommodation with Germany. But for me, at that moment, in the month of June, the question was: Will Great Britain hold on through the summer of 1940? When one left for England in June 1940, one left for the war. That was the motivation of those who wanted to leave. There were few such people around me.

D.W. – Exactly what was your feeling regarding Marshal Pétain at the moment of the 1940 armistice?

R.A. – I want to be honest: neither indignation nor rage. Pétain seemed to me to be the expression of the dominant feelings of the majority of Frenchmen. When I arrived in Toulouse, when I found my wife and friends again, the atmosphere was totally different, because the people around me were already Resistants. There was Canguilhem, for example, who was a great Resistant and who was against the armistice as early as June 22nd or 23rd. But he was in a city where people did not perhaps yet understand the national disaster that I

had experienced in one *département*[13] after another, in full retreat, in the midst of soldiers and civilians.

J.–L.M. – When you were part of the general retreat, did
you have the feeling of having been overtaken by events, of
not understanding what was happening?

R.A. – No, not at all. From the moment we realized that the
best French divisions had been lost in Belgium, it was clear
that the defeat was complete. It was known ten days after the
fight began. The battle was lost in four days. People without
information, like myself, knew it at the end of ten days. The
Somme River resistance could not succeed. The Germans by
then had a very evident superiority in numbers and equipment. The battle was lost because we dashed into Belgium
and Holland with our best divisions. They were not defeated
in battle, but surrounded. From that moment on, it was all
over.

J.–L.M. – How could a force as powerful as the French
army lose a battle like that in four or five days?

R.A. – Confronting Napoleon at Jena, the Prussian army
disappeared in twenty-four hours. In 1940, there were 100
French divisions, a considerable force. But from the moment
the army's spearhead was destroyed in Belgium, the battle
was lost. It was the result of a classic encirclement maneuver.
In 1914, the Schlieffen plan was designed to encircle the
whole of the French army by crossing Belgium. In 1940, Marshal von Manstein had the idea of passing through the Ar-
dennes plateau, which made it possible to cut off the French
and British units from the rest of the army. What followed is
of little importance. Besides, one mustn't forget that the Russians, in the first two weeks of battle, lost more divisions than
the French even possessed, between 100 and 150 divisions.
The truth is that the German army outclassed all the others. It
was finally defeated, like the French army of 1812, by the
winter, by geography, and by the still primitive character of
the Soviet Union.

D.W. – When you arrived in England, what did you find?
Panic?

R.A. – No, not at all. I had come from France, where the
population was aimlessly fleeing along the roads, amid the
ruins and in despair. I hardly spoke any English at that point. I
nevertheless understood the words of encouragement of a

confident Englishman who said to me, "We'll get your country back for you by Christmas." The English were then in their "finest hour," but most of the population didn't understand the danger. The lawns were impeccable, as always. On their island, the English were very tranquil. But, for me, coming from France, it was a shock to find such tranquility in a country so threatened.

D.W. – When you decided to leave for England, had you heard General de Gaulle's appeal mentioned? In other words, did you leave for England or did you join General de Gaulle?

R.A. – I didn't hear the appeal personally. I think that someone told me about it when I passed through Toulouse. And on the boat, yes, I certainly heard about it. But at the time, it was not a question of leaving to join de Gaulle or simply leaving for Great Britain: One either wanted to be with those who were continuing the war, or one stayed in France, resigned. That was, of course, a mistaken concept, since France was not destined to accept resignation. There was the Resistance and there were other events. But at the particular moment, the choice was to help those who were carrying on the fight, or to return home. I chose the first course, in agreement with my wife.

D.W. – How did you leave France?

R.A. – I left my detachment which was near Bordeaux and went to Bayonne, where I stayed overnight. I slept in a train that held all the stocks of the Paris Stock Exchange. This seemed extraordinarily comical to me, and even had a philosophic side: the futile nature of stocks became evident in the moment of catastrophe. It was the only time I ever got close to stocks.

From Bayonne, I went to Saint-Jean-de-Luz, probably by car. There, a Polish division was leaving; very officially, for Great Britain. With a few dozen other lost souls like myself, I slipped aboard the boat among the Poles. The boat's name was the *Ettrick*. While on it, I heard the announcement of the armistice. It was no surprise. From the moment negotiations begin, an armistice is almost necessarily the result. Then London, Olympia Hall, where a few thousand French soldiers of every origin were assembled. We were shortly transferred to a camp where English officers asked each of us, "Do you wish to be repatriated to France?" "Do you wish to stay in England as a civilian or as an English soldier?" "Do you wish to join the Gaullist movement?" Naturally, I joined the Gaullist movement. It was the beginning of July, I think.

J.–L.M. – And the other Frenchmen? Did many wish to remain in England?

R.A. – Among those who were present, only a very tiny majority. Almost everyone wanted to return to France. For them, the war was over. France was defeated, occupied. Well, it was over. They hadn't left for England or for de Gaulle; they had been brought to England, either from Dunkirk, or from one of the other ports on the Channel or on the North Sea that had been surrounded by the Germans, thus making a retreat to France impossible. So, how many did remain? I can't say, but not many. I joined a company of assault tanks. There were at least two men there who have become very well-known. One was François Jacob, a future Nobel Prize winner, then a medical student. The other was the minister, Galley. I chose the tank corps because I still remembered those weeks of unbearable inaction. But they decided I was too old for tank service. Since I knew how to write and count, they made me company clerk. For a few weeks, I added pounds, shillings, and pence. I acquired a certain skill in those calculations that were relatively difficult for a Frenchman. But I found the job exasperating.

J.–L.M. – How did you get out of that?

R.A. – During the war, and perhaps during my whole life, my destiny has constantly changed as the result of an encounter. One of the section heads in the technical department at de Gaulle's headquarters, a man named André Labarthe, whom I did not know, had read my books. One day, he wrote me with an invitation to visit him in London. The General had given him the responsibility of creating a monthly French periodical. I went to see him three days before I was due to leave for Dakar with the few French soldiers in London who was assigned to win over French West Africa for de Gaulle. Everyone knew we were leaving for Dakar! In London, Labarthe went all out to persuade me. "Anyone can handle the paper work in a tank company. But a French periodical is indispensable and we cannot do it without you," and so on. I asked for permission to think it over. I was torn between the two options. The first was that I had come in order to fight.

The other was the fact that a periodical at that moment had a certain significance because there was no longer a French presence outside of France. Rightly or wrongly, for motives I cannot figure out myself, I decided to join the periodical.

D.W. – Can you recall its title for us?

R.A. – *La France Libre*. The periodical quickly became important because of the stir it created in Great Britain and its worldwide circulation, and also because for a few years almost nothing came out of occupied France. Jean-Paul Sartre published an article on it in *Combat*.[14] A few days ago, I met Alfred Cobban, well-known in France as the finest English historian of the French Revolution. He said to me, "I have already met you once; I called upon you at *La France Libre* during the war. For me, your monthly was at the time France's only intellectual presence." He had been a reader for years. At the start, it was a periodical of the Gaullist movement. But it soon began to take a certain distance. "What we appreciated in that periodical," Cobban told me, "was that it was not propaganda."

D.W. – Did you direct it?

R.A. – No, Labarthe did. I just worked more than he did. He was a specialist in public relations. It was a monthly; for the most part, two or three people put it out. There was Staro—that is what we called him. He was a Czech, from Teschen. He had fought in World War I, had been a Communist for a long time and had, since, become very anticommunist. He had a kind of genius and his knowledge of military affairs was exceptional. He was always citing Clausewitz. Through his intervention, this was the second time that I came into touch with the thinking of Clausewitz (the first was during my stay in Germany, before the war). Staro's pieces were the best military articles published in England. The specialists read him attentively. He wrote in German, twenty-five to forty pages sometimes. I translated, adapted, rewrote. In the first issue of *La France Libre*, there appeared an article on the French defeat; the inspiration for the article came from Staro; the style was mine. General de Gaulle read it. I have saved the typescript with the marginal notations of the General himself.

D.W. – Did he approve the analysis?

R.A. – Yes. When there was a felicitous phrase, he would, like a professor, note B in the margin. That meant it was *bien*.

He had written B, for example, for a phrase that said, roughly:
France had the best road network and a static army.

D.W. – Were there any T.B.'s, that is, *très bien*?

R.A. – No, No. His approval never exceeded B.

D.W. – So, you and Staro were there. And who else?

R.A. – Labarthe, and a lady called Lecoutre. She had a genius for public relations. Also, she read and corrected all the articles. For each issue, I wrote an editorial and an article. These articles were reproduced in my book *L'Homme Contre les Tyrans*, first in the United States, then in France. There was a chronicle of France, analyzing what was happening inside the country. These texts became my book *De l'Armistice à l'Insurrection Nationale*. There was the military article in it, as well as others we were able to unearth here and there. It was in this process that we found in London—but later, in 1943—two writers, Jules Roy and Romain Gary. I was, I believe, the first reader of Romain Gary's initial novel *L'Education Européenne*, a book about which I was enthusiastic. We have kept up our friendly relations that began in that period.

J.–L.M. – Morally, what were your feelings toward occupied France?

R.A. – In the winter of 1940-41, it was not morally embarrassing to be in London, because at that time we were being bombed while the French were no longer subject to air raids. However, in 1943, when I talked with Jules Roy or Romain Gary, I had a feeling of humiliation, of course. As pilots, they were making sorties over France, risking their lives while I was in no risk at all. From that point of view, the least unpleasant time of the exile was during the blitz, the period of intensive bombing raids.

D.W. – Why? It was nonetheless a troubled and violent period.

R.A. – No, it wasn't bad. It was all exaggerated. It was disagreeable because London was bombed nightly. But compared to the Allied bombings of 1943 and 1944, it was almost nothing. The two big bombings of London during this period amounted to 500 tons. But in 1943 or 1944, 500 tons was only an average bombing. Moreover, in a city like London the risk for an individual was very slight. In fact, I used to stay in bed, "protected by the law of averages," as one of my friends said.

J.–L.M. – You didn't go down to the air raid shelters?

R.A. – Never. I have never slept so well as under the blitz, for reasons that a psychologist could explain immediately. When someone sleeps badly, as I do, it's because he is neurotic. During catastrophic events, a neurotic sleeps better. So I slept better.

b) De Gaulle and Pétain

J.–L.M. – How was your relationship with General de Gaulle at that time?

R.A. – At the beginning, the relationship was good. I stayed in the background.

D.W. – Why?

R.A. – Because I was a Jew. I didn't think it desirable to push myself up front. Moreover, I had to sign my articles with a pseudonym. The French administration was not supposed to know that I was in London because my wife had stayed in France and she continued to receive my pay. It was naturally Labarthe who had closer relations with General de Gaulle. At the beginning, those relations were very amicable. But they gradually became execrable. He was very close to Admiral Muselier and because of that was involved in the quarrels between Muselier and de Gaulle. I was also caught up in those problems and still have a disagreeable memory of them. They were typical exiles' problems. But there were serious political differences in the background. I personally felt that between the time when the armistice was signed and the Allies' landing in North Africa it was not desirable for the Gaullist movement to transform itself into a government. I obstinately retained the vague hope that once the Allies arrived in North Africa—I was convinced they would begin the reconquest of Europe there—a good part of the Vichy government, or of the forces linked to Vichy, would make contact with the Allies and resume the war at their side. So, I felt that, in its most extreme form, Gaullist propaganda, which denounced everything that was linked with Vichy in one way or another, tended in the direction opposed to what I sought, with little real hope. It was desirable to avoid civil war through a reconciliation at the right moment between the French who were on one side and those who were on the other. Finally, that happened; but in North Africa. The French army based there linked up with and joined the Gaullists.

On the other hand, in London, I was in touch with one of the rare diplomats who was simultaneously accredited to Vichy and to London. This was Dupuy, the Canadian ambassador, who regularly kept me abreast of the conversations he had in Vichy, and of the different Vichy factions. That lasted until November 11, 1942. You must not forget that in 1940 all the great powers were represented at Vichy. This was true of the Soviet Union as well as of the United States. Thus, on one side there was General de Gaulle who claimed to represent French legitimacy with only a few thousand Frenchmen, but also with his name and oratorical powers. On the other side, there was the navy, the empire, the administration, Marshal Pétain—so that General de Gaulle's claim to the legitimacy that, in retrospect, he was accorded, was at the time difficult to accept.

J.–L.M. – Basically, your disagreement with de Gaulle concerned the Vichy Regime's legality?

R.A. – No, because the legality of the Vichy regime was difficult to contest, since it had received the vote of the National Assembly. Nevertheless, it was a debatable legality, because the German army was very close. It was not that vote that was decisive. More decisive was the fact that almost all nations recognized the Vichy government, as did the officer corps of the French army, what remained of the navy, the empire. These were the elements that had to be rallied to the Allied cause and not left to Vichy. But, after the war in Syria, most of the French who had fought on the Vichy side and against the Gaullists did not want to join de Gaulle. The vast majority wanted to be repatriated to France. Obviously, in this sort of civil war between Vichy and de Gaulle, the blame was not de Gaulle's alone; it would be absured to say that! The French are prone to civil war, so they initiated it immediately, beginning at the end of June 1940.

D.W. – I don't understand. You were in England, you were with a monthly called *La France Libre*, a Resistance, Gaullist periodical. But you, were you Gaullist, or were you a defender of the Vichy regime?

R.A. – No. What I said was that the Vichy people were not, by definition, traitors. I said also that, with the armistice signed, it was necessary to wait for the right moment to reenter the war, the moment when the Allies would have arms to give us. I said, therefore, that for the time being, the best one could hope for was for the Vichy government to hold on to what was fundamental. That was the navy, North Africa, and what remained of the army. It would have been senseless to ask the Vichy government to enter the war without the means, without waiting until the balance of forces between the Allies and Germany was modified.

J.–L.M. – But de Gaulle's approach had as its purpose to rally the vital forces of the nation; now, one doesn't rally the vital forces of a nation by saying: on the one hand, there is Vichy, that must be preserved, and on the other hand, there are the Free French.

R.A. – I was not General de Gaulle. I was a political writer. I didn't disagree with him on the essential point: France must be on the side of the Allies. But I hoped, I repeat, I hoped that there would be no civil war; and, also, that there would be on the Allied side, not only General de Gaulle with the few thousand Frenchmen he had recruited early on, but also those who might later join that side.

With reference to our periodical, it was considered everywhere as the Gaullist magazine, that of Free France, *par excellence*. It had a certain quality that General de Gaulle perhaps did not overly admire: it was a publication more analytical than propagandistic. But what was more useful for the cause of Free France? A propaganda magazine like a number of others, or a magazine marked by a high intellectual level, as Cobban described it to me recently?

D.W. – In the final analysis, you were Gaullist?

R.A. – In my own way. I didn't appreciate the personality cult that had begun immediately. I even wrote one or two articles that, today, I wish I had not written, particularly one that was rather good, but had aggressive implications. Its title was *"L'Ombre des Bonaparte."* There developed immediately a kind of Gaullian or Gaullist fanaticism that was not in harmony with my own feeling, which was different, as I've told you, on the armistice and its consequences. This is why I did not participate in Maurice Schumann's propaganda program, possibly the most effective, and certainly the extreme form of Gaullist propaganda, which partly explains the fact that he was rated number two in the Gaullist hierarchy. I can in no way compete with his achievements, which I respect, without having been part of them.

I hoped that the propaganda would not be such as to blemish the honor of the civil servants and, above all, of the military. However, it did give the soldiers and officers on the Vichy side guilt feelings, hence their reluctance to join de Gaulle. Could they really be reproached at the beginning for being loyal to Marshal Pétain, a figure of national glory, rather than to General de Gaulle, whom no one knew? So be it; I was wrong. The French—at least some among them—being as they are, and war being what it is, one could only be extremist. But when someone refused to play the game, as I did, one can only write books and remain more or less isolated. . . . What I wanted, however, coincided with what the French thought. They believed that, basically, Marshal Pétain and General de Gaulle had the same objectives and that their quarrel was not irreconcilable. Most people ardently hoped for an accommodation between the two men. When the Allies landed in North Africa, de Gaulle himself said to his associates, "If Pétain goes to Algiers, we will amount to nothing." That was not true. He would have been Pétain's successor. But it is quite true that if Pétain had gone to North Africa in November 1942, as General Weygand and some of his ministers begged him to do, he would have been a national hero for all the French. In my view, the gravest accusation against the Vichy government and against Pétain was the failure to have understood in November 1942 that they could have saved everything; that is, saved French resources in the war and assured the unity of France. In November 1942, the difference in sensitivity between many Gaullists in London and myself was that they were worried, not to say disconcerted, at the thought of the Vichy government's departure for North Africa. As for me, although I had little hope, I desperately wanted it to happen. I felt that if Pétain went to Algiers, everything that was essential would be saved and French unity reestablished. Only the collaborators would remain, and they would no longer have any importance if they were not protected and, in a way, justified, by the Marshal. The day the Marshal joined the other side, the whole of France would be on the right side of the fence. Of course, you can say that, in fact, Pétain did not go to North Africa, that there was never any chance that he would go there and that these were nothing more than the musings of an intellectual.

For me, the clear-cut, final rupture came in November 1942. From the moment the armistice was signed until then, it was necessary to act decently, something that the Vichy people did not always do, and above all keep alive the opportunity to reenter the war. But after November 1942, the Vichy government and Marshal Pétain brought infinitely more disadvantages than advantages to France. The legend which held that the person and the presence of Marshal Pétain protected the French people no longer made sense. Instead, he provided a kind of sanction to the most detestable activities.

J.–L.M. – You mean to say that there was a kind of third avenue possible between resistance and collaboration?

R.A. – No, I am not saying that. What I am saying is that, beginning with the armistice, through a series of accidents, the French government possessed a certain number of trump cards. It had retained its navy; it had retained North Africa, and some forces there that had been neutralized. Now, these neutralized forces could join one side or the other. The interest of France was to have them join the right side at the right moment. In this sense, between the armistice and November 1942, an *attentiste* policy was justifiable. But General de Gaulle was a man of passion who detested *attentisme* above all. He could understand those who played the German card, but he was unable to accept the kind of cowardliness that, in his eyes, the Vichy government represented. His judgment was possibly sound as it applied to those on the highest level of responsibility, but open to argument in so far as it concerned soldiers, officers, generals who could not go off to war from one day to the next. For those people, it was a question of the timing of their choice. That question was posed in November 1942. But Pétain failed to seize that occasion to leave for North Africa where he would have become a national hero and reconciled the whole French people. It was necessary to explain this, and I have done so. But it looks as if history proved me wrong because the adherents of an *attentisme* that could have been useful to France lost out. But, as always in the most difficult situations, I try to find a way to avoid the worst—and the worst thing that can happen to a country as far as I am concerned, is civil war. It was with this concern in mind that, much later, I took a stand in favor of an independent Algeria.

D.W. – What is striking about you is your obsession with disunity and civil war.

R.A. – That's true. It began with me in the 1930s, upon my return from Germany; then, in 1934, in 1936, and during the war in Spain. I always had the feeling the country was about to begin a civil war precisely at the moment when it would have to confront the critical dangers of war abroad. I was always obsessed with the need to avoid civil war, and I lived in an era when we were always close to it. So, if you will, I reacted to events, partly with my viewpoints that were always categorical, and, intellectually, with the desire to make those who shared my convictions understand that the others, those on the other side of the controversy, were not necessarily traitors. I have done that all my life. It has been, let us say, a modest mission that I assigned myself.

J.–L.M. – May we return a moment to the armistice, a date so important for the historic sensibilities of the French. You understood it, you tell us. But did you approve it?

R.A. – Yes; I told you it was difficult to criticize the armistice after having traveled across France in the midst of the refugees, in disorder, and collapse. However, as far as I can recall, my emotional reaction had been hostile to it, by dint of rather primitive arguments: you don't argue with Hitler—you either resist him or you are crushed. It was a spontaneous reaction, not thought through; but in my case, first reactions, even emotional ones, are immediately counterbalanced by more complex and detailed reflection. I asked myself first the questions: What were the provisions? What is to happen to the fleet? To North Africa? A logical fear was that North Africa and the fleet might fall under the enemy's control. Another question linked to the armistice: Did we have the means to resist in North Africa? From the beginning, my feeling was that if we wanted to go to North Africa, the decision should have been made at the latest by the beginning of June, rather than doing the opposite, that is, bringing the North African divisions to France. Although some people left at the last moment for North Africa, we didn't have much to defend it with. The British had nothing at all and the Americans were giving the little they had to Great Britain. In order to have a substantive opinion about the armistice, one would have to be able to answer these questions: What were the provisions? What were our chances of resisting in North Africa? When all the factors did become known, my inclination was to think that the June armistice was practically inevitable. Later, I thought—just as Churchill himself thought, but the way—that the armistice turned out well, particularly for the Allies, if not for France.

As a matter of fact, if France had resisted in North Africa—that is, if there had been an important Anglo-French force in this zone menacing Italy—Germany would have inevitably been forced to go to its ally's assistance. There would have been a great Mediterranean battle in 1941. As a result, the attack against the Soviet Union would, in all probability, have been delayed. Now, Hitler's fatal decision was to attack the Soviet Union. In a way, the French armistice helped turn the Germans toward their ambitions in the East. Obviously, the Frenchmen who favored the armistice weren't thinking so far ahead. But that was without doubt the consequence. The result, by the way, was that no court, even at the time of the Liberation, used the armistice as an article of indictment against the collaborators.

J.–L.M. – Yes, it was for that reason that you said the armistice was an answer to the German-Soviet pact.

R.A. – Yes, I wrote that, and in a way the armistice was historically, in fact, a response to the German-Soviet pact. It is an irony of history. After all, what, precisely, was the pact between Hitler and Stalin? It was an invitation by Stalin to the French to fight to the last man for the Soviet Union. The French responded courteously: Why don't you do the same thing for us? Naturally, they didn't think in those terms, but that's what they did.

D.W. – In your opinion, France was saved by the speed of its defeat?

R.A. – That's a phrase you've borrowed from one of my books and it's a different question. France had been terribly weakened by its losses in the first World War: one-and-one-half million men. I thought that another hemorrhage, another loss of one to two million men could be fatal, that she would not be able to recover from it. Now, if the French army had held firm in 1940, instead of being defeated in a few weeks—

if it had been conquered only a year or so later, in 1941—the losses would have been much greater. To put the matter brutally: there is a demographic factor in all wars. In this sense, the disaster that did occur, with its tragic moral and material consequences, nevertheless made possible, by its very rapidity, the later demographic, economic, and political recovery of France. It is hardly agreeable to think or to say that we were saved by a disaster; it is even shocking. It is nevertheless something I profoundly believe, even if these arguments seem a little paradoxical.

J.–L.M. – The speed of the disaster was perhaps useful from a demographic point of view, but was it useful on the moral level?

R.A. – That is what I was telling you. While the armistice was perhaps useful to the Allies and perhaps favorable in terms of the demographic future of France, it had nevertheless certain disastrous consequences, notably in the way it divided the French. Inevitably, it created an incipient civil war. If there had been no Vichy government, if there had not been a Pétain to protect Laval, French unity against the Germans would have been rapidly reestablished. In this sense, the negative impact of Vichy was considerable. It cut France in two, and this division has persisted to this day. Everyone who lived through the period was on one side or the other. You, who did not live through it, perhaps find my subtleties outmoded.

J.–L.M. – We were taught a more Manichean view of history.

R.A. – Well, let me repeat to you a phrase from Malraux. "It's true, politics is Manichean," he said, "but one shouldn't overemphasize it." We shouldn't overemphasize it, particularly in the history we have lived through: The depression years, 1938, 1939, the armistice, 1942, 1944, Algeria. Each time, one could have reflected in a Manichean way. There had to be someone who refused to think in a Manichean manner. Today, there are many such people. And to a very large degree, on many points the multi-faceted presentation of these events has become virtually historic opinion, except on the Vichy government, about which most historians are more severe than I.

D.W. – How did the French live in London?

R.A. – That depends. There were some Frenchmen who lived in England and who did not return to France. They were, in the majority, passionately Gaullist. There were others who were purely and simply Gaullists. And there were people like Roger Cambon, for example, the number two in the French Embassy in Great Britain before the war, who stayed in London after the armistice, but who never became a Gaullist. Also, Alexis Léger,[15] in the United States, never became a Gaullist because he was against the idea of creating a provisional government in exile. In London, those who wrote for the newspaper *France* were not Gaullists because they were prototypes of the men of the Third Republic. They quickly suspected de Gaulle of despotic and dictatorial intentions. In their eyes, he was a military man, philosophically close to Maurras, therefore they were not Gaullists. There were also people like Pierre Bourdan, a man of great repute, who was to die tragically one or two years after the war. He, likewise, was no Gaullist, but neither was he anti-Gaullist. So there were all shadings. Those people used to meet frequently to talk and argue. They constituted a kind of political France in microcosm, somewhat ridiculous, carrying on politics typical of exiles. They discussed in the abstract problems that would not become real until after the liberation of France: what kind of government de Gaulle would create, what the new makeup of the political parties would be, etc. And then there was the scission inside the Gaullist movement that I have mentioned, the quarrel between Admiral Muselier and General de Gaulle, and Muselier's departure for North Africa. It was during that period that Labarthe, with Admiral Muselier, sided with General Giraud. There were all kinds of quarrels that those in metropolitan France never imagined. They were uninteresting or at least seem to me to be no longer interesting.

J.–L.M. – And daily life in London?

R.A. – After the blitz that I mentioned earlier, and from the moment Hitler attacked Russia, bombings of London became rare. Life in London was considerably different from usual because the city was, for the first and last time, the capital of continental Europe. One met Czechs, Poles, Belgians, Dutch, etc. All the European problems were discussed endlessly. There was a kind of European society within greater London.

Then, in 1944, there was the period of the V1 rockets and that, too, was not as tragic as it was alleged to be. Even when a hundred V1s fell on the capital in a single day, you could continue to work in peace. First, you could hear the V1s coming. If you were cool-headed enough, you could calculate whether a bomb was going to fall close to you or further away. If it threatened to fall too close, you could crawl under a table. I did that once. The V1 must have fallen very close, since my windows were broken. But because air blast was the dominant effect, a table often sufficed to protect you.

D.W. – The Germans invaded the USSR in June 1941. Did you have the impression that the course of the war had changed?

R.A. – I am not a war historian, but we had the feeling that Hitler was opening up a two-front war, although he had sworn never to repeat this error after the experience of World War I. Following Pearl Harbor, when the Japanese attacked the United States—a still more important date—Hitler, for reasons that remain even today obscure and incomprehensible, declared war on the U.S. Recently, there has appeared a remarkable book on Hitler, *Bemerkungen zu Hitler*, by the German writer Sebastian Haffner. The author cites Hitler's declaration of war against the United States, though nothing in his treaty with Japan obliged him to do so, as one of Hitler's errors or crimes. Now, Roosevelt would have had some difficulty in convincing the American people to declare war on Hitler if the latter had not declared war on the United States. Since 1940, Hitler had patiently accepted from the United States a way of practicing neutrality that was absolutely contrary to the rules of international law. The United States acted, in fact, as a semibelligerent. Hitler nonetheless stubbornly refused to enter into war with it. Suddenly, he made the decision. We had the feeling then that the war was won; it was only a question to the number of years. From the moment all three powers, the United States, Great Britain, and the Soviet Union, were in the war, our optimism was no longer simply one of faith and determination—it was now based on persuasive reasons. The first defeats sustained by the Soviet Union at the beginning of the campaign naturally aroused doubt and uneasiness. But after the 1941 winter, it seemed probable that Germany had lost the war.

J.–L.M. – During those war years, you carried in *La France Libre* a monthly analysis, "*La Chronique de France*," on the situation in Vichy-France. Why? What was so interesting about Vichy for a London Resistant?

R.A. – Listen, perhaps I would have done better to remain a clerk in my tank company. But as chief editor of a periodical for which I had to write at least two articles a month, I knew there was one subject that could not fail to have interest for both French and English readers, and that was what was happening in France. I discovered that, even with a censored press like Vichy's, one can find out almost everything. When you know the country and read the print media—it was the only time in my life when, for three or four years, I truly read the whole press—you can reconstruct a good part of what is happening. Today, those articles have no more than anecdotal or historical interest. There are now books by historians who have had access to archives that I lacked. But my analyses were not all that inaccurate, given the information I had at my disposal. It was not without value to be able to explain what happened on December 13th, when Laval was dismissed; to explain to the French and the English who the political people were in one place or another and what their positions were *vis-à-vis* Great Britain or the United States; to explain Vichy's internecine struggles. We were able to find out about all those things and I tried to analyze them. I also analyzed the French economy, and on that there was a great deal of information available. Why not do it? It was a normal function of that periodical: to maintain contact between the French abroad and those in France, and, to the extent possible, with a maximum of objectivity, though remaining aware, of course, that we were on one side and Vichy leaders were on the other.

D.W. – What is striking when rereading the collection of chronicles is that, until November 1942, you analyzed the Vichy regime without anger. You accepted it as a fact. It is rather strange.

R.A. – The same reproach again. I admit that I just don't like people who fume as soon as they have a piece of white paper in front of them. First of all, let me remind you that we published an article in *France Libre* by René Cassin, who denied the very legality of the Vichy government. At the beginning, there was also an article against the armistice. But from the moment the armistice was signed, and the Vichy government formed, I tried to understand what was happening. That attitude, it is true, did not meet everyone's approval. In London, I was considered too indulgent toward the Vichy government; this indulgence was explained away as overcompensation by a Jew, who could not be other than anti-Vichy. Some people realized that it was simply my style. In general, I prefer to understand and analyze my adversaries rather than vituperate them.

J.–L.M. – Vichy France was also France. But which one? May I describe it this way: a strong fascist-leaning, corporatist, anti-Semitic group that acceded to power, but had already existed before the war?

R.A. – Well, yes and no. Marshal Pétain's first government was dominated by followers of Maurras. Raphael Allibert, the legal counsel at the outset of the Marshal's government, was very much a Maurrasian. But, *L'Action Francaise*[16] had not been able to have a single deputy elected in France for years.

An important corporatist movement? There were sects, groups, there were intellectuals who spoke about corporatism with reference to Italian fascism. But that was all very fuzzy.

No, what happened was that, with the defeat, a number of people came to power. Among them, at the beginning, were some Maurrasians. But, there was also Pierre Laval, who, to the best of my knowledge was neither a disciple of Maurras, nor much of a corporatist.

There were also some survivors of the Third Republic, some Socialists, some leaders of the Popular Front government—Spinasse, for example. So there was a gathering of political personalities from different milieux, who found themselves in agreement, after defeat, with the government as it was—in agreement to accept the defeat temporarily or definitively.

As for anti-Semitism, yes, it existed and it was Maurras. But in the final analysis, I would be reluctant to accept your phrase, asserting that Vichy brought to the surface profound forces that existed in France. Vichy did bring to the surface movements, groups, ideas and men that existed, but did not represent a majority in the France of the Third Republic.

D.W. – All that concerns Vichy at its beginning. But what strikes me is that even after the return of Pierre Laval to the government in April 1942—largely under German pressure, it is true—and even after November 1942, you remained just as temperate in your *"Chroniques de France."* Nevertheless, you knew very well that Vichy was not going to change, that it was sinking deeper and deeper into collaboration. Again, I ask: Why this indulgence?

R.A. – I don't quite understand why you reproach me for writing in my normal style, even when treating events that I obviously detested. Although, my articles continued to be written in the same style, they described and analyzed the worsening of the Vichy regime. I was tireless in demonstrating that. At the end, I wrote an article called *"Les Gangsters au Pouvoir."* Perhaps I should have written in a different style, but others took care of that. The other publications were always written in the style you seem to prefer, full of adjectives, indignation, and rage. One has to choose: Either one finds the tone of a Bernanos, which requires a special talent, or, if one lacks the talent, one must avoid stooping to vulgar invective.

D.W. – I must insist, because I notice in you a constant attitude, whether it is a question of the Popular Front, the Resistance, or the Vichy regime. You make your choices, but you give the impression of not adhering to them. This need, or this capacity to remain out of phase with your own choices— where does it come from?

R.A. – Have you read the great political writers, such as de Tocqueville or Machiavelli? Did you observe any evidence of facile indignation in their works? Never. Their feelings become evident through ironic phrases and the use of certain words. My feelings were easily discernible. But I wrote for the French who were outside of France, for Englishmen who wanted to understand and who had no difficulty at all in deploring what was happening in France. All right. . . . If I had been Bernanos, I probably would have written differently.

There is another reason why I had no business writing tirades of indignation. In the tranquility of London, it seemed to me insufferable. It would have been too easy to play the hero. It seemed to me that I had the duty and the right to say to myself, thinking of the French living in France, "What would I do in their place?" You found in my war chronicles my usual style. I think that many of those who read my articles at the time were grateful that I retained, let us say, a certain decency of expression and that I didn't let myself be carried away by facile emotions—emotions that I indeed felt.

I have already mentioned to you something about this attitude concerning the French and Pétain. You speak of an IFOP poll of September 1944 in which, before Pétain returned from Sigmaringen in Germany, 58% of the respondents refused to envisage that he might be tried and convicted. I am not convinced of the validity of the poll. On the other hand, I repeat, I am persuaded that the great mass of the French did not think of Pétain as a traitor, that many clung to his image, to his past glory, to a great man who, as they saw it, sacrificed himself, let's say, to spare the French greater suffering. They respected this old man who remained with them in their moment of trial. Some of the French hated Pétain. The Resistants detested him. But there was, I think, a France, deep-seated and silent, that was both Gaullist and Pétainist. This is what I was saying and writing. Why deny reality? The French were not forty to fifty million heroes. You can't imagine today the extent of the country's defeat. The French were stricken. De Gaulle was unknown and far away. Pétain had been the glory of a previous day. He was there; they needed him and they accepted, to a certain degree, the myth of Marshal Pétain protecting the French in the same way that a good number of the French, later, accepted the myth of General de Gaulle having represented French legitimacy as early as June 1940, at a time when he was almost alone in England. You will say that's a lot of myths in a short time. But myths play an important role in politics. And then, in times of great misfortunes, but also, as was the case later, in moments of great happiness . . . truth is prosaic and insufferable. The proof: You find it insufferable that I tried to describe the reality of Vichy. You would like to have the heroes on one side and the villains on the other.

D.W. – It was often this way that we were taught this story. Still, I continue to find it difficult to distinguish between what you understood because you analyzed it, and what you approved or disapproved.

R.A. – It's not sufficient to understand in order to excuse. It is a question of understanding and explaining. That does not mean that one doesn't condemn. But I don't like to play at being the world's conscience. I find it indecent. Many of those who write on politics, write either with rage against their adversaries—when it comes from a Bernanos, it's tolerable— or they pose as interpreters of the conscience of the world.

Jean-Paul Sartre played both roles at once. He criticized su-
perciliously the positions of some and, at the same time, he
wrote terrible things about people he didn't like. I speak
without any resentment, because I continued to have for him
both admiration and friendship, despite everything. As for
me, I am neither one nor the other. I was sometimes severe
with French writers close to the collaboration, in some cases
too severe, but I was not tempted to be severe with the
French for what they are. Some peoples were more heroic
than the French—the Poles and the Danes, for example. But
the French are what they are. Since that time, films have been
made and books written that heap reproof about them. . . .

c) The Holocaust

J.–L.M. – As a matter of fact, this brings us to anti-Semitism
in France. The government passed laws against the Jews. But
one doesn't find in the periodical *La France Libre* any reports
on Vichy's policy against the Jews. Why?

R.A. – That is true. I should have spoken about it. The anti-
Jewish laws were issued on October 30, 1940, before the Germans demanded them. It was a Vichy initiative. And then
there was the exhibition: *"Les Juifs et la France."* And above
all, the roundup of the *Vélodrome d'Hiver*[17] in 1942. Why did
I not comment on these events? I am tempted to tell you that
I do not know why, myself. Upon reflection, I find a number
of reasons. The first is that we were French Resistants in London. As Frenchmen, we were obviously hostile to all anti-
Jewish measures. But there was a kind of agreement to talk
about them as little as possible. Probably because I was myself
a Jew, I spoke about them as little as possible.

There is perhaps another, deeper reason, one that is not to
my honor, but is understandable: all the measures that the
French might take against the Jews touched me deeply precisely because I am French, if I may put it this way, before I
am Jewish. It was a kind of emotional precaution for me to
think as little as possible about what some Frenchmen were
doing to the Jews. That's why I spoke less than I should have
about this aspect of reality, less than about other aspects of
French reality.

There is still another reason to explain why relatively little
was said of the Jewish question in the English and American

newspapers. Hitler's propaganda machine repeated cease-
lessly that it was the war of the Jews. As a result, there was a
kind of unspoken agreement that I, consciously or uncon-
sciously, respected. There were also anti-Semites on the Allied
side. One of the easiest and most simplistic ways to parry
Hitler's propaganda was to avoid proclaiming that the war
was being fought to liberate the Jews. The war was being
fought to liberate France, it was being fought against totalitarianism, against despotism, and not for the Jews. It was an attitude, mine and that of many others—today, I judge it rather
severely—that led to our speaking less about the fate of the
Jews than we should have.

Churchill and Roosevelt failed to denounce the extermina-
tion of the Jews for the same reason. An American diplomat
wrote a book, *Quand les Juifs Mouraient*. He tells of his ef-
forts to have Roosevelt and Churchill pronounce the words
that might have saved a certain number of Jews. In vain. The
men who led the war wanted to do nothing explicitly for the
Jews. They did not say to the Nazis, "You will pay if this ex-
termination continues." Similarly, the Pope, who tried to take
action discreetly, almost clandestinely, said nothing in public.

J.–L.M. – What kind of information reached England on the
genocide or "final solution"?

R.A. – The truth is that I am not sure exactly what I did
know. I knew, of course, that there were persecutions. I am
sure that I did not know while I was in London the existence
of the gas chambers. Did I know that millions of Jews were
exterminated? I believe I did not, but I am now tempted to
think it was a form of emotional comfort. I did not want even
to imagine it. I naturally knew that Jews from the West were
deported to the East. I knew there were concentration camps.

D.W. – You knew it?

R.A. – How could one not know it?

J.–L.M. – But genocide itself?

R.A. – I never imagined genocide. I had lived in Germany. I
knew that people. I expected the worst from the Nazis, but I
must say honestly to my shame that I never imagined the ex-
termination of a people, just like that, in cold blood. . .Jews,
Gypsies, why? In England, two Polish socialist Jews committed suicide because of the indifference of the English and the
Allies to the fate of the Jews. We knew that in London. But we

were probably guilty, like all the others, of not having known more. To be severe with myself, I will say that I could have known it if I had wanted to.

D.W. – And in your opinion, why did people not want to know?

R.A. – In part, it's incomprehensible. However, they did not want to fight the war for the Jews. It is a rather monstrous thing to say, but I think it is true.

Of course, the English and the Americans disapproved of the Nazis' conduct regarding the Jews. It is even possible to say that, to a degree, Germany lost the war because of the way it treated the Jews, for it chased the great Jewish scientists from Germany and created in the United States and even in England profound emotion against anti-Semitism, against German anti-Semitism. But, as I said, there was a covenant of silence during the war. There was disapproval, but at the same time, there was a kind of intellectual or emotional cowardice on the question of the fate of the Jews. When Himmler proposed the exchange of some tens of thousands of Jews for trucks, the Allies refused.

D.W. – Then it was relatively generalized behavior?

R.A. – I think you could even drop the word, "relatively."

There were many things the Allies did not want to know, even at the Nuremberg trials. The Soviet Union was an ally. The English and Americans knew very well who exterminated the 10,000 Polish officers in the Katyn forest. It wasn't the Germans, but the Soviets. The break in relations between the Polish government in London and the Moscow government took place on this occasion. Terrible crimes occurred in the Soviet Union itself.

Finally, when did I know with certainty about the genocide? In France, later, when it was published, when it was written down.

J.–L.M. – What were your reactions then?

R.A. – Can you accept it? No Jew can say, in a definitive way, that he has accepted it. The only thing I can say, to bear personal witness, is that since then I consider myself a survivor blessed by good fortune. The rest of it is impossible to articulate. You belong to another generation, but for you, Jewish like myself, the catastrophe continues to exist as if it were still close. That has not made of me a hunter of Germans or other culprits. I am not the world's conscience. It is simply that the tragedy remains very close to me.

D.W. – Why didn't you write anything about it after the war?

R.A. – What can one write? Have you read Poliakov's *Le Bréviaire de la Haine*? It is written in precisely the same style that you reproach me for in respect to my writings on Vichy. It is an analysis. One senses that the writer has warmth and that he is deeply affected by what happened. But it is a history book. I think that unless one has a touch of genius, one can write about those tragic events only by analyzing them. Anything else is useless. I have spoken about those events several times in my courses at the Institute of Political Studies, but in such an emotional way that I would never have dreamt of writing about them. My writing style falters in the face of events of such magnitude. As for writing in order to cleanse one's self of those emotions, of all those horrors, it isn't possible. They remain. Nevertheless, Jews must overcome them and live, not as if those tragedies had never happened, but not obsessed by the memories, either.

J.-L.M. – What about Sartre's book, *Réflexion sur la Question Juive*?

R.A. – It's a fine book, but Sartre was not knowledgable about Jews. He thought that all Jews were like his schoolmate, Raymond Aron, who was totally unreligious, thoroughly French, who largely ignored Jewish tradition, and thus, only Jewish because others called him Jewish. Sartre wrote a book that misses the reality of the Jews, of those who are authentically Jews—it should be understood that those who were no more Jewish than I were persecuted like the others. For this reason, those who did not consider themselves as Jews before, became, for the most part, consciously Jewish again when they discovered they had to share the destiny of their coreligionists who had remained Jews.

J.-L.M. – And Zionism? What is your reaction to the Zionist movements that have developed actively since 1945?

R.A. – I have never been a Zionist and never will be, first because I am not a believer, and then because I have always thought that the creation of the state of Israel in the Near East would be the origin of a series of wars. I believed that once again the Jews had settled, not in a place that was accursed,

but in an area where peace would be preached but not prac-
tised. I recall having spoken of this question at the University
of Jerusalem when I received the doctorate *honoris causa*
there. I said, "Jerusalem, sacred city for the believers of the
three religions of the Book, Jerusalem that was the theater of
so many wars, Jerusalem that resounds still to the cries of the
vanquished," etc. But Israel exists, and will continue to exist,
I hope. In a certain way, I am attached to Israel, but I am a
French citizen.

D.W. – At the end of the war, you said that the tragedy is
too ghastly for one to write about or for one to comment
upon. But wasn't the support of the state of Israel the only
way to inscribe it in history?

R.A. – Jews have the liberty to choose to be Jews in the Diaspora. They can choose, also, to be Jews in Israel. But if they
choose to be Jews in France and citizens of France, if they
claim equality of rights with their French compatriots, then
they must accept the fact that their fatherland is France and
not Israel. It is possible to have a physical fatherland and a
spiritual fatherland, in the way that Christians are French and,
in a sense, are Christians before being French. Except, Israel is
not a religious state; it is a half-religious state and military
state. Therefore, because I am a French citizen, I conduct my
political criticism as a Frenchman and not as a Jew.

I went to Israel for the first time in 1956. You can ponder
that point, also. In 1948, the year of Israel's creation, my feelings were of course with the Israelis. But that was no great
spiritual experience for me. I admit it, because it is true. Today, my reaction is different: I rather regret not having been
more emotionally involved in 1948. I was deeply upset by the
outbreak of the Six-Day War in 1967. I thought for a moment,
mistakenly as it turned out, that Israel was in mortal danger.
Since then, I made peace with the Israelis, who like me and
accept me as I am: A friend of Israel, but not a Zionist; not an
Israeli, but a Frenchman. However, I have a greater sensitivity
toward the state of Israel now than in 1948. In a way, the
tragic events of World War II have progressively penetrated
deeply into my being. They have more meaning for me today
than in 1945-1946. It's paradoxical, but that's the way it is.

J.–L.M. – One has the impression that there goes on in you
a slow process of sorting out ideas. In 1930, there was Ray-

mond Aron, the Jew fully integrated into French society, completely secularized, whose identity with Judaism was very weak. Then there was the contact with German anti-Semitism, followed by the Holocaust revelations of 1945, all finally leading to such a transformation that you have stopped playing the card of integration.

R.A. – I have not stopped. Not at all. I am not advocating anything at all. I think that every Jew is free to choose who he wants to be. I have decided once and for all that I am French, despite Vichy, despite anti-Semitism, and I remain a French citizen, with, however, a perfect right to have contacts with other countries. But I am not less integrated into French society; on the contrary, I am more integrated than ever. First, because of age, then because of what is known as fame. This is what I always reply when I am asked questions about anti-Semitism: "Personally, I am not at all affected by today's anti-Semitism, but I am now in France a little like those who were once called 'court Jews'." Once an individual has achieved a certain social status, he is no longer perceived as a Jew. Today, I am not very much perceived as Jewish in French society. It is well known that I am. But basically, I am known as Raymond Aron, incidentally Jewish, with unexpected reactions to events.

D.W. – Do you lay greater claim to your Judaism today than thirty years ago?

R.A. – Certainly. When a tragedy like that of the Rue Copernic[18] happens, some television station is bound to ask me to comment upon it.

III
THE DISILLUSIONMENTS OF LIBERATION

a) National Renewal

D. Wolton. – When you returned from London, how did you find the French? Were they changed?

Raymond Aron. – Let's begin with my friends. I got together again with Malraux, who had become passionately anticommunist. My last conversation with him had taken place during the "phony war." In the course of a dinner, I beseeched him to break with the Communist party. We argued all evening, but he refused to make the break. "I would do it if Daladier had not imprisoned Communists," he said.

I saw Sartre again. In the intellectual and literary world, he had become the great man that he was not back in 1938 or 1939. At the same time, he was much closer to the Communists than before. He was now politicized, whereas, earlier, he had not been. There was a reversal of attitudes between Malraux and Sartre, two men who did not like each other. I liked them both, but never both at the same time because there was practically no conversation possible between the two.

As far as the French are concerned, to judge them after years of war didn't make any sense. Living conditions were very difficult. The war was still going on. It was the period of the black market. However, when I met Resistants, I had an inferiority complex. As circumstances would have it, my decision to leave in 1940 assumed, in retrospect, an entirely different significance. I thought to myself as having avoided the suffering and risks of those who had remained in France—something that was manifestly not my desire, nor the significance of my gesture in June 1940.

J.–L. Missika. – How did you judge your friends who published during the occupation?

R.A. – I think I've already told you: It is not my habit to make moral judgments of other people. Since I neither suffered nor ran any serious risks during the war, I did not believe I had any right to make moral judgments on the behavior of one person or another. Moreover, my close friends had done nothing of a culpable nature. Well, Sartre had one of his plays staged during the occupation, but for those who could read between the lines, the play was anti-Vicky and anti-German. The *Figaro* journalists were more or less Vichyites until November 1942. But it never occurred to me to criticize them, the less so since I had written in *La France Libre* an article praising what was being written in *Le Figaro Littéraire*. The magazine defended French literature against those who, at the time, mouthed abuse against France and the excessive intelligence of the French, attributing to that intelligence their lack of character and the military defeat. So, for my part, despite some articles that I did not like, I always put *Le Figaro* on the good side of the barricade.

J.–L.M. – And the purge?

R.A. – What can I say? I have written nothing about it. First, I didn't have the opportunity. The purge took place chiefly in 1944-1945. At that time, I was still writing mostly for *La France Libre* and a bit for an illustrated weekly, not very seriously. Besides, I just didn't consider myself enough of a moral authority to take a position on the question. Personally, I detested the purge, but I knew that something like it was inevitable. I wrote a few lines on the subject as part of the conclusion to the *"Chroniques de France"* in *La France Libre*. I was rather favorably disposed to Mauriac's position, except that for certain people, like the Resistants and the Jews, it was more difficult to accept Mauriac's views.

D.W. – What was the atmosphere like when peace came, in May 1945?

R.A. – There, I must go back very far, to November 1918, when I was thirteen years old. I lived in Versailles. My parents brought me to Paris. And there I lived the unique, unforgettable day of a people unified in joy. What Paris was on Armistice Day and the day after the Armistice could not be imagined; it had to be seen. People embraced each other in the street. Everyone, the bourgeoisie, the workers, office clerks, the young and the old; it was the madness of the crowd, but a joyous madness. There was no hatred; more than anything else, there was a kind of elation and relief. Everyone repeated again and again, "We beat them." But, above all, there was happiness.

In May 1945, on the contrary, Paris was mortally sad, as I experienced it anyway. I recall a conversation I had with Jules Roy that day. He was struck just as I by the sadness, the absence of hope. It was the end of the war, but it was the victory of the Allies more than that of France. There was nothing comparable to the outbursts of enthusiasm of November 1918. I have only one precise memory of May 8. I was walking in Paris, because I did want to share the experience with the Parisians. I saw—I forget where—General Giraud. He was alone. He walked along sadly, as if lost. I went over to greet him as a kind of gesture; then I saw him walk away without saying anything. It was the sadness of a man who could have played a role, but who failed despite his courage. No one remembered him that day. Political life is like that.

J.–L.M. – Woe to the conquered.

R.A. – In politics, you must win or stay away.

D.W. – Didn't France at this time want to forget the five years of war, during which the behavior of the French had not always been praiseworthy?

R.A. – It is difficult to say. I am not sure the French would be able to answer. It must not be forgotten that General de Gaulle, who was president of the provisional government, had immediately transformed the nature of the events of that period. He considered himself as the permanent legitimacy of France. Because he had always been on the right side, perforce France had also been on the right side. In a striking manner, a number of events of the years 1940-1944 were, so to say, erased.

I recall a conversation with Sartre. We asked ourselves: Why has there not been a single article, not even one, saying, "Welcome to the Jews upon their return to the French community"?—not even an article by Mauriac. The underlying reason for this silence was that one had in a sense blotted out what had happened. There were many Resistants among the Jews. In the Resistance, the Jews had been Frenchmen like the others—to such an extent that no one thought of writing that article. The French settled down again in their

France as if the Jews had never been cast out. I took this phenomenon as evidence of a determination to forget, and also as a kind of return by France to its old self.

J.–L.M. – Did France refuse to make an examination of conscience, as the Germans, for example, did to a greater degree?

R.A. – Was there an examination of conscience in Germany, except under the constraint of the defeat and of its conquerors?

J.–L.M. – Whether under constraint or not, there was a certain self-questioning.

R.A. – French responsibility was not comparable to that of the German people. And then, wasn't there really an examination of conscience? Many Frenchmen made it, probably as individuals. But there was something more important: the transformation of the atmosphere in France, the transformation of the French people, after the war. Beginning in 1944-1945, the France that I have known has been totally different from that of the 1930s. The Right was not the same; neither was the Left. Something gave me hope; the people around me (my generation) were motivated by a genuine passion, it was of nationwide scope. We had in us the memory of the decadence of the 1930s, about which I have spoken. In 1944 and 1945, a truly profound determination for national renewal became evident.

D.W. – That appears very clearly in your articles in the newspaper *Combat*. In those articles, there was an optimism and a will to modify conditions that were extraordinary. What led you to *Combat?*

R.A. – I began there in March 1946, after having spent two months as Malraux's *directeur de cabinet* in the second de Gaulle government, where I had my initial experience as, let us say, an official personality, at a modest if not mediocre level. I learned a bit about how things are done in a ministry, and it didn't make me anxious to stay there!

First, one had visits from people for eight to ten hours a day. The newspapers were the focus of attention. By the time I arrived, at the end of 1945, pretty much everything had been done. The newspapers had either been recreated or eliminated. Resistants and non-Resistants had taken over the old newspapers with the titles more or less modified. I had visits from personalities linked to the old newspapers, who had, correctly or unjustly, been considered collaborators. Chastenet visited me; he had been the director of *Le Temps*. I told him what I thought—that I didn't like all that, but that there was absolutely nothing I could do about it.

The only thing I tried to do and would have succeeded in doing if General de Gaulle's government had lasted a few more months, was to prevent the birth of the company—later created by Defferre—that was to group all the printing plants confiscated by the state. The proposal of having one company control all those plants seemed stupid to me. I was convinced that the national company would be incapable of managing them, and that they would go to pieces in a few years. So I refused the proposal drawn up by the ministry's legal counsel and had a totally different text drafted. My proposal would have the printing plants transferred as rapidly as possible to their directors, to the newspapers, and so on. I saved this text for a few years and finally threw it in the wastebasket. Nothing remains of this program that, in my point of view, was reasonable and would have avoided several of the disadvantages of the other decision. Otherwise, I didn't do much. Nonetheless, Malraux and I authorized the creation of *Le Figaro Littéraire*. And then, from time to time, there were discussions on the allocation of paper. One day, we received a telephone call from Palewski, General de Gaulle's *directeur de cabinet*. He told us to cancel the authorization to publish. At the time, as a matter of fact, there existed a system of authorizations to publish. But there wasn't much point in authorizing newspapers to publish without having any paper to give them. The same question was repeatedly discussed: how to allocate the paper stocks. Allocation was based on unsold copies. The greater the number of unsold copies, the less paper a newspaper was entitled to receive. So, when there were a lot of unsold copies, a paper began a decline that carried it still lower. It was a very bad system, though inevitable. A large number of newspapers were created, but many disappeared in a year or two.

Paper was not the only problem. People visited us with various requests for things one can have in a prosperous society without asking. But at that time, everything was scarce, including gasoline. None of that thrilled me, but it educated me a little and amused me to some extent. Moreover, I had the feeling that working eight or nine hours in a ministry office was less tiring than reading the *Critique of Pure Reason* for three hours. The work was enervating and irritating, but it didn't require any intellectual effort.

b) The Political Virus

D.W. – Let's return to your journalistic activities. You started writing for *Combat* in March 1946.

R.A. – Hold on. Before that, I should mention a decision I took, whose consequences for my life were almost unlimited. I think of it today as perfectly irrational, but I took it in full awareness: I returned neither to the University of Toulouse, to which I had been nominated in August 1939, nor to the University of Bordeaux, where I was a substitute before the war, and whose faculty of letters offered me the chair of sociology.

I refused, first, because I was intoxicated with politics. The political virus. I have since lost it. But at the time, I was truly intoxicated. Also, I wanted to live in Paris. I had been in exile for a number of years, all my friends lived in Paris and the idea of living in Bordeaux did not appeal to me. As for living in Paris while teaching in Bordeaux, I told myself that it wasn't the right thing to do. But it was only a rationalization. I think the real reason was twofold: on the one hand, politics; on the other, the feeling that teaching sociology in Bordeaux to a few dozen students was not really a way to work for the revival of France. I had the illusion that a quasi-political activity in Paris would be more effective, a more direct contribution to what we are trying to achieve. It was a bit naive. The result was that my university career was set back by ten years, which is of no importance; but of more importance is the fact that I became a journalist, something that would never have happened if I had accepted the chair at Bordeaux. I had never written a single newspaper article. My war pieces were periodical articles, rather academic, something between journalism and serious work. I wrote my first newspaper article for *Combat*.

I said that my decision was irrational. Upon reflection, I am not so sure. It is extraordinarily difficult to know myself whether I chose well or badly. Were thirty years of journalism at *Le Figaro* a contribution to French political life? A meaningful contribution? It's not for me to say. However, if I had remained a full-time professor, I would have been nominated to Paris, very probably to the Sorbonne, in 1947, rather than in 1955.

My journalistic career began essentially because I had to earn a living. I didn't have a cent. I had rejected the university position, the life of a peaceful civil servant, and I had to earn my way. Malraux was a close friend of Pascal Pia, the director of *Combat*. . . .

J.–L.M. – What was the atmosphere like at *Combat*?

R.A. – It was a marvelous institution, typically French, a little crazy. There was an exceptional density of gray matter per square inch in the rooms of *Combat*. Seven or eight people who wrote the short news items became university professors, people like P. Kaufmann, Merleau-Ponty (cousin of Maurice), etc. As for me, I started out by writing a half-dozen articles on the several French political parties. I don't know why, but they met with a great deal of success in Paris circles. After that, I became one of the two editorial writers. The other was Albert Ollivier. So, I began my journalistic career immediately at the top.

At the time, that amused me. And then there is always the question of pride. I arrived as a professor of philosophy who had written obscure books that few had read. Therefore, I wanted to demonstrate that I, too, could handle this profession. But once I had demonstrated it, I was much less excited after a few weeks or months. A number of philosophers who also wrote for *Combat* said to me, "It's curious that you prefer to write articles rather than the *Introduction to the Philosophy of History.*" I thought they were right, but there was this intoxication with politics, as I've told you, and the idea, or the illusion, or the will to participate in political life, in the recovery of France. So I stayed at *Combat* between March 1946 and April 1947, the era of the first political struggles. I was one of those who led the campaign against the first Constitution, defended by the Socialist and Communist parties. I remember my editorial written the day after the referendum rejecting the Constitution. Its title was, *"Sauvé par la Défaite."* I discussed the Socialist party, that was, deep down, very happy to have been beaten in the referendum. It had no desire to find itself part of a duo with the Communist party.

There existed something then that has since died out: debates among editorial writers. They existed during the Third Republic and returned after the Liberation, thanks in part to Camus, Ollivier, and perhaps to myself, and to Mauriac, on the other side, and to Léon Blum. The debates were at once political and intellectual, perhaps too intellectual, but I think their level was often about right. Today, there is no longer a daily "editorialism," nor any dialogue among editorialists. When I write an article or notice one article or another in *Le Monde,* it doesn't seem to be part of a normal dialogue, but, rather, a kind of assault.

At the time, there was real discussion: on the purge, on General de Gaulle and his provisional government, on daily events, on the future of France. That is why the recollection of my time with *Combat* is more agreeable than all my other memories of journalism. It was much more lively than today. There are now only monologues or insults.

D.W. – There was another interesting milepost during this period. With Jean-Paul Sartre, Simone de Beauvoir, Marleau-Ponty, Malraux, you were one of the founders of the periodical *Les Temps Modernes.* What did you expect of it?

R.A. – It was Sartre's magazine. He had already written novels, books on philosophy, plays. He wanted to take part in the political action. That is why he conceived *Les Temps Modernes* as a periodical that was, I won't say essentially political, but quasi-political—that is, from the very beginning, a periodical much less literary in nature than action-oriented. So, he asked friends like me, and also some outstanding intellectual personalities like Jean Paulhan and André Malraux, to serve on the editorial committee of *Les Temps Modernes.* My recollection is that neither Paulhan nor Malraux ever came. I wrote three or four articles for *Les Temps Modernes,* one of which was relatively good. It was on Pétain's trial. It wasn't at all conformist, but *Les Temps Modernes* ran it without any fuss. My other articles didn't amount to much. I left *Les Temps Modernes* when I entered Malraux's cabinet. I didn't return. The illusion of the Liberation had faded away: the assumption that all the Resistants would constitute a single corps and that there would be republican unity for the reconstruction of France. There were Communists in the Resistance bloc and in view of the kind of relations that immediately developed between the Soviet Union and the United States, I was absolutely convinced a break would occur rather rapidly inside the Resistance group.

I constantly tried to explain at the time—to Sartre, for example—that there was such a close connection between international relations and French domestic politics that Resistance unity wouldn't last in the event of tension between the superpowers.

Besides, the near-break inside the Resistance began before the cold war. If the illusion of unity persisted for some time at *Les Temps Modernes,* it was due to the fact that there were no Communists on the editorial committee. But Sartre liked to say, and Merleau-Ponty, also, "My problems with the Communists are just family quarrels". . . an expression I found rather naive.

Moreover, I had immediately developed an overall image of the world. As early as the end of 1945, I was convinced the Soviets would remain in East Germany. Consequently, the reconstitution of a united Germany was excluded; there would be two Germanies. I concluded that the Franco-German alliance was practically sealed. I was only a bit ahead of events.

D.W. – Let's return to *Combat* of that time. It was a successful newspaper and yet it collapsed very quickly. Why?

R.A. – I often said, jokingly, "In Paris, everyone read *Combat;* unfortunately, 'everyone' amounted to only forty thousand people." It was true. One could say that in the political and intellectual world, everyone read the editorials of Camus, Ollivier, perhaps my own. The paper was a great success, but an intellectual one, which meant it did not have enough readers. On top of that, it was characteristic of a super-intellectual newspaper and of the climate of the period that everyone wrote what he thought. So, there were often contradictions from one article to the next. Here is an example. Concerning the referendum on the second Constitution, I wrote a long editorial in which I said, with regret, that it should be accepted because we could not continue writing constitutions and rejecting them. The next day, Albert Ollivier wrote an editorial with the title, *"Pourquoi pas, 'non'?"* But newspaper readers want, from their regular newspaper, less to be educated or informed than to have their opinions reinforced—I found that out later. From the moment a newspaper supports contradictory opinions, it can perhaps continue to exist as a newspaper of opinion, with a limited public, but it cannot expect to keep the 200,000 readers *Combat* had in its heyday. In this sense, the decline of *Combat* was the inevitable consequence of the qualities, or rather, the peculiarities of a newspaper administered and written by intellectuals.

There were crises. Camus left and returned. The relationship between Camus and Pia was difficult. The various *Combat* journalists reproached each other for the loss of readers. For some, Ollivier was responsible; for others, Raymond Aron; for still others, this one or that one. In fact, we just didn't know. It was probably a combination of everyone. Each was acceptable to part of the readership; together, they always exasperated some of the readers.

Moreover, the director was himself an intellectual, a novelist. We also had difficulties with the printers. I remember one time when the union members said to us very firmly, "We need a boss!" The printers perhaps looked upon our ideas with favor, and perhaps they looked favorably upon intellectuals—that's not so certain—but they were workers, they expected their pay and they wanted the opportunity to discuss with someone the enterprise, salaries, etc. However, it is indeed possible to find a manager among intellectuals. Later, Jean-Jacques Servan-Schreiber, who was in his way an intellectual, was also, without any doubt, a manager.

J.–L.M. – General de Gaulle quit the government in January 1946. Did you approve of his departure?

R.A. – It wasn't my business to approve or disapprove. I understood his reasons. He was in a situation he considered intolerable. He did not want to govern France in the parliamentary framework or to conduct endless discussions and negotiations with the political parties, even though he had extraordinary talents as a parliamentarian. I heard him once or twice at the Consultative Assembly. If he had wanted to, he could have governed France as prime minister, in view of his historic stature and his talents as a debater. But he did not want to govern France in this fashion.

I knew, however, that he had the desire, hope, and conviction that he would return to power. I remember André

Malraux telling me, after a conversation with some people in General de Gaulle's entourage, "We'll be back in six months." It took twelve years. At that time, I saw no imperative reason for his return. I believed that, for what it was worth, the parliamentary regime could last. In *Le Grand Schisme,* I wrote, "The Fourth Republic can last; it cannot innovate." That's pretty much what I thought. It was a piece I wrote in 1947 and it was published in 1948.

D.W. – Concerning General de Gaulle's departure, we have found an IFOP poll. In March 1946, 40% regretted his departure; 32% were satisfied; 28% were indifferent. People were far from unanimous about de Gaulle!

R.A. – It is important to note that the first de Gaulle government wasn't very different from a government of the Third or Fourth Republic, except that on this occasion the head of government was an exceptional personality. However, General de Gaulle was not responsible for the economic and parliamentary difficulties, and he could not eliminate them, either. So, in withdrawing in 1946, he didn't leave behind him the memory of an exceptional head of state, neither among the French in general nor in the political class. When someone would make the observation to me, my reply was always, "Yes, he arrived in power and he had all the power, it's true, but he lacked a telephone." That was a little bit the French situation in 1944 at the Liberation. On the other hand, in 1944-1945, de Gaulle was already obsessed with foreign policy, while the French were more concerned with food supply problems and reconstruction. But in terms of domestic policy, de Gaulle didn't do anything in 1944-1945 that was substantially different than any other prime minister would have done. What's more, in the argument between Pleven and Mendés-France on the economic program, the intellectuals were the Mendés-France. Were they right? In my opinion, what Mendés-France wanted to do was right, but he lacked the means to realize it. In any case, de Gaulle had chosen Pleven, with the result that he lost some prestige in the eyes of those intellectuals aware of French economic conditions.

In power, de Gaulle was accepted, just as Pétain had been accepted in 1940. But because he came to power, not in order to suppress political activity, as Pétain had done, but to restore it, the political parties inevitably became active again. Some of the French were on the Right, the others on the Left:

Socialists and Communists. To the degree that a party was for or against de Gaulle, party members were themselves more or less in agreement with, or against him. De Gaulle was above and beyond parties, but he could not avoid restoring the party system, though he detested it, because he had decided earlier that, upon returning to France, he would reestablish the Republic and democracy, and he could not do otherwise. But since he did not wish to govern with the parties, he left. It seems to me his decision was logical. So that, in 1946, there were three groups: The Communists, the anticommunists, and a third, a personality who constituted a group by himself, General de Gaulle.

There was, on the one hand, the battle between de Gaulle and all the parties; on the other, there was the battle inside the parties between the Communists and the rest of the members. That was at once the curse and the singularity of the Fourth Republic, which could have lasted longer if it hadn't been for Algeria. But to try to resolve Algeria and hold out against de Gaulle at the same time was too much for the Fourth Republic.

D.W. – You say, "It wasn't my business to approve or disapprove of General de Gaulle's departure." But it is a fact that you were in the government at that time. Furthermore, why did you want to take that step, that is, to enter the political arena, when you could have influenced events as an intellectual, or journalist?

R.A. – My friendship with Malraux was a factor. I was very close to him. We had a long talk before his first interview with de Gaulle, let's call it something like the meeting between Goethe and Napoleon. I was involved in Malraux's conversion to Gaullism, a logical move, it seemed to me. After the war, he was affected, like others, by a national, almost a nationalistic, feeling. At the same time, he had ceased to be a revolutionary, and the only political poetry possible in postwar France was General de Gaulle. Now, Malraux was interested in politics only in their historic or poetic sense. So, it was perfectly normal for him to become a Gaullist.

As for me, I was never a Gaullist in the same way as André Malraux. De Galle said so himself. One day, I wrote an article displeasing to the General, *"Adieu au Gaullisme."* The next day, he said to Malraux, "He has never been a Gaullist." If being a Gaullist meant being General de Gaulle's vassal, or believing in him whatever his opinions, then, indeed, I was not a Gaullist. No more so after the Liberation than before. When I was in the RPF,[19] I continued to express opinions totally different from those of General de Gaulle on a number of questions. However, in one sense, and on several occasions, I was a Gaullist. At the time of the Liberation, I thought that General de Gaulle's government was much the best and that it was necessary to support it. In 1958, I thought that de Gaulle's return to power, even though the circumstances were unpleasant, was rather desirable because, with him, there was a chance that France might be able to take a decision on Algeria. But my manner of being a Gaullist could not be satisfying to him. To be truly Gaullist, it was necessary to have faith in de Gaulle and to be ready to change one's own opinions to agree with his. I could not do it, but that didn't prevent me from being André Malraux's *directeur de cabinet.*

J.–L.M. – But this friendship with André Malraux was really astonishing. Your personalities were very different. It was the difference between hot and cold!

R.A. – Absolutely. But do friendships generally spring up between people with similar personalities? André Malraux was eminently cultivated, and we had in common many subjects of conversation: Literature, history, politics. When he wasn't chasing a will-o'-the-wisp, he was a very acute analyst of political matters. From time to time, his romantic attitude toward catastrophes got the better of his sense of reality. That was true between 1946 or 1950, but we could generally discuss French and international politics with a great deal of pleasure and purpose. Moreover, in friendly relations between two people, there are factors at work that are quite outside the analysis of personalities. There is the chance that something will click between the two individuals; at the same time, the reverse is also possible: that they will be like two ships passing in the night. Between Sartre and Malraux, there never was a "click." I found myself between the two. In a way, I acted quite differently with one than with the other. I didn't have the same kind of conversation with each of them. Each was glad to speak about the other, but not always in the most friendly way.

Unfortunately, my friendship with Malraux didn't last until the end. He gradually became very closed, very solitary. As one of General de Gaulle's ministers, he was often irritated by what I wrote. I still saw him from time to time, and I retained the same admiration and friendship for him that I had felt over the years. But as we grew older, problems of distance, separation and sadness weighed upon us. A little bit the way it was with Sartre. For men of our generation, it seemed impossible to sustain friendships when political choices did not coincide. Political affairs were probably too serious and too drama-filled for friendships to overcome differences. In the case of my relations with Sartre, that was very clear. As far as Malraux was concerned, I don't think it was my non-Gaullism or the inadequacy of my Gaullism that was at the bottom of our gradual separation. There was something else, more personal. It would be necessary to talk about the last part of Malraux's life. But this is not the time.

D.W. – This political virus that you spoke about; how long did it grip you?

R.A. – If by that you refer to the inclination to be a politician, the virus never affected me very much, and, in any case, I was able to rid myself of it very quickly. But if by political virus you mean a permanent attention to political events, then the contamination began during the war and I have never been cured. To the extent that I commented upon events in *Le Figaro* over a period of thirty years, between 1947 and 1977, I remained permanently a quasi-political person. I have not considered myself a political activist because I was never a candidate for anything. But I was a political journalist or a political writer, who commented on daily events and simultaneously wrote academic works.

I have used the words "virus" and "contamination" because I still remember the philosopher I was before 1939 and the opinion I held at the time of the Ecole Normale graduates who drifted toward politics. I didn't think well of them. I have occasionally, but very rarely, kept a diary. I found there once a few sentences in which I denounced in advance what might happen to me, that is, to find myself drawn toward political activity. Before 1939, I aired my editorials in conversations. Later, I wrote them. Well, that's the way it worked out.

c) Yalta: The Legend of the World's Partition

J.–L.M. – At Hiroshima, in August 1945, the first atomic bomb exploded. How was this event perceived at the time?

R.A. – It was immediately perceived as a landmark event. The discovery of nuclear explosives was a turning point in universal history, and people began to speculate. Did it mean that there could be no more wars? Did it mean that humanity was going to commit suicide? And so on. It is important to emphasize that people immediately began to reflect upon, and write about, the event; no one failed to understand its importance or its historical significance. On the contrary, people rapidly went too far. They began to hope that war would disappear simply because a single bomb could destroy half a city. We didn't know then that the Hiroshima bomb, with a yield of 20,000 tons of TNT, was a very small thing. Today, we talk about megatons.

J.–L.M. – Was it perceived as a hideous thing?

R.A. – There were no protest movements. The Communist party was enthusiastic. On the whole, it was accepted by public opinion. The American generals were relieved. Thanks to the atom bomb, it was not necessary to invade the Japanese islands. The generals had told President Truman that the invasion could cost as many as 500,000 lives in the first weeks. Hence, there was no moral or spiritual revolt against this weapon. It was much later, with the advent of the cold war, that the arguing began, with the Americans accused of having used the weapon needlessly, just to scare the USSR.

D.W. – However, is it not Hiroshima that partly explains the reserve, even the hostility, of Europeans with regard to the United States?

R.A. – I do not believe that at all. Don't forget that peoples, or governments, after four or five years of war, are capable of committing the worst atrocities without being aware of it. The bombing of Dresden was just as terrible, and perhaps worse than, Hiroshima. There were 300,000 deaths in one night. The city was crowded with refugees. The great bombing attack on Tokyo, in the course of which the city was burned, cost ninety thousand lives. Everyone accepted these bombings, this blind destruction, as a natural form of war. It was only when people emerged from the delirium of war, from the paroxysm of violence, that they realized men had done things that were, if not comparable to Hitler's actions, nonetheless absolutely terrible, unjustified and unnecessary for winning the war.

Even if the senseless principle of unconditional surrender

had not been adopted, Japan's imminent defeat was clearly spelled out. The country had no more warships, no more freighters; it was a prisoner of its islands. If there had been a willingness to negotiate, obtaining satisfactory peace terms would have been very feasible. But Roosevelt wanted unconditional surrender, a notion that went back to the Civil War. At that time, the formula made sense because it was the very existence of the United States that was in balance. Those who seceded had to capitulate and accept federal authority. Unconditional surrender made sense in a civil war. In a foreign war, it was absurd. Hiroshima was partially the result of the unconditional surrender precept.

D.W. – Let's come back to Europe. Would it have been possible to avoid the gradual domination of a part of Eastern Europe by the Soviet Union in 1945-1946?

R.A. – First, one saw the gradual Sovietization of the Eastern European countries. The Americans protested because they felt that at Yalta the USSR had committed itself to democratic reconstruction. But democratic reconstruction had a different meaning for the Russians than for the Americans.

Then, one noted that there gradually developed a more or less impassable line of demarcation between the areas occupied by the Soviets and those occupied by the English and the Americans.

Could it have been prevented? My first remark: It was not because of Yalta that Eastern Europe became Communist.

D.W. – Nevertheless, people say that it was Yalta that determined the partition of the world.

R.A. – No, that's the legend.

D.W. – Then what did happen at Yalta?

R.A. – First of all, there was an agreement about the date and the modalities of Russian intervention against Japan. The date was set at three months after the end of the war in Europe.

The borders of the German occupation zones were also confirmed. These zones had been fixed by an ambassadors' committee in London and the confirmation took two minutes. So, the occupation zones of Germany were not really discussed at Yalta.

There were other discussions on reparations and secondary questions. And there was one decision whose consequences were considerable. This determined the line at which troops coming from the East and those coming from the West would stop. It was the fixing of this line of demarcation that has mistakenly been considered as the decision on the partition of Europe.

As far as Europe's future was concerned, there was a final decision on the terms for the democratic reconstruction of the continent. Neither the Americans nor the English had agreed that the countries liberated by the Soviet army would be reconstructed on the Soviet model. Perhaps they should have understood that it be done that way, but they did not believe they had accepted it. The best proof is that the difficulties between the United States and the USSR began on the question of the Polish government. At Yalta, the Soviets had accepted an enlargement of the Lublin Committee, then wholly Communist. A number of Polish political figures came over from the West, theoretically to broaden the Communist government. But after a few months, they were obliged to leave.

In the short term, even in Czechoslovakia, that had been liberated by the Soviet army, free elections were held. The elections in Hungary were also relatively free because the party of the small landowners, absolutely not Communist, obtained a majority. In Czechoslovakia, the Communists received 38% of the vote, thus falling well short of a majority.

So, when people say that the world, or Europe, was partitioned at Yalta, it really is a legend. Before Yalta, an agreement—a secret agreement—had indeed been made between Churchill and Stalin. But the Americans rejected it. Percentages had been set. Ninety percent of Greece would be under British control and 10% would go to the USSR. For Romania, I think, 80 or 90% was to go to the Soviets and 20% to the Allies. This wholly cynical deal was not discussed at Yalta. It was the movement of armies that brought about the partition, not of the world, but of Europe. The West could have foreseen that the point at which their troops stopped would also become the outermost border of Western-type democracies. But they didn't think about it ahead of time and they did not agree ahead of time to what the USSR ultimately did.

The USSR did in Eastern Europe what it had the intention of doing. Stalin had said to Djilas, "In a war like this one, the victors bring with them their ideas and their regimes." The West tolerated this Sovietization because there was no way to prevent it. Once Soviet troops are in place, you either bring pressure on Moscow by a threat or an ultimatum, that is, if you have the forces to push the troops back; or else you declare that it is unacceptable—in other words, that you accept it.

That is what happened in 1945 and 1946. The West declared that Soviet conduct in Eastern Europe was unacceptable. But because the Americans had demobilized their troops immediately, they tolerated it, though they protested, and there was some diplomatic tension.

J.–L.M. – Did the West purchase its tranquility by sacrificing the East Europeans?

R.A. – That's a formula the East Europeans use frequently. Perhaps it is an expression that Solzhenitsyn also uses. It seems to me that the truth is less simple. Soviet troops arrived and occupied a part of Europe, the Western countries took note of this Sovietization that they didn't like, and that was not in their interest. But they lacked both the possibility and the political courage to use drastic measures to prevent it. It is easy, after the fact, to say that they should not have accepted this development. But how could they convince their peoples that the Soviet Union, that had contributed so importantly to the victory over Hitler's Germany, had suddenly become the danger, the menace—the devil. A democracy never allies itself in war with the devil. So, because the war had been fought with the Soviet Union, the war had been fought, perforce, with a democracy and not with a totalitarian regime. . . . As long as the Soviet Union was an ally, it could not be considered totalitarian. There would have been a kind of moral revolt against the fact of having fought a war against one devil, alongside another devil.

Again, it is easy, using hindsight, to condemn the government leaders. Perhaps Roosevelt would have acted differently if he had known better the Soviet Union and Europe. But basically, what took place corresponded to the logic of that war, because it was won by potential enemies; and each of these potential enemies took a half of Europe. But one half was Sovietized and the other half had the opportunity to rebuild itself thanks to American aid, although a number of Frenchmen continue to think that the American influence in Western Europe was (or is) the equivalent of the influence—if it can be called influence—of the USSR in Eastern Europe.

D.W. – But surely people knew what the Soviet Union's concept of democracy was.

R.A. – You are speaking in 1981. But in 1945 it wasn't known. Some people knew; Roosevelt didn't. Roosevelt didn't believe all that. Churchill was better informed; he had had long experiences as a European statesman. He had no doubt that the Soviets would try to transform the countries it occupied into satellite countries. But he saw no way of preventing it. Was it possible? In a sense, it was, but in the abstract. The United States was much more powerful than the Soviet Union. The Soviet Union was exhausted from the war. It didn't yet have the atomic bomb. But you must remember that the United States had only the two atomic bombs it used against Japan. It didn't have any others in 1945 or 1946. It knew how to make them, but they were not yet made. Furthermore, as I have said, when the war ended following Japan's capitulation, the Americans, as is their habit, hastened to demobilize. From that moment on, their ability to influence Soviet decisions was, at the very least, reduced.

It took a few years for the Americans to understand fully what, you could say, every Swiss hotel doorman had immediately realized. That is, the moment Germany was eliminated and there was a void in Europe, that void would be filled by Soviet power. It would have been the same if the Soviet Union had not been Communist. It would have been enough to have an overpowerful Russia with nothing in front of it for there to be a danger.

But there was the aggravating circumstance that Russia was, in fact, the Soviet Union; it was clear that the void had to be filled. First, it was necessary to rebuild those countries that were "victors on paper": Great Britain, France, and the others. Then, it was necessary to rebuild the vanquished. The need to reconstruct Germany became evident very rapidly to those with any political acumen. It took two or three years for the others to understand that, and they did so only with difficulty, even then. De Gaulle himself had trouble with it, for he repeated incessantly, "Never again the Reich."

D.W. – In the final analysis, was the partition of Germany and its occupation by the various armies an error? What should have been done?

R.A. – We could not force the Soviets to leave East Germany. Some thought there was a chance to create a unified and neutral Germany. I never believed it, for the simple reason that, as early as the autumn of 1945, the Russians began to Sovietize East Germany. From the moment they began to do so, their intentions to remain there were clear. It was and still is a basic principle of Soviet diplomacy: What is ours must remain ours; the rest can be negotiated. So, the chances of de-Sovietizing East Germany were very slim, while the liberation of Austria, on the other hand, was possible because the Russians did not try (or were not able) to Sovietize that country. It was the sign that they contemplated leaving some day. That is why I thought this liberation would take place in Austria and not in East Germany. Concerning Austria, 250 negotiating sessions were held, with no results. One day, the Communists decided to leave. Only twenty sessions were needed to wrap it up.

But as soon as it was realized that intervention in East Germany was impossible, the reconstitution of West Germany became imperative. Of this, I was immediately convinced and quite categoric. I wrote, as early as 1945:

> The historic conflict between France and Germany has ended. For Germany, the 1945 defeat is equivalent to 1815 for France. In the foreseeable future, Germany cannot again be the major danger. The great power in Europe now is the Soviet Union and its satellites. If an equilibrium is to be reestablished, the American presence in Europe is necessary and, additionally, Western Europe must be reconstructed. And Western Germany cannot be reconstructed without West Germany.

That is why, when General de Gaulle, who was no longer in office, drafted a message against the tri-zone, which signalled the beginning of the Bonn Republic, I wrote in favor of the tri-zone. I considered that the creation of the Bonn Republic was necessary. My belief was that, precisely at that moment, we stood the best chance of creating new and personal relations between the Germans and the French. The Germans were at their lowest ebb. And it is when the enemy is beaten that the conqueror must show generosity, that he must not use his superior power, that he must create new ties with the vanquished.

So, I returned to Germany, beginning in 1945-1946. I gave a lecture at the University of Frankfurt in 1946 and resumed my contacts with the Germans immediately. People said to me, "You're lucky, you can do it because you are Jewish." It was the only time in my life I was told I was lucky to be Jewish. But it is true that at that particular time, a Jew could write in favor of reconciliation with Germany more easily than others.

D.W. – The Gaullists and the Communists were against reconciliation. Who was in favor?

R.A. – Privately, all reasonable men. Publicly, a few. Nonetheless, a few. The MRP,[20] Camus, many others, thought the same thing. The difference was that I thought of the reconciliation in a much more political way than the others. But many did find it necessary. All you had to do was to look at the map. The Soviet zone reached to within 200 kilometers of the Rhine River. Very clearly, West Germany was not a great power. Today, it is a great economic power, but not a great military power. However, because the Federal Republic of Germany exists, we are, for the first time, not on the front lines. To the degree that a danger exists, Germany lies between the great threatening power and France.

All of that was evident. Soviet expansionism could leave no one in doubt. The USSR had already Sovietized Poland. It was very rapidly transforming all the countries of Eastern Europe into Soviet regimes. But it is true that for three, four, or five years, it was extraordinarily difficult for the French to accept the fact that, from then on, the danger no longer came from Germany, but from the Soviet Union.

By the time the Korean War began in 1950, I would say that the idea was accepted by the majority of Frenchmen. As for Germany, people had, despite everything, accepted in 1947 its participation in the Marshall Plan; that is to say, they had accepted the idea of cooperative and almost friendly relations between the countries of Western Europe and West Germany.

J.–L.M. – The war resulted in the triumph of two great powers, the United States *and the* Soviet Union. Europe was weakened; France in particular was no more than a regional power. Was there an awareness of this on the part of political leaders and public opinion?

R.A. – That was not something to say out loud, but, of course, people were aware of it. You must understand, the 1914 war began as a European war. It became a world war toward the end, with U.S. intervention. The 1939 war began as a European war, won by Nazi Germany in 1940. But, beginning that same year, a second war began which became truly worldwide, first with the participation of the Soviet Union, attacked by Germany, and then with the participation of the United States and the entry of Japan into a great war in Asia. It became thus the first great war that was truly worldwide in scope.

So, the idea of European entente belonged to the past. In the European entente, France had been a great power. In the world entente, France, with forty million inhabitants in 1945, was manifestly not a great power.

J.–L.M. – However, we have two IFOP polls that are not in accord with what you say and that give the impression that the French were dreaming a little. In December 1944, 64% felt that their country had recovered its position as a great power. In March 1945, 70% thought France should annex the left bank of the Rhine.

R.A. – The first poll: We had been accepted as one of the five permanent members of the United Nations Security Council. We are still there. In this legal sense, we appear to be a great world power.

Second poll: That was an opinion shared by a large number of the French in 1918. And beyond that, people remembered the events of 1936, that is, the reoccupation of the Rhineland, the turning point. The French and de Gaulle himself continued to be preoccupied by the question of Germany for a few years. De Gaulle wanted reconciliation with Germany, but with a Germany that would not have a central government, that would accept a special status for the Ruhr and, possibly, for the Rhineland. With these reservations, he offered his hand to the Germans.

My own thinking was that it was contradictory to take so many precautions against a danger that belonged to the past, and, at the same time, propose reconciliation with Germany. This reconciliation could not take place with the *Länder* (the regions) as separate German countries. The *Länder* without a central government didn't make sense. Reconciliation was necessary with a West Germany that would indeed have *Länder,* but also a central government. Now, when people said, "No Reich," that clearly meant: no central government.

That made no sense . . . but it was General de Gaulle's doctrine, and that of André Malraux, until 1950 and later.

J.–L.M. – And the first misunderstandings between France
and the United States? Don't they date back precisely to the
period of Liberation?

R.A. – The relations between General de Gaulle and President Roosevelt were always difficult. Roosevelt played the Vichy card for a long time and did not accept General de
Gaulle's legitimacy. As a result, there were resentments on
both sides. It must be said also that the Americans were very
disagreeable toward France with regard to Indochina.
Roosevelt was against the French return to Indochina. Unfortunately, he didn't succeed in preventing them from returning, which would have been better. But at the time, we were
certainly not grateful to him for his attitude. Finally, it is true
that Roosevelt, who had earlier been rather pro-French, was
so shocked by the French defeat that he had no faith in the reconstruction or in the future of France.

So, there were tensions almost immediately. But most of all,
and almost by definition, relations could not be easy between
a victorious superpower and a humiliated ex-power seeking
to regain its former status. The relations between the two
countries were destined to be unpleasant, whoever the men
in power.

D.W. – Yes, but at the same time, one has the impression
that at the Liberation, the French had almost more gratitude
toward the Russians than toward the Americans.

R.A. – Mostly, perhaps, because they didn't see the Russians, but did see the Americans!

Secondly, American bombings had caused damage outside
their targets. There were emotional reactions when American
planes dropped their bombs from very high altitudes, in theory very precisely, but in fact less so, thought many Frenchmen, than the English. Also, there certainly existed a Soviet
mystique at the time, justified to a degree by the enormous
losses suffered by the Soviets. The Americans had suffered a
few hundred thousand deaths, which is certainly a lot, but
was nonetheless a limited sacrifice when compared to the
millions and millions of Soviet soldiers and civilians who had
been killed.

Curiously, the French didn't want to admit that Stalin

refused France a zone of occupation in Germany, or that he was even less willing than Roosevelt to have General de Gaulle at the Yalta conference, or that he spoke of the French with still more contempt than the Americans might have done. However, I don't think that when Europeans, even the French, had the choice of taking refuge either in the Soviet Union or in the United States they were tempted to go East, no.

D.W. – Another poll, taken in November 1944, therefore before the end of the war, underscored once again the good opinion the French harbored for the Soviet Union: 61% thought the Soviet Union had played the most important role in the German defeat, and only 29% the United States.

R.A. – On that subject, I can recall for you a conversation I had with Pierre Brisson, director of *Le Figaro*. "Clearly, it was the Americans who won the first World War," I said to him, "because if they had not begun to arrive in 1917, we would have lost the war." To that, he burst out, "But they did almost nothing; they arrived at the end. Just compare what they did and what we French did." And I answered, "Agreed; our was the heaviest, the costliest burden of the war; we were heroic beyond all expression, but those who arrived at the end and won the war were the Americans. Those who win a war are not necessarily those who most merit the fruits of victory; they are simply those who arrive at the end." As far as World War II is concerned, the Soviet Union would have had great difficulty in hanging on to the end if Great Britain and, above all, the United States, had not kept it supplied. On the other hand, even if the Soviet Union's contribution to victory was superior to the Americans' in terms of lives lost, in the last analysis, for us, it was the American contribution that was decisive. I think the American effort was decisive because Great Britain could not have kept up the struggle if it had not been for America's engagement. And even suppose, and it is an at least dubious supposition, that the Soviet Union, with Great Britain—but without the United States—had won the war; in such a case, the whole of Europe would have been Sovietized.

J.–L.M. – Did the intellectuals share the same favorable prejudice toward the Soviet Union?

R.A. – Yes. There have been cycles in France, periods when the Soviet Union held an attraction for a fairly sizable group of intellectuals and workers.

There was an early period of attraction between 1917 and 1919, which led to the breakup at the Congress of Tours.[21] The Socialist party's majority accepted the Third International's charter.

In 1936, the restructuring of the unions occurred under Communist direction. Communist party membership increased after it became part of the Left majority.

Then, after the war, the memory of the heroism of a good number of Communist Resistants played a role. The Communists entered the Resistance in large numbers, beginning in 1941, when the Soviet Union came into the war. The phenomenon was such that many Frenchmen tended to mix up in their thinking the courage of the Communist Resistants and the courage and heroism of the Soviet soldiers. At that time, I said to Malraux, who subsequently adopted the phrase, "The Soviet myth today is the Red Army, rather than Marxism."

So, at the end of the war, there was the distant greatness of the Soviet Union, heroic and victorious. And then in a few years, people rediscovered the nature of the Soviet regime, especially because Stalin was, after the war, super-Stalinian, if I may put it that way. For example, all the Soviet prisoners, civilian or military, repatriated to the USSR against their wishes, were put in concentration camps. You are aware that the British and the Americans repatriated them forcibly. One learned about it, but slowly, very slowly. That was among the things one didn't want to know.

D.W. – It was at that time that you entered *Le Figaro.* Your first article was dated June 29, 1947. Can one say that Raymond Aron chose the Right at that time?

R.A. – No, he chose between *Le Monde* and *Le Figaro.* I've told the story several times. When I left *Combat,* I had proposals and, I'll say it now, financial proposals, that were about the same from both sides, each just as modest as the other. I hesitated. It was Malraux who determined my choice. He said to me, "You will have less difficulty getting along with André Brisson than with Beuve-Méry." He was right.

There was another reason, a little silly. At *Le Monde,* I

would have had to do my journalistic work in the morning. But I wanted to save my mornings for serious work, university work. So I preferred to write for a morning, rather than for an evening, newspaper.

However, let me add that if *Le Figaro* was traditionally considered a newspaper of the Right, Brisson voted for the Socialist party after the war. And he favored the Labor party in England. The fact is that I would have had a great deal of difficulty in agreeing with Beuve-Méry on the big foreign policy decisions. Nevertheless, I don't know. . . . In 1977, when I was hospitalized, I received a letter from Beuve-Méry that touched me deeply. He told me that he had very much hoped I would join *Le Monde* and that even now (at the time of my illness) he regretted my decision. He thought that if I had gone to *Le Monde,* the evolution of that newspaper would possibly have been different and the conflicts between *Le Monde* and *Le Figaro* would have taken a different turn. In any case, that was in 1977, and I had made my decision in 1947, thirty years earlier. I was at *Le Figaro* exactly thirty years, between the spring of 1947 and the spring of 1977. A long story.

Section Two

Democracy and Totalitarianism

I
THE GREAT SCHISM, 1947-1956

a) Who Won the Cold War?

D. Wolton. – Let's return to *Le Figaro*. You began there, we have learned, in the spring of 1947. Was it your way of taking part in the cold war?

Raymond Aron. – Absolutely not. I entered *Le Figaro*, as I told you, after having chosen between that newspaper and *Le Monde*. At the beginning, there wasn't much difference between the two. *Le Figaro* had the reputation of being more rightist, but the director, Brisson, had decided to give the newspaper a different orientation. Before the war, it was considered to be rather academic, with a circulation of about eighty thousand. Right after the war, because its name was known, it become a great national newspaper, something it had never been before. It is true that there was not much love lost between Beuve-Méry and Brisson. But they were still on speaking terms. In any case, my choice of *Le Figaro* was certainly not linked to the cold war.

D.W. – In terms of time, however, didn't your choice coincide with the beginning of the cold war?

R.A. – When did it begin? Historians argue about it. Some say, in 1944; others, in 1945. Generally, it is set at the beginning of 1947. At a point of fact, let's say that the civil war in Greece was already a cold war episode. In 1945, quarrels broke out between the United States and the Soviet Union over the conditions in which the new Polish government was constituted. Later, there were interminable negotiations on Germany. I think the most symbolic act was the breakup of negotiations between the West and the Soviets on the German question. That finally happened in 1947. There was first the recognition that agreement was impossible; then, the Western decision to rebuild West Germany, first, by joining the English and American zones and then by adding the

French zone. From that moment on, from 1947, that is, it was clear that a new West German state was going to be created, which meant the at least temporary, and possibly definitive, division of Germany. For me, it signified the acceptance of a division of the former Germany—at the time, I took bets for at least a generation. At the end of twenty years, I still kept my bet. I continue to keep it today. Now, if there were two Germanies, there were also two Europes. When I gave a lecture at the University of Frankfurt in 1950, I told the audience, mostly students, "Germany will remain divided as long as Europe is divided."

Germany seemed to be at once the symbol, the origin, the cause, and the reality itself of this division. With the Soviet Union keeping for itself a part of Germany, the evident result was that Europe would be divided into two areas; one governed in the Soviet manner, the other governed in the manner we call democratic.

J.–L. Missika. – 1947 was also the year of the Marshall Plan. Was this plan a factor in the division of Europe, or was it a consequence?

R.A. – The Marshall Plan was a reaction to the situation observed in Europe: the misery, the Sovietization of the eastern part of Europe. It expressed a determination to erect a dam—not a military, but a political and economic dam—against Soviet expansionism. The idea was that it was necessary for the countries of Western Europe to be able to resist Soviet propaganda and, for France, to resist the Communist party. The necessary condition was the economic reconstruction of Europe. Because it was decided to reconstruct Western Europe, it was necessary to have Germany participate. It was through the Marshall Plan that the Germans found their place in the common European and Atlantic organizations.

At the same time, the Marshall Plan was also offered to the Soviets and the acceptance depended solely upon Stalin. As you know, the Czech government had accepted it before the Soviet interdiction. Those who conceived the Marshall Plan were not hostile to participation by the Soviet Union, but they judged it improbable. My friend Bohlen, who later became ambassador to France, was convinced that the Soviet Union would refuse to participate. On the other hand, if the Soviets had accepted it, would the United States Senate have approved the plan? In the final analysis, experts on Soviet politics were not surprised by Stalin's refusal, even though some of them were astonished that he didn't want all those dollars offered him. But he could not accept them, probably for the following reason: It was planned that the Europeans would decide among themselves on the repartition of the funds placed at their disposal by the United States. Now, such a European Council, in which the Soviet Union and the countries of Eastern Europe would have to participate, was unacceptable to Stalin.

D.W. – Grave events marked those cold war years: In Europe, the Prague coup, in February 1948; Stalin's Berlin blockade from May 1948 to May 1949; the revolts crushed by the Soviets in East Berlin in June 1953, and in Budapest in October-November 1956. In Asia, there was the triumph of the Chinese revolution in January 1949; the Chinese-Soviet friendship treaty of February 1950. There was also the war in Indochina, and the Korean War that began in 1950.

At one moment or another, did you ever have the feeling that a world war was in the offing once again?

R.A. – At certain moments I had some worry. But most often, I doubted that there was a very great danger of a generalized war in those years. I said that at the beginning of the cold war in my book *Le Grand Schisme*, published in 1948. The title of the first chapter was *"Paix Impossible, Guerre Improbable."* The rivalry in Europe and in the world between the USSR and the West would last for years. A real peace between the two worlds was not forseeable; it was even unlikely. On the other hand, neither the United States nor the Soviet Union had a desire or an interest in turning to war. It was the beginning of the nuclear age. The Soviet Union was probably just as expansionist as Nazi Germany had been, but its expansionism was of a wholly different nature. Stalin had always been a prudent man. Even during that period, he continued to be relatively cautious. For example, the Berlin blockade was never proclaimed; it was simply a fact. First, the Soviets claimed that railroad repairs were necessary, and then, that the canals had to be repaired, and so forth. So, gradually, a blockade came about. If the Americans had responded differently, Stalin would probably not have gone as far as a blockade.

J.–L.M. – Responded differently?

R.A. – The Americans should have told the Russians that their pretexts were not plausible, that making repairs would not prevent the use of the railroads, or the circulation of barges on the canals, and so on . . . An English leftist politician, Aneurin Bevan, claimed immediately that the blockade was a Soviet bluff and that there was no reason for fear. It would have sufficed, he said, to send a military convoy through East Germany to Berlin and the blockade would be ended.

In fact, because the United States had demobilized its army and there were few military forces in Europe, the Americans accepted the blockade. But the manner in which they overcame it was probably a more brilliant victory than if they had broken it with military force. They showed that, through an airlift, a population of two and a half million could be supplied almost normally. The airlift became a remarkable political and technical achievement and created lasting ties of affection between the Berliners and the West. Something of it remains. This was in a sense one of the great moments of the cold war. An important battle that cost only a few deaths, all accidental.

D.W. – The Soviet Union exploded its first atomic bomb in July 1949. Did this increase the risk of war, with the equilibrium of forces having been modified?

R.A. – There, we are in fact approaching a moment when the Europeans really feared a war; this was in 1950, when the Korean campaign began, especially during the first few weeks of U.S. military reversals. I recall having received from Concarneau a letter of André Malraux in which he said of the French, "A strange people that prepares for war by accumulating stocks of sardines."

In fact, there was a near-panic, an unreasonable fear of war. It was caused in large part by Soviet propaganda. When, for example, North Korea invaded the South, East German newspapers said, "It will soon be West Germany's turn." Korea gave people the impression of being the equivalent of divided Germany. What happened in Korea might happen in Germany. But the comparison was not valid. South Korea did not have the same significance as West Germany and in Korea it was possible to fight a limited war, which is what the Americans did.

J.–L.M. – At the time, you expressed astonishment in your *Figaro* articles. In substance, you said, "These Americans are strange, they permit communism to triumph in an immense country like China, and they go to war for tiny Korea."

R.A. – They were right. If they had tried to prevent the communist victory in China, it would have been a much greater catastrophe than Vietnam. We would have had a Vietnam to the nth degree. However, they intervened in Korea because, if they hadn't, their passivity would have had considerable symbolic significance. I think that was the decisive motive of President Truman and Secretary of State Acheson.

I had a conversation in Washington with the secretary of state in early December 1950. He told me that the basic reason for his advising Truman to intervene was the following: It was the first occasion the United States had to demonstrate to the world that it would stand up to its commitments. If it did not support South Korea, which had been attacked by the forces of North Korea, the whole world would doubt American promises. The Americans fought the Korean War in large part to reassure the Europeans. Moreover, South Korea had been created under the aegis of the United States and the United Nations. To let this republic that had organized more or less free elections be destroyed by North Korea—which had refused all contact with the United Nations—would have been a political defeat and a real moral disaster for the United States. So I think that, if you keep the overall world situation in mind, the American intervention in Korea was wholly justified.

However, we probably gave the North Korean attack a significance it didn't really have.

We know today that the attack was mostly the idea of Kim Il-song, the head of North Korea. Stalin certainly gave the green light, but it is by no means certain that the initiative was his. As for Mao Tse-Tung, American historians today believe he wasn't even aware of North Korea's intentions. It is known now that China did not at all want to enter the Korean War. The Chinese attack came because the Americans failed to take their warnings seriously. The Korean War became an event of highest importance because of a series of misunderstandings between the two sides.

D.W. – And the Indo-Chinese War? Officially, its start is linked to the failure of the Fontainebleau accords. What did you think about it?

R.A. – It began, in fact, in December 1946. The Fontainebleau agreements were not the real cause. The reasons were numerous, but the most directly decisive event was the bombardment of Haiphong harbor by French guns. That was an unjustifiable act that cost several thousand lives.

D.W. – It was condemned at the time. Did you denounce it?

R.A. – I thought it was senseless. I believe I wrote an article in *Combat* the day the war began in December 1946.[22] It expressed my perplexity and my contradictory feelings. It was clear that I did not favor the reconquest of Indochina by military means. As much the Gaullist as he was, Malraux himself said, "It would take ten years and 500,000 men to retake Indochina." He was mistaken in that neither ten years nor 500,000 men sufficed. Despite all that he felt that he had to say or write in the 1950s, Malraux, who knew Indochina well, had exactly the same opinion as I. He judged that the French effort was destined to fail, and that it was wholly unreasonable in view of France's poverty at the time, its reconstruction needs, etc.

But French patriotism at the time was such that the abandonment of a part of the empire was, it seems, unacceptable to public opinion in general, and especially to the public I was addressing. Thus, there was a certain discrepancy between what I wrote and what I felt, which was not very honorable. In fact, I wrote very little in the media on the Indochina war, but I clearly said what I thought in my book *Les Guerres En Chaîne*, published in 1951.

I said that, strictly speaking, the war could be justified in the framework of worldwide containment of communism. But, as far as France was concerned, its intervention in Indochina was madness. It is necessary to note, however, that as early as the end of 1946, the government tried to negotiate. But it lacked the courage to go all the way, that is, to accept Vietnamese independence. Also, as early as 1947-1948, it was no longer a question of maintaining the French empire, but of resisting communism. In 1949, the United States had changed its position. It had been hostile to France's return to Indochina, but because Indochina had become part of the free world, a curious definition, it supported the French Indo-Chinese policy that it had earlier opposed.

D.W. – So, in 1946, you were not in favor of France's return to Indochina. But you hardly took a stand at the time. Why? Was it difficult to state publicly?

R.A. – It wasn't so difficult; it was mostly just totally useless. In 1946 or 1947, I was unknown. When I took a position on the Algerian question, the pamphlet had a resounding impact because it was signed by Raymond Aron. But who was Raymond Aron in 1946 or 1947? A curious figure who had written some books on philosophy, who had disappeared for five years during the war and who, instead of returning to the university, was writing articles.

It is true that I immediately acquired a certain status in journalism. But you know, to have a little more than a certain status, is not so much a question of talent, as one of time. Anyone can write a good article—it is more difficult to write articles consistently that accord with reality.

J.–L.M. – So, for you, the criterion is effectiveness? You do not take a stand if it's not effective?

R.A. – No, no. It's not that. But simply to write that the Indo-Chinese War was unreasonable didn't make much sense. Everyone agreed on the principle. The minister of foreign affairs and, particularly, the colonial minister, supported the idea of a French union; that is, a program transforming colonial ties into relationships of equality. As for writing about the negotiations, that was much more difficult, because at the time I did not know the details. Moreover, one has to choose his role: If I were one who took positions based on morality, idealism, great principles, then I should indeed have written more on Indochina questions between 1946 and 1949. In fact, I wrote nothing, for or against. I told everyone, however, how unreasonable I found it to commit the greater part of French troops to Indochina.

If I had written articles, I suppose my reputation would be better. But it never occurred to me to write articles with my future reputation in mind. I wrote what seemed to me to be possible and useful to write at the time—and, at the time, to write articles on the Indo-Chinese War was not very useful.

Again, when the Chinese troops reached the frontier, it became evident to everyone that the French presence in Vietnam was doomed. As early as 1950, the successive French governments were privately convinced, but they were in a corner, they didn't know how to get out of Indochina.

Americans sometimes asked me if the French government would hold to its Indochina policy. My response was, "The French governments are too weak even to retreat."

A lot of courage was needed to beat a retreat in that kind of affair. When you are deeply involved in a war, when billions have been spent, when thousands and thousands of soldiers have died, it takes a great deal of courage and authority to say, "We were mistaken, we are going to pull out." To persuade René Pleven, for example, that it was time to withdraw was an easy matter. I knew very well that he wanted to pull out, but how?

J.–L.M. – And it was useless to write all that?

R.A. – No, it was useful, but about half the French commentators were writing about it. However, if you want me to admit that it would have been better if I had written more on the subject, I would agree with you readily. But I have no remorse, because I am persuaded that the few articles I might have written against French policy in Indochina would have changed absolutely nothing, given the fact that, through private conversations, the men who counted knew exactly what I thought.

D.W. – Let's return to the cold war. In the 1947-1956 period, who was winning? The Soviet Union?

R.A. – The expression "cold war" implies that there existed the equivalent of a war, which one side might have won, and the other side lost. At the time, I very often used a different expression, a "warlike peace," and the warlike peace has lasted to this very day. If you define the cold war as the limited period between 1947 and 1953 that extends from the breakup of the Big Three over Germany to the death of Stalin (which marked the end of the extreme form of the cold war)—during that period, the West made errors, but it won. In any case, it didn't lose. In the Berlin blockade, it won. As far as Korea is concerned, it didn't lose; and it could have won more if it hadn't pushed its armies too far north. Finally, it demonstrated that it wouldn't tolerate military intervention beyond the demarcation line, thus reassuring Westerners in general, and Europeans in general, about the constancy of American resolve.

J.–L.M. – And the Prague coup? And the crushing of the workers' revolt in East Berlin?

R.A. – Concerning Prague, there was no Soviet military intervention. There was a Communist party ultimatum, and once again, there was a concession or capitulation on the part of the President Benes. It meant the transformation of a democracy that was half "popular" into one totally "popular." What could the West do? It didn't have any armies to send to Prague. Besides, there existed a recognized semi-legal government that transformed itself by expelling its noncommunist members. It was not a coup d'etat that the Allies could prevent.

Also in Berlin in 1953, the West could do nothing. The popular uprising was outside its area of influence. It lacked the military means to intervene in East Germany to prevent the repression. Can you imagine the president of the United States sending an ultimatum to Stalin—or to his successor—forbidding him to repress a worker revolt?

It was certainly an important insurgency. But at the time, it was already known that the Soviet regime was not popular in Eastern Europe; it was already known that East Germans were leaving by the hundreds of thousands for the West. As the saying goes, they were "voting with their feet" for capitalism over "socialist liberation." It must be said that the regime Stalin imposed on Eastern Europe at that time was much worse than the present situation. In the years 1949 through 1952, an exceptional capacity for ignorance was necessary for one to be in favor of the socialist regimes of Eastern Europe. Everyone was aware of the extent to which the USSR-dominated area of Europe was badly treated, partly on purpose and partly because the Soviet Union, as a consequence of the war, was terribly impoverished and tried to extract the maximum booty from Eastern Europe and from Germany in particular.

J.–L.M. – To return to the North Atlantic pact. On that subject, you wrote a great deal and you were almost a militant.

R.A. – I fought for American intervention in Korea. The day we learned of the North Korean attack, I wrote "*Epreuve de Force.*" So, I supported American intervention in Korea.

Concerning the Marshall Plan, there was really no conceivable reason to be against it: essentially, it consisted of giving the European countries the dollars they needed. Even today, they would accept them. As for the North Atlantic pact, it was a relatively vague treaty concerning the collective security of the Western countries, with the promise that, in the event of unjustified aggression from the outside, each country would take measures to assist the country attacked. But, against the North Atlantic pact, there were two kinds of propaganda attacks: One inspired by a desire for European neutrality; A second that emanated mostly from Gaullist circles, but also from among the neutralists. This propaganda faulted the pact's text as being too vague, as not having spelled out precisely U.S. commitments and promises to Europe. Personally, I felt that the details of the text were less important than the pact itself.

NATO was not explicitly mentioned in the North Atlantic Treaty text. It was created as a military organization after the beginning of the Korean conflict, in the perspective that the Korean War might extend to Europe. Its institution was based upon an assumption that proved to be inaccurate: the supposed existence of a "master plan," or a Stalinist global strategy of aggression, that, after beginning with the war in Korea and Asia, would later spread to Europe.

It was in these circumstances, then, that the military organization was created, but the North Atlantic pact itself basically provided what the Europeans had hoped of the Americans after World War I, that is, a promise to intervene if the Europeans were attacked. Even today, I find it difficult to understand those who rejected the North Atlantic Treaty.

J.–L.M. – But in 1949, the neutralist theses were based on more noble motives: French independence. Didn't you feel at all concerned?

R.A. – That's a strange way to present the problem. If we had had an alliance with the United States in 1939, do you think that would have been contrary to France's independence? The North Atlantic Treaty did not reduce French independence. First, the treaty concerned only one part of the world. So, elsewhere, we could do exactly as we pleased.

Also, the treaty did not limit France's diplomatic autonomy. It contained reciprocal promises or commitments to go to the assistance of a country attacked. How did that reduce national independence?

D.W. – Didn't it diminish our military freedom? In an integrated organization, we were no longer autonomous.

R.A. – Those are two different things. The integrated military organization was created in 1950, not at the time of the North Atlantic pact. The first, certainly, was based on the idea that the defense of Western Europe could only be collective in nature. Consequently, it was necessary to have plans established in advance. It was not new. In 1939, when France possessed the bulk of the military forces, it was the French government, it was the French generals who were responsible for military operations all over France.

However, as far as NATO is concerned, it was not to act or intervene except in case of war. Furthermore, plans had to be established by unanimous agreement. Consequently, the French government was free to reject any plan judged to be contrary to French interests. NATO called for planning in the event of war and for the integration of the Alliance's military forces. So there were, and there are today, some arguments for not being a part of the integrated organization. Nonetheless, if France wants to participate in the defense of Europe in case of war, it must establish plans, in peacetime, with the other participants of the North Atlantic Treaty Alliance.

I would add that as far as our nuclear forces are concerned—they did not exist at the time—France would have precisely the same freedom of action that it has today, if it had remained in NATO.

However, the NATO problem belongs to the past, in my opinion. We are outside the unified command and French public opinion is resolutely opposed to a return to NATO. It would be without purpose to try to recreate a public debate on a question that has become academic. We are in the Alliance and outside the NATO unified command, with certain favorable consequences and others that are less so.

D.W. – At the time, why was the NATO debate so heated between those who were called neutralists and the others?

R.A. – Because that was not really the subject being debated. One of the major arguments against the North Atlantic Treaty concerned the rearmament of Germany. Beuve-Méry, for example, several times wrote that the seeds of German rearmament were in the North Atlantic Treaty like the chicken in the egg.

The other argument concerned the drafting of the text: U.S. obligations were allegedly not sufficiently precise. But, to the best of my knowledge, there were no protests against the idea of preparing plans in advance in case war should break out. General de Gaulle's opposition, particularly, did not concern that. De Gaulle, rather, remembered certain experiences from the earlier war; for example, the planned evacuation of Strasbourg that he prevented despite Eisenhower's orders. General de Gaulle was always obsessed by the idea that the loss of a portion of our military autonomy meant running the risk of accepting orders that might be in the general interest, while not being in the specific interest of the French nation. He was always emphatic on this point. With one reservation. There was a moment, with the threat of war seeming very imminent, when he envisaged a unified command for Europe. But in 1949 or 1950, his criticism of the North Atlantic Treaty concerned above all the inadequacy of the American commitment. French military force was so weak and power was so great on the American side, that what he wanted at the time was an American decision to commit all U.S. forces to the defense of Europe. He feared that, once again, the United States would not be present at the beginning of the war, but only at the end. This is a polemic that seems to me no longer to make much sense.

D.W. – In 1951, you published *Guerres en Chaîne*, analyzing twentieth-century wars. What astonishes the reader is your appeal for Europe to abandon its defensive strategy. At the end of the book, you wonder whether the cold war is a preparation for total war, or a substitute for it. Looking back, do you think that the cold war was a substitute for total war?

R.A. – It was an extreme form of rivalry between the two worlds, but until now this rivalry has continued without total war. So, it really has been a substitute for total war. Solzhenitsyn claims, on the other hand, that this war without war has brought a series of defeats and disasters to the West. He believes that the decolonization is one aspect of the West's defeat. The fact that a number of the decolonized countries have gone over to the Soviet side seems to him the symptom, or the proof, of Western decadence.

Personally, I consider that decolonization was, first of all, inevitable and, second, that it conforms to the values the West defends. As for the decline of Western Europe, it is incontestable, but it was written in the great book of history right after World War II. Europe could not keep its empires; a Europe protected by the United States could not remain an imperial power; that was evident.

At the beginning of the century, Europe was the center of the world. Great Britain was the center of a powerful empire that covered a considerable portion of the planet. Today, Great Britain is a small power, a second-class power. France was a great power in the European context; today, it is a power only in a regional context. But even without the two world wars, this decline would have intervened, if more slowly, less brutally. However, the rivalry between the West and the Soviet world is not yet resolved.

D.W. – The rivalry continues, but are not the power relationships changing? Since the beginning of the cold war, what is the balance sheet?

R.A. - After the war, the United States was a superpower and there was no other. Economically, American production must have represented over half of the world's total. At that time, there was a difference in nature between the standards of living and the productive capacities of Americans on the one hand, and Europeans on the other. Today, standards of living and work productivity are comparable in the United States and Europe. So there has been a relative decline of the United States with respect to the Europeans, revealing the extent to which American domination—so to speak—has failed to prevent the recovery and progress of Europeans.

Concerning military forces, in the period 1945-1947, the United States was the world's leading power, with an overwhelming nuclear superiority. Today, the world's leading military power is the Soviet Union. The United States is only the second power—equal, let us say, to the Soviet Union in nuclear arms, perhaps slightly superior in its naval and air forces, but quite inferior to the Soviet Union in terms of ground forces. Moreover, the Soviet Union has developed in recent years an ability to intervene all over the world. As the Americans say, they have acquired "the capacity to project their military power throughout the world." In this sense, if we compare the 1947-1948 situation with that of 1980, it is quite evidently the Soviet Union that has made the greater progress as a military power. But, conversely, in economic, ideological, and moral terms, it has lost a great deal.

By now, almost everyone recognizes that the Soviet economic system is inefficient, and that the standard of living in Eastern Europe is much lower than that in Western Europe. Even today, in scientific production, creativity, and in the dynamism of its civilization, the West represents 90 percent of what is created in the world. The Soviet Union has lost a great deal of its ability to exert ideological influence. Today, it is an economic failure, a great military power and perhaps a great imperial power.

J.–L.M. – Isn't this change in the military balance surprising, in view of the economic superiority of the West?

R.A. – It is not so surprising. Between 1962-1963 and 1972, the Americans spent a great deal on the Vietnam War, hence much less on other things. Furthermore, probably beginning about 1962, the Soviet Union decided to make an exceptional military effort and since then it has increased its military budget by 3 to 5 percent each year. In a way, it is a military economy; military production has priority. The people get what is left, as in wartime, to simplify a bit. But, despite everything, there are limits to increases in military expenditures.

D.W. – The cold war made it necessary to rethink the Western military system. At the time, why did you favor Germany's rearmament?

R.A. – For a relatively simple reason. The security of Western Europe at that time could be conceived in two different ways:

—First, the United States solemnly declares that any attack against Western Europe will be considered as an attack against itself, and we are no longer concerned with our self-defense; the European military void is accepted, but the American declaration suffices to preclude direct military aggression by the Soviet Union. . . .

—Alternatively, we consider that this declaration of a faraway country is insufficient; the Korean experience incited reflection about the desirability of exclusive reliance on an American declaration of war. In this case, we decide that a minimum of self-defense capability with classic weapons is necessary.

Once Great Britain and France decided to rearm, it was very difficult, for both economic and military reasons, to conceive of West Germany as not participating at all in this collective European defense.

So, it was not that I wanted German rearmament as such, but German rearmament was made inevitable by European rearmament in general.

It was not accepted with much pleasure. When in the autumn of 1950, during the Korean War, Secretary of State Acheson proposed the rearmament of Germany to the English and French ministers, the first reaction of the French was to delay the decision as long as possible. Pleven, perhaps prompted by Jean Monnet, proposed the EDC, both as a way to delay German rearmament and to encourage European union.

J.–L.M. – As a matter of fact, a long debate on the EDC, the European Defense Community, took place in France between 1950 and 1954. Just what was this EDC?

R.A. – There were several debates. The first centered on the question: Neutrality or Atlantic Alliance? The Communists, of course, were on one side, but most of the population accepted the Atlantic Alliance, because it was a sort of guarantee of American protection. Neutralism, the policy of neutrality as such, was extremely difficult, because its defenders added: armed neutrality. That was the point of view of *Le Monde*, of people like Etienne Gilson and Beuve-Méry. Since we were not armed, it was difficult to have rearmament and neutrality at the same time. It was a utopia. It answered very profound feelings, the desire for a distinctive, independent Europe, separate from both the Soviet Union and the United States. This desire still exists. It is an authentic aspiration of the French population, but at the time, in 1949-1950, it didn't make much sense.

Then, there was a second debate: on rearmament. It centered upon the rejection of German rearmament and on the measures entailed by European rearmament, that is, the EDC. Roughly, the EDC was the European army. A number of those who wanted this European army had at the same time all kinds of mental reservations about Germany and German rearmament. It reached the point where they were not satisfied with the idea of German, French, Belgian, Dutch divisions under a single command, but wanted national groups of the smallest size possible, the guideline being the fusion of units. Only the smallest detachments would remain national.

Besides, there was one overwhelming obsession: Prevent the rebirth of a German general staff. There was to be no commanding general, no supreme command. Finally, the EDC was to take the form of a ministry of European armies. This ministry was, first, to establish a merger of the armies of the six partners and bring this European army to a state of readiness. Then, it was to place it at the disposition of the Americans or under NATO command. Thus, the EDC adversaries would claim "the EDC effectively destroys the French army and rebuilds the German army; not only will the French military give up its autonomy, but it will be placed at the service of foreigners in a twofold manner: First, under a European ministry; then, under a supreme American command."

D.W. – Was anyone in favor of the system?

R.A. – Except for the hard-core proponents of a European union, that is, those faithful to the ideals of Jean Monnet, the project's adversaries multiplied. Some were antagonistic to German rearmament itself. Others were hostile to the system chosen. At the time, public opinion polls were taken on those questions. But they really made little sense. If people were asked, "Is it preferable to rebuild a German national army, or to rearm Germany without an autonomous German army?" they obviously chose the second. If they were asked, "But should the autonomy of the French army be forfeited?" they naturally responded in the negative.

In other words, the discussion was carried on in the utmost confusion. The choice was not clearly explained: there were two acceptable ways to rearm Germany; the first, create a European army; the second, reconstitute a German army that would immediately be placed at the disposition of NATO.

D.W. – And what did the Americans think?

R.A. – They were wholeheartedly in favor of the EDC that the French had conceived, and were to reject—and they spent their time saying there was no other solution, an idiotic thing to say since there obviously was another solution. When the European Defense Community was rejected, after the Geneva conference—that is, after the liquidation of the Indochina War, another solution, that everyone had already been aware of, was found: the creation of a German army that would have no general staff and that would immediately be put under NATO command. First, with Mendès-France as prime minister and then with Edgar Faure, the French Parliament accepted the second solution because the first had been rejected. If the alternative finally approved had been presented first, it is possible that it would have been rejected just as the EDC had been. Deep down, the Parliament was hostile to both solutions; it was unfavorable to German rearmament in any form.

J.-L.M. – With the failure of the EDC, didn't Europe miss its chance?

R.A. – A minority of the French say, in fact, that the EDC, which gave Europe, at least on paper, the ability to defend itself, represented the only important chance to preserve European autonomy. But I've always had reservations, because the European army was basically conceived against the German danger and not to create an effective army. I found it absurd to reduce the national units to the point envisaged. The idea of launching an enterprise as important as a collective European army with so many reservations, so many precautions, so much uneasiness—it was all not very convincing.

D.W. – And today? Are the chances for a European army better?

R.A. – There is no chance at all. We now have a French army, a German army, a Belgian army, etc. What is conceivable, is an integration at the command level.

D.W. – In the 1950-1954 debate, the Communists succeeded in monopolizing the peace theme. All the others, those who were partisans of the EDC or of German rearmament, were painted as warmongers. How do you explain that phenomenon?

R.A. – It was not the first time, nor the last, that the Communists monopolized the peace theme. In 1950, only five years had elapsed since the end of the war. The rapidity of the reversal of alliances, the very short time span during which we passed from an obsession with the Nazi menace to an obsession with the Soviet menace—it was all so rapid that a large part of the French population found the change difficult to accept. The contrary would have been surprising. Well, there were some people who used this adjustment problem for political purposes. Others, like myself, who were not very numerous, thought that German rearmament was less dangerous at a time when the Germans themselves didn't want it. The best course, I thought, was to accept them as allies at a moment when they were tempted to isolate themselves; creating ties between the new Germany and France, while putting the past behind us. But I was in the minority. The majority would have simply preferred that the question not be posed. It should be added that *Le Figaro*, through the articles of Pierre Brisson, was fervently in favor of the European Defense Community. I was not. At the very beginning, in 1950, I thought it was an error. I did not believe the French would accept that solution. One day, I said to Robert Shuman, "It's a strange concept all the same; you do not want to accept the Germans as allies, but you are ready to accept them as compatriots." He smiled and responded, "After all, why not?"

I focused on the dangers of the European Defense Community in a few articles. I didn't campaign strongly against it. Most of all, I said to everyone, to the Americans as well as to the French, "German rearmament is inevitable. The question is not whether you are for it or against it; the question is whether you prefer to have the European Defense Community or to have the German army in NATO." I rather favored the second solution.

b) In the *Rassemblement du Peuple Francais*

J.–L.M. – Let's turn back a bit. In 1947, a surprising thing happened in your life: you became a member of a political party, the RPF.

R.A. – Yes, but I had already been a member of a political party once, as I believe I told you: the Socialist party, when I was at the Ecole Normale, to do something for the people. Well. . . I joined the RPF in 1947, in fact. Everyone has asked me why and no one has understood why.

For the record, the RPF was the *Rassemblement du Peuple Français*, a parliamentary movement supported by General de Gaulle. "Raymond Aron followed in my footsteps," André Malraux said, "It is because of our friendship that he became a member of the RPF." There is something to that, but nevertheless, my friendship for him didn't go as far as my taking a position contrary to my convictions.

I believe there were two reasons for my joining the RPF. The first was that I had a rather bad conscience for not having participated to a greater extent in the Gaullist movement in London. I regretted the dogmatic and excessive positions I took against General de Gaulle; I have mentioned them earlier. After the fact, I felt I should have joined the Gaullist movement when the Allies landed in North Africa, because, beginning at that moment, there was no alternative to Gaullism.

I recognize that a number of distinguished Frenchmen, like Alexis Léger, frowned upon the creation of a government outside France. But, today, I thing Léger was wrong. The moment Marshal Pétain failed to establish his headquarters in Algiers, General de Gaulle had to create the provisional government of liberated France. I would have been more useful if, instead of remaining outside with my criticism, mental reservations, suspicions, I had joined the Gaullist movement—if I had *"mit machen,"* as the Germans said in 1933, accusing me of being incapable of *"mit machen,"* that is, of associating myself with historic movements.

The second reason was that I was very much against the Constitution and the way the Fourth Republic functioned. I believed that, over the long term, the Fourth Republic was incapable of presiding over the reconstruction, or the restoration of France, and I thought that the RPF represented the only chançe for having the Constitution revised.

It should be added that this was the period when de Gaulle was closest to Parliament because he was heading a parliamentary movement. It was also as the head of this movement that he was the most anticommunist, that he propagandized most against the Communist danger and that he termed the Communists "separatists." So, on the two essential points, the Communist or Soviet problem and the problem of the Constitution, I agreed with him.

But I disagreed with him on a great many other questions.

D.W. – What is strange is that you joined the RPF, which was violently anticommunist and anti-Fourth Republic, although you have told us many times that you like neither factionalism nor civil war. Yet for four years, from 1947 to the legislative elections of 1951, you were to belong to the RPF, a movement that had no parliamentary representation and that sought to weaken the Fourth Republic.

R.A. – There was no atmosphere of civil war between the RPF and the Fourth Republic. Between 1947 and 1951, there were few Gaullist deputies in Parliament. So, it was not principally the RPF that disturbed the functioning of the Fourth Republic. Let me add, even, that the fact that those in power were threatened by General de Gaulle, had as a result—it was both logical and paradoxical—that they argued less among themselves. If you study the history of the Fourth Republic, you will find that when the de Gaulle threat temporarily ceased after the RPF's breakup in 1952, the Fourth Republic functioned less well.

D.W. – The fact remains that, from 1947 to 1951, the RPF carried on a policy of destabilization, something that does not correspond well with your personality.

R.A. – That is true, but I repeat that, between 1947 and 1951, the RPF had no parliamentary presentation. It was, then, a verbal opposition, accompanied by public demonstrations. It didn't prevent the parties from reaching agreements; on the contrary, in creating a danger for the normal operation of the parties, the RPF helped give the parties more coherence than they had before or after.

D.W. – On the whole, then, you believe that General de Gaulle's opposition to the Fourth Republic, through the RPF's activities, was almost a factor of stability for the regime!

R.A. – The phrase is yours. I mean that, in point of fact, the RPF made the continuance of the Fourth Republic rather easier between 1947 and 1951.

After 1951, the RPF had become a party that played a destabilizing role, but it had no chance of succeeding. The RPF's opportunity would have been the possibility to constitute a majority with the Communists. If there had been sufficient Gaullists and Communists to make up a majority, the third force—the Fourth Republic's center parties—would have been doomed. They would have been forced to accept a revision of the Constitution. That was the project, so to speak.

But since there was no Communist-Gaullist majority, thanks to the system of party alliances, the Fourth Republic continued after the RPF's dissolution, but it was more incoherent than before. General de Gaulle continued to work toward his return to power, while ceasing to oppose the Fourth Republic in an ostentatious way. He recognized that the RPF was finished. He waited out events and, depending on the days, he would say, "They'll never let me return," or, "I will certainly make it back some day."

D.W. – Did your relations with de Gaulle improve during this period?

R.A. – They were good during the lifetime of the RPF. I went to see him several times. We had political chats that I found interesting. I was impressed by his way of reacting to things. We even had some personal conversations because, on the occasion of a death in my family, he wrote me a very touching letter. I saw him about that time, and he spoke to me about his own misfortunes.

During those few years, our relations were sincere, without his ever having thought that I had become an orthodox Gaullist or a vassal. When, for example, I sent him one of my books, I would receive from him, as many other authors did, a handwritten, interesting letter.

J.–L.M. – You were an RPF militant. What was it like for you to be a militant? You were about forty-three or forty-four years old. Did you put up posters? . . .

R.A. – I was a militant, yes, but not to that point. I recall a big public assembly of RPF intellectuals at which I gave a talk. It worked out rather well. I succeeded in silencing the Communists in the hall by poking fun at them. I criticized the newspaper *Franc-Tireur* which was more or less neutralist. When the Communists tried to keep me from speaking, I said to them, "But I thought you would be happy since I was attacking *Franc-Tireur*." The newspaper was, in fact, one of the bugbears of the Communists. The audience broke out in laughter and all of a sudden, the small clique of Communists became quiet.

And then I was a member of the studies committee that met weekly for a year or two. Other members were Pompidou, Palewski, Chalandon, etc. We made plans for General de Gaulle's future government. I was even a reporter on the question of labor-capital association, now called *participation*. But within the RPF, I was considered a bit too skeptical. That was true, but I attempted to translate that generous, if vague, idea into practical, viable measures. That was known in the RPF as Aronian skepticism.

D.W. – One easily recognizes Raymond Aron there. But if you were a skeptical militant, you were also a journalist. Were you able to reconcile the two points of view?

R.A. – As a journalist, I said what I thought about everything, whether I agreed or not with the official RPF articles of faith. I wrote in *Liberté de l'Esprit*, the RPF periodical, as freely as in *Le Figaro*. However, there were a few difficult moments on both sides, particularly when the RPF newspaper, *Rassemblement*, attacked *Le Figaro*. *Rassemblement* had cited a number of unfortunate wartime articles in *Le Figaro*. I said to Pierre Brisson, "If you want my resignation, all right, I will leave."

D.W. – Do you have a happy memory of that time?

R.A. – You know, I am not a born militant. But, contrary to what most of my friends and adversaries think, I have no regrets about that episode. I continue to think it would have been more desirable for General de Gaulle to return to power at a calmer moment, rather than through a near-coup, as he did in 1958.

J.–L.M. – Exactly how do you account for the failure of the RPF?

R.A. – I have told you. The parliamentary representation of the RPF would have had to obtain either an absolute majority—which was impossible—or make up a majority with the Communists. But it could not have governed with the Communist party. So, it had to obtain from the center, or "third force," parties a sort of concession or capitulation. But it failed to achieve that.

J.–L.M. – Did you stay with the RPF to the end?

R.A. – There was a schism within the RPF. One group joined Pinay. I stayed with Malraux and General de Gaulle. Shortly afterward, de Gaulle said he was indifferent to the fate of the RPF. Thus, I, too, became indifferent to the fate of the RPF. It was no spiritual disruption. Had I hoped during this period to participate more actively in political life? Vaguely, but not in any clear-cut way. When you want something, you have to ask for it.

D.W. – And, there, you were not strongly resolved?

R.A. – That's it.

D.W. – I see still another paradox in your RPF participation. The RPF was hostile to what was called the two blocs, the socialist bloc and the capitalist bloc. You were not. You were against one, not the other.

R.A. – You want to demonstrate that I have a complex personality? All right. But, you know, during that period between 1949 and 1951, I had a number of conversations with General de Gaulle on that subject. To some extent, he believed that a war was in the offing and he was determined to have a close alliance with the United States. He realized that in order to maintain European equilibrium and to protect Europe, as well as France, America's cooperation was essential. During the big crisis, that of 1950-1951, there was no question of rejecting both blocs.

Later, it is true, that did come up. But I never took those slogans very seriously. There was a difference between the philosophic views of General de Gaulle in the opposition and what he actually did when he headed the government.

D.W. – The RPF was also somewhat cold to the idea of European unity, while you rather favored it.

R.A. – No, that is not correct. In 1949 or 1950, Michel Debré wrote a pamphlet in which he reproached the center parties for not unifying Europe rapidly enough, and totally. In fact, he drafted a program for a federal constitution of a united Europe in which a president of the "Republic of the United States of Europe" was to figure. During the war, also, Michel Debré had been an Atlanticist to the nth degree; in 1949 or 1950, his dream was to see General de Gaulle as president of the European Republic.

If there was opposition to the European unity idea, it was against the kind of Europe conceived by Jean Monnet. There was even personal animosity between Monnet and de Gaulle. The latter felt that Jean Monnet was no longer French, but supranational, or at least beyond nationality. He was deeply hostile toward Jean Monnet until the end. Monnet was no less a good Frenchman and just as good a patriot, but he was convinced that it was necessary to go beyond nationalism and the nation-state. And he thought that only through organizations, supranational institutions, would it be possible to do that. In General de Gaulle's eyes, supranationalism had come to symbolize the end of France. Between the two men, both of whom merit respect (in different tonalities), there had developed an implacable antagonism—with the reservation that Monnet remained, as always, unimpassioned. He was convinced that there was a great task for this generation to accomplish: create the institutions of a united Europe.

D.W. – And your position between the two?

R.A. – I would have hoped that a united Europe, as Monnet conceived it, might be possible. But I didn't believe very strongly in the possibility. I've always preserved a strain of Lorraine patriotism. So, I leaned toward one side or the other, according to circumstances—but always remaining favorable to a kind of unification of Europe, for which I worked hard, both before and after the RPF. However, I was skeptical about the possibility of effacing a thousand years of national history. France had been to such a degree the European nation *par excellence*, it had always been so opposed to empires, that I never ceased to doubt, unless it was right after the war, that France would become anything else than the French nation. But I passionately hoped for a reconciliation with Germany and close cooperation with it. And, basically, we have probably obtained what was possible and what is, today, a reality for the young people of France and Germany: they belong to the same civilization. Historical boundaries no longer mean very much. That's already very important. It's absolutely not what Monnet dreamed of. It's probably closer to what General de Gaulle had in mind. It was the historic probability.

c) The Opium of the Intellectuals

J.–L.M. – The cold war had important repercussions on the French intelligentsia. The East-West split repeated itself inside each country and divided the intellectual world in each country. This was particularly true in France, where it even broke up friendships. In 1955, you published *The Opium of the Intellectuals,* analyzing the myths of the leftist intellectuals. It was the culmination of eight years of polemics, and it was a fundamental debate for three reasons. First, it was the most important debate of the postwar period and it was destined to keep the French intelligentsia divided to this day. Then, it was to radicalize the Left-Right cleavage and transform the postwar debate into a dialogue of the deaf. Finally, the animators of this debate were Jean-Paul Sartre, Maurice Merleau-Ponty, Camus, and Raymond Aron. You say it was the attitude toward the Soviet Union that marked the dividing line between the intellectuals. What themes divided them regarding the Soviet Union?

R.A. – First, I would like to say that, as the sole survivor among the four, I would prefer as far as possible not to settle old scores again. I would like to try to remember the other three with the friendship I felt for them over a long period of time.

Indeed, as I saw it, the principal question concerned attitudes, on both the diplomatic and intellectual levels, toward the Soviet Union.

Diplomatically, the question was posed in the following manner: The USSR Sovietized half of Europe. To preserve the equilibrium of Europe, American cooperation is necessary, hence the Atlantic Alliance is a necessary element in the diplomatic balance.

Many intellectuals refused to accept this proposition that seemed to me at the time almost self-evident. The refusal can be explained by the existing antipathy regarding American civilization and by the warm sentiments the Soviet Union inspired in them—or, perhaps, by the attraction they felt toward the official "socialist country," the nation in which the proletarian revolution had triumphed. Thus, the diplomatic question—should we accept being part of the Atlantic coalition with the United States?—was inevitably linked to the other problem: Which of the two countries, the Soviet Union, or the United States, is preferable?

Personally, I felt the United States was the offspring of Europe, of liberal Europe. One can detest the mercantile society of the United States, but American civilization is a liberal civilization. When the United States exerts an influence in Europe, it's generally in the direction of institutions cherished by the majority of intellectuals, that is, liberal institutions. So, the refusal to accept these evidences was difficult to understand.

D.W. – But it is a fact that few intellectuals made the same choice as you at the time.

R.A. – That is true. Sartre detested bourgeois society. In those years, he wasn't as close to the Communists as later. He had created, with David Rousset, *Le Rassemblement Démocratique Revolutionnaire,* an enterprise that I felt was destined to fail. Joining the two adjectives "democratic" and "revolutionary" seemed contradictory to me. It is possible to make a revolution with democracy as the goal, but a revolution is not normally made through democratic means. The French Revolution was rarely democratic during the years of turmoil. And the Soviet Revolution has never become democratic in the Western sense. But, at the time, Sartre wanted to place himself between the Soviet Union and the United States. He wanted a "revolutionary movement," but he didn't want a revolution like that in the Soviet Union. So, he was heavily criticized at the time by the Communist party journalists and writers.

There was no reason for a break between Sartre and me on account of the *Rassemblement Démocratique Revolutionnaire*. But he considered that my pro-Atlantic position and my writing for *Le Figaro* demonstrated that I had joined the bourgeoisie and the American alliance, both of which he loathed. So he thought that friendly relations between us no longer had any purpose. And there were also incidents of a secondary nature that don't seem to me to be worth recounting. Finally, beginning in 1947-1948, we had an official falling-out, as the phrase went—we were no longer on speaking terms. Sartre broke successively with me, with Camus, with Merleau-Ponty. But he showed more fury toward me, and wrote articles more disagreeable about me, than about Camus or Merleau-Ponty. After the deaths of Merleau-Ponty and Camus, he wrote touching articles about each. I don't think he would have written with such warmth about me.

Another reason that explains his exasperation with my viewpoints must always be recalled: Sartre was a moralist. He could not admit that my views, that might of course have been erroneous, were not also willful. As a moralist, he found it difficult to accept the arguments of someone who took a political position radically different from his own. So, he censured me morally. I have always thought, by the way, that he was more a moralist than a political activist. And I think he was often lost in political affairs, precisely because he was essentially a moralist, but with a style very different from the usual kind: an inverted moralist, a moralist of truth and not at all of bourgeois conformism, which horrified him. This explains, for example, his feelings toward his father-in-law, who was both a bourgeois and a polytechnician. A bourgeois poly-technician was too much for him.

J.–L.M. – Did the break with Sartre bother you deeply?

R.A. – It was, if you will, the sadness of an adult who loses the friendships of his youth. Yes, losing friends means losing part of oneself.

J.–L.M. – But how could a political difference about the Soviet Union lead to jeopardizing your friendship?

R.A. – It was because what I thought about the Soviet Union was intolerable for Sartre. I thought of it with its concentration camps, its despotism, its expansionism. Moreover, I tried to explain that the Soviet Union had become what it was, neither by accident nor because of Stalin, but because, from the beginning, there was a conception of revolutionary movement that inexorably had to culminate in what became the Soviet Union. If I had limited myself to saying that the Soviet Union was Stalinist and not Marxist, Sartre probably would have tolerated it. But if the socialist movement itself were put in doubt—there, one was tampering with something that was basic for him. As a matter of fact, he wrote on several occasions, "Only a participant in the socialist movement, in the revolutionary movement, can denounce the Soviet Union." He also wrote, "All anticommunists are bastards." Although he was not a Communist himself, he considered it morally reprehensible to be anticommunist.

For me, to be anticommunist when one was not a Communist seemed to be something quite natural, since the Communist were saying at the time, "Either you are with us or you are against us." It seemed to me natural to say, "Since we are not with them, since we judge them to be detestable, well, we are against them." But Sartre would reply, "You do not have the right to criticize the communist movement, because you are outside of it. You must be in sympathy with the movement to have the right to criticize it." Since I thought the movement, from the very beginning, would lead to the results it did, I naturally could not accept this interdiction of criticism.

J.–L.M. – The role that the Soviet concentration camps played in the debate is astonishing today. In *The Opium of the Intellectuals,* you say, "The dividing line passes between the intellectuals who do not deny the camps' existence and those who denounce the camps. And it is the change from one position to the other that marks the break.''

R.A. – That's the side of the debate that is a little bit French. In *The Opium of the Intellectuals,* I don't argue with the Communists. I discuss or I argue with my friends who recognize the existence of the concentration camps, who are not Communists, yet who do not want to be anticommunists. To a large degree, *The Opium of the Intellectuals* was a dialogue with Sartre and Merleau-Ponty, a dialogue between men who began at the same place, who were to an extent impregnated with the same philosophy, existentialism, who had gone through the Marxist stage, who had been antifascist, who had been close friends for years, and who became almost implacable enemies, because some called themselves noncommunists, and the others, anticommunists.

It was practically the same quarrel between Camus and Sartre. Sartre did not deny the existence of the concentration camps. He once wrote an editorial in *Les Temps Modernes* in which he admitted that there were probably about ten million prisoners in the camps. However, he failed to denounce the Soviet Union.

D.W. – But how could people simultaneously admit the existence of the camps and still support the Soviet Union?

R.A. – Ask the question of those who did precisely that! There was an intellectual movement in France that had practically no equivalent elsewhere. There were those who were in between: who were so attracted to the proletariat, socialism, history, revolution, the Left, that they could not accept the consequences of a break with communism. They could not admit that the break with the Soviet Union necessarily led to my choice: the acceptance of the Atlantic Alliance and the anticommunist coalition.

D.W. – What was the source of the fascination of the intellectuals with revolutionary ideas, with the proletariat as the agent of history, with the kind of violence that was to enable people to overcome their antagonisms, with the theme of the construction of the ideal society?

R.A. – I don't want to repeat my book. I tried to answer those questions in *The Opium of the Intellectuals.* To simplify, let's say that the Left-Right split exists in France. Those who were resolutely anticommunist were classified as Rightists. Those who did not want to be classified as rightists, who wanted to stay on the Left, tried desperately to avoid being either Communists or anticommunists.

From there, they clung first to the myth, or the reality, of "being on the Left." Then, they clung to the idea borrowed from Marxism that capitalism was inherently bad and was to be radically condemned, that the bourgeoisie was detestable and contemptible, and that one could not be on the side of the bourgeoisie.

They wound up with positions that were extraordinarily subtle and difficult. They were not with the anticommunists and they were not with the Communists. Merleau-Ponty said, "I am 'acommunist'." The discussion, by the way, remained in the domain of ideas. For example, Camus wanted Sartre to admit that he recognized what the Soviet Union had become and to take a resolute position against that country. But in his book *L'Homme Revolté,* while he took a position clearly against the Soviet Union, Camus failed to draw any conclusions of a diplomatic nature. As far as I can recall, he never wrote on the Atlantic Alliance, never proposed to do this or that, never took a position for or against the Korean campaign. I was much more political than the others, much less ideological, if you will.

The glorious battle or debate between Sartre and Camus was really typically French, because they argued while being very close to each other on many points, one being noncommunist and the other, anticommunist. Besides, there were other concepts in the discussion, like Camus' Mediterranean idea and the way he wrote his *"Lettre au Directeur des Temps Modernes"* to attack, not Sartre, but Jeanson, who had written the review of *L'Homme Revolté*. Underneath all that there was also a writers' feud.

D.W. – But all those ideological involved more than a handful of people. There was a wider impact.

R.A. – Let's take the Parliament first. This cleavage had no equivalent there: there was a single bloc that extended from the Socialists to the Right. This bloc was defined by its opposition to the Soviet Union. Also, according to the polls, there were people who voted for the Communist party, and who were more or less favorable to the Soviet Union. The two concepts were not identical, because many voted for the

Communist party without being overly convinced of the virtues of the USSR.

On the other hand, the majority was, on the whole, Atlanticist, but with many reservations concerning the United States. Between these two groups, or two blocs, if you will, there were let's say, 10 or 20 percent of the French who were profoundly neutralist and who allocated their criticism of the Soviet Union and the United States more or less equally. To a degree, they found their abstract, intellectual, philosophical expression in that group of men (Sartre, Merleau-Ponty, who were in agreement for awhile, then separated) who did not want to be anticommunist and who did not want to be Atlanticists, but who wanted to be revolutionaries in a revolution that, it seems, didn't exist.

In fact, Sartre and Merleau-Ponty confined their discussion largely to the vocation of the proletariat, to the historic rationality linked to the truth of Marxism, etc., in strictly philosophic language incomprehensible to ordinary Frenchmen and even to most politicians.

J.-L.M. – Then, retrospectively, why was this debate so important?

R.A. – First, I am not sure that today there isn't a certain reaction. Among the young people, some say, "In the final analysis, all that had absolutely no significance." To the extent that those debates do continue to have some meaning, it is because of, first, Sartre's personality and that of a few others; then, because what was put in question was a certain philosophic interpretation of Marxism. This went out of style a few years later, that is, toward the end of the 1950s and the beginning of the 1960s, and the intellectuals in search of Marxism, such as Althusser and his disciples, found a version different from the existentialist or Hegelian interpretation that Sartre and Merleau-Ponty had drawn, and more or less popularized, from Kojéve's thinking.

D.W. – However, this debate that you characterize as of basically little importance was renewed with structuralism. The same questions continue to be asked: What is history's agent? What is historic reason? What is the ideal society? And they continue to stimulate the political parties of the Left. The same thing is true of the debate about the nature of the Soviet Union.

R.A. – Yes, but you are confusing two debates. There is a debate, that continues to this very day, on the nature of the Soviet regime and on the possibilities of its transformation. On the other hand, there is an intellectual debate on the philosophic interpretation of Marxism, the relationship between Marxism and Hegel, and so on.

It is true that this debate continues to have a great influence in the Latin countries. In Italy, it remains of current interest. In Latin America, too, because debates on the philosophy of history are traditional there.

In the Anglo-Saxon countries, there is renewed interest in Marxism, but in a Marxism very different from that of Sartre or Merleau-Ponty. It is a Marxism drawn from the least philosophic writings of Marx. It concerns less the question of the historic vocation of the proletariat, or the question of reason in history, than the following problem: Do the forces of production determine, or condition, relationships of production? Is there a succession of social regimes that can be reconstituted on the basis of the relationships of production or the forces of production? The Anglo-Saxon countries are turning back to the old discussions that were frequent in the Second International, but they are doing it on the basis of writings unknown before 1940 and through the use of analytical philosophy.

D.W. – What was strange in the 1947-1955 period was that quarrels among intellectuals were very heated at a time when French political life was much more pragmatic, the dividing line between Left and Right being rather fuzzy.

R.A. – To tell the truth, all those big intellectual debates that so titillated the Parisian or French intelligentsia had no influence, at least short term, on the pursuit of daily life in France. The most striking phenomenon of the 1950s was not the march toward revolution, but the economic recovery of France.

The recovery took place despite the colonial wars and the divisiveness they engendered in the very interior of all the political parties. As a matter of fact, not all the Atlanticists were in favor of the Indochina War or of the Suez expedition. Nor did they all approve the war in Algeria. The debate should have concentrated on strictly French problems. But in fact the French debated in a way that was typically, narrowly

French, while deluding themselves that they were challenging the universe and cosmic values.

D.W. – Aren't you underrating that debate a little?

R.A. – No, I think it is dead now. The discussion about what socialism can be, or what it is in the Soviet Union, remains of permanent interest. But typical of our debates was the phrase of Merleau-Ponty, "If Marxism is false, there is no meaning in history." It was a way to transform an argument on the nature of political regimes into a philosophy of history that soared high above reality and the problems political leaders had to resolve.

D.W. – Why did those intellectuals show such little interest in the extraordinary transformation of French society, such as reconstruction, the rural exodus, industrialization, and the beginning of economic growth?

R.A. – Why would intellectuals who were philosophers be interested in those aspects of reality? They wanted to dream about a different society, boundless, universal.

D.W. – Why were you interested?

R.A. – My conversion took place a few years earlier when I realized that political philosophy could not ignore reality: one could not be a socialist without studying political economy and acquiring an idea of what socialism really meant.

But Merleau-Ponty, who was a philosopher of stature, an admirable human being, had never really studied economic questions. In his *Humanisme et Terreur,* a strange book about the Moscow trials, there is a minimum of detail on, say, the nature of the Soviet regime or on the essence of a democratic-capitalist regime. The discussion was very philosophic and far beyond the common sense arguments that a more or less positivist sociologist could challenge him with, even if, as in my case, one is not precisely such a sociologist.

J.–L.M. – It would appear that during those years the existentialists, or the leftist intellectuals, had a sort of monopoly on thought. Why?

R.A. – The extent of the monopoly should not be exaggerated. But it is true that there was a phenomenon and an important one: Jean-Paul Sartre. He was a philosopher, an authentic one, who wrote plays, novels, newspaper articles, and who concerned himself with politics. He acquired a kind of monopoly in all forms of the expression of thought. And then, his was a personality of considerable breadth because of the diversity and exuberance of his talents and because of the influence he thus exerted on the professors of philosophy who were at the time an important segment of the intelligentsia.

D.W. – Yes, but in your own way, didn't you help shape the image of Jean-Paul Sartre? Because if one examines the evolution of the intellectuals' positions, it is all more complex. From 1947 to 1950, Jean-Paul Sartre was not close to the French Communist party (PCF); he was neutralist at the time and was not to come close to the PCF until 1952 or 1953. On the other hand, Albert Camus broke [with communism] rather early, in 1952, but, basically, he didn't interest you very much. And Maurice Merleau-Ponty broke in 1955, but you were barely more interested. One gets the impression that in the period of *The Opium of the Intellectuals,* and in the books that followed, you retained a privileged adversary who was Jean-Paul Sartre, as if only his opinion counted.

R.A. – Oh, no, it was not really I who manufactured Sartre. But what is true is that, in my interest for Sartre, there was, beyond the permanence of friendship, the fact that he was the very prototype of an attitude that was neutralist and rather close to the Communist party. With regard to Camus, I had worked with him at *Combat,* but he was not a close friend, as Sartre had been. I never had any reason to argue with him. It is true that in *The Opium of the Intellectuals,* there was an unpleasant page about him that I regret. He wrote me a letter about it. I answered, giving him the reasons why I had written those disagreeable remarks, and I added, "in future editions, I am going to drop the section because it is unfair." He wrote back: "Do not take the section out; it really is not important." Our personal relations ended with these wholly reconciliatory letters.

Concerning Merleau-Ponty, I did indeed argue with him in several articles. We never had a falling-out, because he accepted disagreement more easily than Sartre, and we kept up friendly relations of an intermittent nature. At the time of the Algerian War, I received some very warm letters from him. A polemical period had existed because I did not like his book,

Humanisme et Terreur, published in 1947, I think. It was an interpretation of the Moscow trials that could be taken as a semi-justification.

J.–L.M. – Between 1947 and 1956, did you have the feeling that you were ostracized from the rest of the French intelligentsia?

R.A. – Well, I felt alone, cut off from friendships of my youth. Of course, I did receive many congratulatory letters, but they affected me very little because they were from strangers. It's true, the French intelligentsia did not have much tolerance for me in that period. When I was elected to the Sorbonne in 1955, the campaign against me was essentially political. I was a rightist, I wrote for *Le Figaro,* etc. I was nonetheless elected, thanks to some friends of my youth who were at the Sorbonne.

D.W. – You have said frequently that you were closer to people who attacked you, than to those who agreed with you.

R.A. – It's true, because my spontaneous system of values that led me to the Socialist party in my ingenuousness, has remained the same. Only, the world had changed and I adapted my opinions to reality. I have tried to serve the same values in different circumstances and through different actions. I believe I have been true to myself, faithful to my ideas, to my values, and to my philosophy. Having political opinions is not a matter of having an ideology once and for all; it is a question of taking the right decisions in changing circumstances. I don't mean to say that I haven't been mistaken rather often. But I have not betrayed the values and aspirations of my youth.

D.W. – Before the war, you were on the Left. After the war, you were classified as a rightist. But you are not the one who has changed?

R.A. – Events and people have classified me. Abroad, where people are more indulgent with regard to the French, it has almost always been said that I was impossible to classify. If I have changed, it is because I was very uninformed before the war, and because circumstances were different. But from 1945 on, I have made, to my way of thinking, no fundamental errors of judgment or of commitment. However, it is true that in 1955 I was different from what I was in the 1930s, and from what I have become since. Always arguing against people who are attacking you creates the danger of drifting too far in the opposite direction. That is a possibility. But it is also possible that I am now freed of those polemics and passions. Why? Because I am old—a reason without merit.

J.–L.M. – You analyzed "the myth of the proletariat." But during the 1950s, the proletariat really did exist. There were grueling strikes and violent street demonstrations. That reality escaped you, didn't it?

R.A. – If you define the proletariat simply as the aggregate of factory workers, it is clearly a reality. The proletariat becomes a myth when a number of philosophers represent proletarian existence as the model of authentic existence, or, still more, when they reproduce a passage from Marx purporting to show that the proletariat is a universal class—and that, to the extent that this universal class takes power, there will be a universalization of the whole of society.

Well, there, we have a more or less simplified image of Marxism, extracted from Marx's youthful writings and, obviously very far from the preoccupations of the French workers, more or less communist, who rebel against their living conditions and who might, one day, at the Communist party's request, protest the arrival of an American general in France.

J.–L.M. – You believe those strikes against General Ridgway were manipulated by the Communist party.

R.A. – It is obvious. But you cannot manipulate strikes and workers unless the latter agree, in a way, with the protest. Worker movements are not the mere product of a party's manipulations. On the other hand, indignation against the arrival of an American general in France becomes the stuff of demonstrations only to the extent that there exists a party that explains to the workers that the arrival of an American general is a scandal, that the general is inhuman, that he is "Ridgway, the plague," etc.

However, no one ever denied the class struggle. I myself wrote a book called *La Lutte de Classes*. The philosophic or sociologic argument on this subject goes as follows: Within a complex society, there are always antagonistic groups; there is competition, rivalry, possibly a fight for the repartition of the national product.

Moreover, there is disagreement about the overall organization of society. The myth, then, consists in representing the workers as bearers of a concept of society altogether different from present society, a society where there will be no more class conflicts. It was just such a mythic representation that, like the Communists, many intellectuals made, Sartre among them. For them, a class society is bad by definition and any revolutionary movement is a step in the right direction.

D.W. – Even if that direction was the Soviet Union's, with its concentration camps?

R.A. – As I've already told you, Sartre did not deny the basic truth of what was later elaborated upon and demonstrated by Solzhenitsyn. It was simply that, like Merleau-Ponty (who, nonetheless, was more hesitant), he maintained that in order to escape class society, to escape from evil capitalism, there was no other movement, no other road, than socialism and that only the Soviet Union and the Communist party opened this road leading to a transformed society. They were not unaware of and they did not deny the cruelities of the Soviet regime. They said it was the price that had to be paid for a better future.

J.–L.M. – You said: No one was unaware of the Soviet concentration camps. But let's take the example of the Kravchenko trial against *Les Lettres Françaises*. All the intellectuals who went up to testify against Kravchenko denied the existence of the concentration camps.

R.A. – When I say, "no one," I exaggerate. I simply mean that in discussions among intellectuals, most, except those who were card-carrying Communists, recognized the basic facts concerning the concentration camps, because Merleau-Ponty and Sartre, who dominated French thought in that period, themselves admitted their existence in the most explicit manner. Those intellectuals who testified against Kravchenko were for the most part Communists or quasi-Communists. Neither Sartre nor Merleau-Ponty testified against him. But you are right. When I say, "everyone knew it," I am wrong. There were those who didn't know, but mostly because they didn't want to know the facts. All I want to say is that the facts were as well known at the time as they are today. There were so many books on those questions that it was very difficult to challenge the evidence, without claiming once and for all that it is preferable to admit, not the reality, but the reality as it would be if it conformed to people's desires.

D.W. – Was the Kravchenko trial revelatory of the atmosphere of the period?

R.A. – Yes, with the reservation that the trial was a bit questionable. Rumors circulated about Kravchenko's personality. It was not an untainted trial. To tell the truth, I was never interested in the argument about the concentration camps because, for me, the facts were clear. My disagreements with my friends didn't concern the existence of the camps. I asked them: Why do you accept all that in the name of an image, to my mind, largely mythic? So, I never wrote anything in particular on the camps.

J.–L.M. – In the face of those facts, why didn't the theme of democracy stir the support of the intellectuals?

R.A. – But everyone talked about democracy. The Soviets talked about democracy. The question was knowing whether the Western kind of democracy—therefore, the American kind—was the real democracy. Would the regime that emerged from the horrors of the war be a parliamentary democracy? No one was enthusiastic about prosaic parliamentary democracy, a system that is never cherished until it has disappeared. There is only one argument in its favor, but a very strong one, it is Churchill's: "Democracy is the worst form of government, with the exception of all the others."

Now, resignation to this form of government that is the least bad, or the best—compared to all the others—did not meet the hopes and enthusiasm of the soldiers and the men of the Resistance who had just come out of the war. It is very understandable. Stalin's regime was fascinating. It was horrible, but it was fascinating. That discipline of language throughout the world, the adoration for Number One, the love for that man—all in the name of humanism, liberty, democracy—it was monstrous, diabolic, and fascinating.

D.W. – How did you acquire your hatred of totalitarianism?

R.A. – I could only detest it. I had the personal experience of totalitarianism in Nazi Germany. As a sociologist and as a student of politics, I had reflected on the possible systems of government for our industrial societies and I felt that the supreme danger, the ultimate evil, was the totalitarian system. And to my way of thinking, the Stalinist regime was the fully perfected totalitarian system. One couldn't do better in that line. And today almost everyone agrees.

J.–L.M.– You have also said that French intellectuals chose totalitarianism to console themselves a little for France's loss of political prestige.

R.A. – Yes. To work toward the goals of the Fourth Republic—with the Fifth, it's another matter—meant setting one's sights within the French hexagon, concentrating on a limited, national task, rebuilding the economy, remaking French society. For me, it was the unique objective, the imperative of the period; it was duty. And I believed it was very important for the French to regain their pride in country. But it seems that the real intellectuals didn't find the task worthy of them. To permit France to rejoin what is today called the "lead group" of modern economies didn't excite them. It didn't excite me, either. But it was nonetheless important to give the French the possibility of not being ashamed of their country. In 1940, we were overcome with shame. Beginning in 1945, we wanted to put humiliation behind us, to construct and accomplish. . . .

J.–L.M. – On the subject of this radical attitude of intellectuals toward society, you have written, "Intellectuals do not want to understand or change the world; they want to denounce it." What explains this change of attitude on their part after the war?

R.A. – I am not sure that it was a change.

D.W. – Also, you often say that the intellectuals of the Left refuse to think politically. You mean that they refuse to build and take action?

R.A. – It means two things. First, they prefer ideology, that is, a rather literary image of a desirable society, rather than to study the functioning of a given economy, of a liberal economy, of a parliamentary system, and so forth.

And then there is a second element, perhaps more basic: the refusal to answer the question someone once asked me: "If you were in the minister's position, what would you do?" When I returned from Germany in 1932—I was very young— I had a conversation with the secretary of state for foreign affairs, Paganon. "Tell me about your experiences," he said. I made a very Ecole Normale kind of presentation, apparently brilliant—at the time, my presentations were brilliant. "All that is very interesting," he said after about fifteen minutes, "but if you were in my place, what would you do?" Well, I was much less brilliant in the answer to that question.

The same story happened to me, but the other way around, with Albert Ollivier. He had written a splendid article in *Combat* against a minister. "In his place," I asked, "what would you do?" He replied, "That's not my job. It's up to the minister to find the solution; my responsibility is to criticize." I rejoined that I did not have exactly the same concept of my role as a journalist. And I must say that, thanks to Mr. Paganon, I have throughout my journalistic career always asked myself, "What would I do if I were in the place of the ministers?"

D.W. – Is that a question intellectuals fail to ask themselves?

R.A. – They rarely ask it. They think that kind of question is for the experts, the technocrats. They are worried, anguished by the fact that there is evil in our system (evil exists in all systems); they thirst for the solution that would provide the "universalizable" society. They indeed have opinions on what should be done to fight inflation, or on the subject of German rearmament, but those are essentially opinions based on imperative or assumptions, not on an analysis of the situation.

II

DECOLONIZATION

D. Wolton. – In 1955, you were elected to the chair of sociology at the Sorbonne. It is an important date in your life. Why this return to the university, when your career in journalism was proceeding so well?

Raymond Aron. – First and most importantly, I didn't have a feeling of self-fulfillment in journalism. So, I simply wanted to find fulfillment and respond to a kind of vocation

There is also a deeper and more personal reason that I want merely to allude to: My father had not realized his ambitions and at the end of his life, when he was unhappy, he always dreamed that it would be I, his third son, who would accomplish what he had not been able to do. I had a kind of debt toward him and I had the feeling that I would not be paying this debt if I were only a journalist or politician. I had to be a professor and write books, books that mattered. So I really wanted to be elected to the Sorbonne. I didn't do any of the things necessary to be elected, but I made it, nonetheless. My most glaring error was to have published *The Opium of the Intellectuals* three or four weeks before the election. But, as I've told you, some friends from the Ecole Normale spoke persuasively on my behalf.

It should be added that the opposition to my election was legitimate. I hadn't played the game. I had not accepted the few years of teaching in the provinces. I had been nominated for a position in the provinces in 1939, but the war had prevented me from teaching there. And as I have told you, when I returned to France after the war, I refused to go to Bordeaux. So, a number of my colleagues who forcefully rejected my election had rather good reasons, beyond the political ones that were probably more compelling.

a) The Algerian Tragedy

D.W. – You were to write many books in the fifteen years following your election to the Sorbonne. But paradoxically, the first, published in 1957, was a political, not an academic, book: *La Tragédie Algérienne*.

R.A. – Yes, but I also published in 1957 a collection of three essays *Espoir et Peur du Siècle*. In one, *"L'Essai sur la Décadence,"* I spoke about decolonization.

D.W. – But the *Tragédie Algérienne* was of a different nature: it was a political pamphlet that made a great deal of noise. You affirmed that Algerian independence was ineluctable. You couldn't have extracts published in *Le Figaro*, so *Le Monde* published them.

R.A. – I think we should review the context: 1954, the Geneva conference and the end of the first Vietnam War; Mendès-France's initiative in Tunis, that is, the beginning of decolonization in North Africa; in the fall of 1954, the onset of the Algerian revolution; in 1955, German rearmament in the NATO framework; in 1956, Khrushchev's revelations about Stalinism. This is a weighty collection of events. For France, the big question was: After the end of the Indochina War, what is going to happen in North Africa?

I thought at the time that I had not written enough, had not sufficiently made my opinion public on the Indochina War, and I decided that this time I would do my best. I tried, for example, to see the president of the Republic after the Suez expedition that I judged to be foolish. He received me in a very friendly manner, and for a little over an hour. He spoke almost all the time, so much, indeed, that he was very pleased by his conversation with me. Tocqueville tells the same story about his interview with Louis-Philippe. The king spoke all the time. Tocqueville concluded: "He was very satisfied with me."

So, this time, I tried to be more effective, that is, to talk first with the politicians. And I noted very quickly that most of them, after the Moroccan episode, were more or less persuaded that Algerian independence was inevitable.

The turning point was Morocco. It brought about a crisis inside *Le Figaro*. François Mauriac left the newspaper at that time. The readers did not accept his opinions: He had said, for example, that it was necessary to send Sultan Mohammed V back to Morocco and to give Morocco its independence. He was absolutely right. My opinion was the same. But, instead of leaving *Le Figaro*, I did the best I could: I served as intermediary between Pierre Brisson, the director, and Edgar Faure, the prime minister. The latter had organized a luncheon, to which I was invited, in order to sound out Brisson, who was a powerful figure at the time, regarding the return of Mohammed V.

J.–L.Missika. – This sort of thing couldn't be done without *Le Figaro's* support?

R.A. – That would be an exaggeration. But Edgar Faure's position was not very strong. And at the time *Le Figaro* was politically powerful. The prime minister wanted to know what the reactions would be. Finally, Edgar Faure succeeded in sending Mohammed V back in an extraordinarily "Faurist" style: No one understood a thing. In the final analysis, it went the way he wished.

After Moroccan independence, it seemed to me clear that the Algerians would not accept less than both neighboring countries had achieved. If I may put it this way, my advantage in the Algerian question was that I did not know that country first hand. I had never been in Algeria. I wrote about the country on the basis of arguments and data that seemed to me to be persuasive.

D.W. – That was an advantage?

R.A. – In this case, I think those who knew Algeria too well had particular difficulty in imagining an Algeria other than a French Algeria. But I had studied the question of French Algeria in the context of the world situation. When the *Front Républicain* won the elections, I drafted a report that I sent to Guy Mollet. This report eventually became the first part of the brochure *La Tragédie Algérienne*. No reaction from Guy Mollet. He didn't answer. For him, it was one study among many. He didn't know me particularly. He must have said to himself, "Well, here's someone who has that point of view."

Later, I talked with many people. I argued that there were only two solutions: either French Algeria or independence. All the suggestions about a liberal policy toward Algeria meant nothing; either the right to independence was accepted or the war would continue. But to say that to one person or a dozen was one thing; to put it in black and white in a pamphlet was another. After some hesitation, I decided to publish the pamphlet. It had the impact of a small bombshell in the political world. Soustelle's pamphlet immediately followed; its title was, I think, *Le Drame Algérien et la Décadence Française, Réponse à Raymond Aron.*

D.W. – What kinds of reactions did your brochure evoke?

R.A. – It was spoken about a great deal for a few weeks or a few months. People in politics found in it what they thought, but didn't dare say. I recall a conversation with Edgar Faure, who mentioned the role he had played in the independence of Morocco. "Well, I 'made' Morocco," he said, "now it's up to someone else to find the solution to the Algerian problem." Around him were Socialists of the majority and Moderates. The dominant opinion was that Algerian independence was inevitable.

Today, I can report a dialogue between Pierre Brisson and Louis-Gabriel Robinet, editorial writer at *Le Figaro.* I was discussing Algeria for the thousandth time with Brisson. I said to him "Ask Robinet what he thinks." He had Robinet come in and asked him, "In your opinion, what will finally happen in Algeria?" And Robinet answered, "Independence, clearly." Most perspicacious people knew that independence was inevitable. But there was strong resistance in French public opinion and among the French in Algeria. That's why I have always said that, to write *La Tragédie Algérienne* required perhaps some civic courage, but the real difficulty was elsewhere. It is relatively easy to say "Independence is inevitable," but it is very difficult to proceed from this philosophic or historic affirmation to action.

Speaking about action, I moved about a great deal, meeting many civil servants. There was one group of higher officials, in particular, that had organized to put pressure on the government. They came to see me.

J.–L.M. – When the *Front Républicain* came to power in 1956, it had campaigned on the theme of peace in Algeria. Did you think it was capable of achieving such a peace?

R.A. – That is difficult to say. The *Front Républicain* government was both Guy Mollet and Mendès-France. You probably recall Guy Mollet's first trip to Algiers. They threw tomatoes at him. He returned to France convinced that there existed both Algerian nationalism and a French nationalism opposed to independence for Algeria. And he found rationalizations for the policy he followed. He even cited Alain, who had written that the essential thing was not a country's independence, but the liberty of individuals within the country. It was a very nice phrase in the abstract but it had no relevance to the problem of Algeria.

J.–L.M. – It is often said today that the French voted for Mendès-France, but got Guy Mollet.

R.A. – Perhaps.... But there were also the Poujadist elections of 1955. The majority was very, very weak. Mendès-France was certainly far superior to Guy Mollet as a political figure, but would he have been able to conduct a policy of independence? Was an intermediate policy possible? Obviously, an intermediate policy would be a preparation for a solution. But the essential condition for a solution was to recognize the right to independence, which did not necessarily mean immediate independence.

D.W. – Although you say that reasonable people in politics recognized independence as inevitable, your *Tragédie Algérienne* was nevertheless attacked violently.

R.A. – Yes—torn to pieces by some. I was rebuked for accepting the idea of Algerian independence and for justifying it on the basis of economic and demographic necessities. I was also faulted for not using the language of ideology, for not solemnly condemning colonization as such, but for handling the problem as it presented itself. Now, the reason I treated the Algerian question that way was because I felt that the problem at hand was to convince those on the Right, who were not responsible to a moral condemnation of colonization. They had to be shown that Algeria was not necessary to France, either for the economy or for prosperity in general. It was necessary to demonstrate that the return to France by a portion, or by all, of the Algerian French would not be a catastrophe, but, on the contrary, a source of enrichment for the country. And that is what actually happened, which didn't prevent some journalists from writing that I wanted to put the French of Algeria in concentration camps.

And then, I chanced a phrase that seemed ridiculous at the time: "the heroism of abandonment." I meant that a politician was being more courageous in accepting Algeria's liberation than in continuing the war for years. In fact, I wrote at the same time that we could not lose the war. We had left Indochina, thanks to, if I dare say it, a military defeat. But there could be no military defeat in Algeria.

What made possible the Geneva conference, that brought the Indochina War to an end, was, first of all, the intervention of the United States and the Soviet Union; but it was also true that the French had finally been convinced by the evolution of military events. But military events in Algeria never made capitulation or negotiations with the FLN necessary. At the moment when General de Gaulle accepted Algerian independence, the French military situation was better than it had ever been before.

D.W. – Was there really no risk of military defeat?

R.A. – French military superiority was incontestable. The French army had succeeded in largely separating Tunisia and Morocco from Algeria by means of electrified fences. There was a small Algerian army in each of the other two countries, but inside Algeria there remained only a small number of guerrilla detachments that had no chance of winning. But that was not the question. It was a matter of knowing whether, once the French army was brought back to the Metropolitan France, French order could be reestablished in Algeria. That was the real question. If we had wanted to stay there with four hundred thousand men, we could have done so. But total victory was also impossible. To win, it would have been necessary to prolong and extend the war against the Algerian troops in Tunisia and Morocco, which seemed diplomatically out of the question.

D.W. – So independence was a kind of political constraint?

R.A. – We had the choice: maintain Algeria French for years through the intermediary of the Frency army—with ever more violent protests from a part of the French nation—or find a political solution. And there were only two political solutions of a lasting nature: Algerian independence at a fixed date, or Algeria as an integral part of France. When the French or Algeria understood that equality for all the Algerians in Algeria proper meant Muslim domination (that was evident, the Muslims were more numerous by ten to one), they conceived the idea of integrating Algerian Muslims in the whole of France. That was the famous formula, "From Dunkirk to Tamanrasset." But at the time, there were only ten million Muslims. It was already a large number, but represented somewhat less than a quarter of the French population. In 1980, Algerians number more than twenty million. At the end of the century, they will be between thirty and forty million. Now, if the thirty or forty million Muslims were an integral part of France, the Chamber of Deputies, the National Assembly, would be 40 to 50 percent Muslims; which is unthinkable.

D.W. – Was integration demographically impossible?

R.A. – Strictly. French social laws were conceived for a population with a low birthrate. That is what I wrote. In France, for example, state financial support to mothers is a way to combat a falling birthrate. But in Algeria, on the contrary, a reduction of the birthrate is sought. So, Algeria's integration into France would mean condemning ourselves to an impossible situation. It is not possible to apply the same laws to populations that do not have religion, birthrates, or lifestyles in common.

D.W. – Summing it up, you favored independence more for economic reasons than for moral reasons?

R.A. – That's not at all the way things should be presented.

D.W. – However, that's the way it was at the time.

R.A. – There was no purpose in my saying that I was against colonization, because others were already saying it. Like them, I was against colonization for reasons of principle, or for moral reasons, if you prefer. But what was important was to convince those who were using the opposite argument.

I recall a former prime minister saying, "When Algeria is independent, France will have an unemployment problem." I explained to him that the fear was groundless. And that was what had to be proved. My pamphlet was not a philosophic treatise destined to be transmitted to posterity. It was a political act. A number of readers decided once again that I was really a man of the Right because I based my policy on reality. But I don't know on what else a policy can be founded. Furthermore, the policy that I recommended could just as easily have been based on moral principles, because they were compatible. But, again, what was important was not to persuade the anticolonialists, but those who were colonialists.

D.W. – But you have told us that all the politicians were convinced. So, just what was the purpose of your action?

R.A. – They were privately convinced. You will perhaps say that they lacked courage. And they would probably answer that it was easier for Raymond Aron to take a position because he wasn't a candidate for anything, wasn't a deputy, and risked only receiving insulating letters or threats. They waited until experience and events had sufficiently evolved to convert French public opinion. I agree with you that they didn't very much encourage events to convert the French. That was when political writers had the duty, and sometimes the opportunity, to say what the politicians didn't dare say.

D.W. – After you wrote your pamphlet, did you go to Algeria?

R.A. – Why?

J.–L.M. – To verify what you were saying. . . .

R.A. – But I am not a reporter. And, then, I knew a large number of Frenchmen who lived in Algeria, particularly drafted soldiers and officers. So, what would I have discovered by going to Algeria? I would have seen that in a number of regions peace had been reestablished. It would have been explained to me, and I would have been shown that a number of French units were doing admirable work in improving the population's living conditions, and so on; but I was persuaded of that in advance and I had even written about it.

J.–L.M. – Above all, you would have seen a million Algerian Frenchmen who didn't want to leave.

R.A. – But I was aware they didn't want to leave. I had been fiercely attacked when I wrote that France's policy could not be determined by a million Frenchmen in Algeria. That was judged to be the most offensive remark. But I also wrote in *La Tragédie Algérienne:*

> We have obligations toward the Algerian French. We must try, through a peace established as rapidly as possible, to give them an opportunity to remain in Algeria. And if it is impossible for them to stay, we can spend on their behalf the money we are now spending in a war that cannot be won.

That created a scandal. But I have talked with a number of French Algerians in the meantime. They told me that, at the time, they considered me to be the personification of evil.

Now, some tell me, "Basically, you were the only one who cared about the French of Algeria."

So, I hadn't written a reporter's account of Algeria. All the newspapers were publishing such articles. Thierry Maulnier, for example, in *Le Figaro*. My purpose was to analyze a political problem in order to demonstrate that a given solution was the least bad; that, to be sure, it was agonizing and extraordinarily painful for some of the French in the metropole and in Algeria, but that the avoidance of a national tragedy, that is, a civil war, depended upon the courage of the politicians. Well. It was a political act. A reporter's feature article on Algeria would have had no significance in comparison to this political act.

J.–L.M. – Did you think that the Algerian French would have been able to remain in Algeria if the war had not been carried through to the end?

R.A. – I was never very optimistic about their chances of remaining in an independent, Muslim Algeria. However, the conditions of their departure—in panic—over a period of a few days or a few weeks, were not inevitable. I foresaw that in *La Tragédie Algérienne*. We would pursue the war for several years, and then, one day, there would be total collapse, and we would leave. That is what happened.

D.W. – After *La Tragédie Algérienne,* you wrote nothing in *Le Figaro* on the question. Why?

R.A. – Because I wasn't authorized to do so. *Le Figaro* had its own policy on Algeria. Thierry Maulnier explained that Algeria was France's California. He wrote what I had not: a report on Algeria, one of excellent quality, in which he pointed out the most persuasive reasons for optimism on Algeria's future and that of France in Algeria.

J.–L.M. – What I don't understand is why you remained with a newspaper that forebade you to write on a subject as important as Algeria. Why didn't you leave?

R.A. – Listen, a newspaper has a certain readership, and I have known for a long time that readers constitute one of the limits on the freedom of the press. Lazurik, who was the director of *L'Aurore,* used to tell an amusing little story: "I have almost always written for newspapers that were in the pocket of some businessman or interest group. Life on such newspapers is tranquil and easy. The businessman who provides the money is sensitive to two or three questions that concern him particularly. You don't touch these questions, but otherwise, you can write anything you wish."

Conversely, when a newspaper has not "sold out" to some interest, you depend upon readers, buyers. Now, most readers of the big newspapers want their paper to champion their opinions. Those who seek only information in the newspapers are probably a minority. So, if I had left *Le Figaro* because of the Algerian question, I would have lost all possibility to express myself in the press. When I was the first to speak of Algerian independence, neither *L'Express* nor *Le Monde* granted that I was right. They found I was too far ahead of public opinion.

D.W. – However, *L'Express* had been created in 1953 and 1954. . . .

R.A. – Well, *L'Express* wrote that my opinions were typical of capitalist capitulation.

D.W. – What did that mean?

R.A. – Nothing. It was just a journalist's phrase. In the same way, Jacques Soustelle wrote that I was the representative of the *Comité des Forges*.[23] As it happened, the president of the *Comité des Forges* told him he didn't know me.

J.–L.M. – After your *Tragédie Algérienne,* you were accused of rightist defeatism. "Raymond Aron's argument is that France doesn't have the financial means to afford Algeria," people said.

R.A. – I thought it was unreasonable for France to ruin itself: first, by waging war, then, by investing in Algeria—to end up finally and inevitably with Algerian independence.

D.W. – Could other things have been done to prepare public opinion, particularly that of the Right, for independence?

R.A. – I don't very well know what I could have done other than what I did. I wrote *La Tragédie Algérienne* in June 1957. After General de Gaulle's return to power, I wrote another book, more serious and detailed, *L'Algérie et la République,* published in the fall of 1958. It ended with the phrase that the 1958 revolution afforded an opportunity for the renewal of France, on the condition that the revolution devour its own. That is indeed what happened.

D.W. – At that time, you were a very influential editorialist. *Le Figaro* was still the major newspaper. What influence did you have on the politicians? Can it be said that you were the counselor of princes?

R.A. – I don't think so. Most politicians read *Le Figaro* in general, and Raymond Aron's article, in particular. Some told me that reading my article was a must. When I agreed with government policy, the ministers were rather satisfied. When I criticized one finance minister or another, they were not always pleased, but, well, that was part of the game. However, I have no illusions. My belief is that a writer like Walter Lippmann in the United States or Raymond Aron in France has more influence over the long term than on day-to-day controversies.

On Algeria, my influence was very limited, but I brought to moderate politicians an overall image of the world that vindicated their policy. I was different from other editorialists in that my judgments of specific events were always implicitly integrated in a certain world vision.

J.–L.M. – Among the politicians of the Fourth Republic, there was one who was termed a statesman: Pierre Mendès-France. But one doesn't have the impression that the relations between the two of you were very good.

R.A. – We didn't have much of a personal relationship, probably because of differences in chemistry. I greatly respected and continue to respect his personality. I rendered him homage when he made peace in Indochina at Geneva. I praised him also when he went to Tunisia.

As for the European Defense Community, I didn't really hold him responsible for the collapse of the European army project. In my opinion, the plan had already failed before he took office. It is possible that, at the time, I wrote articles critical of him on the subject, but, later, I said that the EDC was dead by the time Mendès-France came to power. However, deep down, he was certainly against the EDC.

D.W. – In 1956, Mendès-France left the *Front Républicain* because he was opposed to Guy Mollet's policy on Algeria. What is strange is that, as much as you tried to work with de Gaulle, one has the impression that you never tried very hard to work with Mendès-France.

R.A. – He had not created a party. He had great difficulties in having himself accepted as the leader of the Radical party.

However, you well know how the Parisians are: there are circles, groups. We were in different groups. That makes me think—if I dare compare us to much greater men—of the speech Guizot gave on the occasion of the reception for Lacordaire, elected to the de Tocqueville chair at the *Académie Française.* "I never really knew de Tocqueville," said Guizot, adding, "Given the compatibility of our ideas, we should have been friends." Paris was that way already. If I didn't have closer relations with Mendès-France, there was no good reason for it except the circumstances of life in Paris. Perhaps, also, we have different temperaments.

D.W. – You could have given chance a nudge.

R.A. – But I never sought out politicians. Everyone assumes that while I was a journalist, I met politicians constantly. It's not true. Even when I was solely a journalist, I led the life of a professor. I saw politicians from time to time, but rarely, much less often than most journalists—I had very little special information beyond the newspapers. I was never really the kind of journalist obliged to rub elbows constantly with politicians.

D.W. – Then, what were your sources of information.

R.A. – The same as everyone's: the newspapers. I didn't try to make journalistic scoops; I tried to analyze problems. My analyses were reflections on events.

When the war between Egypt and Israel broke out in 1973, a journalist from *Le Figaro* wrote that the Egyptians had fallen into a hornet's nest, an Israeli trap. The next day, I wrote exactly the opposite: that it was the Israelis who had been surprised by the Egyptians. I didn't have any special information. But all one had to do was to think. In peacetime, Israel has only a very small standing army. So we knew the army had not been mobilized when the Egyptians attacked. Everyone should have known there were not more than six hundred soldiers on the famous Bar-Lev defense line and along the Suez Canal. Consequently, it was difficult to defend this line. It was simply a matter of being informed about something that everyone could have known.

J.–L.M. – Let me go back to Algeria. You have written that the French army fought in Indochina and Algeria to wipe out the memory of the 1940 defeat.

R.A. – That is an exaggeration. But there is something to it. There was, I think, in French public opinion, in the French nation, and particularly in the French army, a will to wipe out the humiliation that I found disquieting. The 1940 defeat could not be effaced in Indochina or Algeria; that was impossible.

J.–L.M. – And the Fourth Republic politicians were afraid of the military? They gave in to them?

R.A. – In Algeria, yes; not in Indochina. But the Fourth Republic was also influenced by General de Gaulle. "France never abandons anything," said de Gaulle. As long as he was in the opposition, he never granted that decolonization was necessary. In 1950, he inveighed against any negotiations with Ho Chi Minh. While in the opposition, de Gaulle made decolonization still more difficult for the Fourth Republic.

J.–L.M. – And General de Gaulle was synonymous with the army?

R.A. – No, no, but de Gaulle represented a part of French public opinion; to decolonize against de Gaulle and against public opinion was doubly difficult.

D.W. – Could the Fourth Republic, in your opinion, have guided decolonization to its conclusion?

R.A. – No, I don't think so. It would not have been capable of granting independence to the FLN. It is difficult to prove. Nonetheless, four years elapsed between General de Gaulle's arrival in power and the end of the Algerian war. De Gaulle himself had to do battle against two revolts. And he had a new constitution to support him and more prestige than the leaders of the Fourth Republic. He had the capacity that was peculiar to him of transforming something that was essentially a defeat into victory; a victory of France over itself. It was what I had been advocating, but someone had to do it and he was the one. He succeeded in convincing those who favored French Algeria that to give independence to Algeria was for France to be itself; that is, to be generous.

J.–L.M. – Before we discuss the Gaullist republic, did the Fourth Republic deserve its poor reputation? What kind of balance sheet would you draw?

R.A. – It was an unfortunate republic, one that began under unfavorable auspices, with a poor constitution that was accepted by only a third of the country. The men of the Fourth Republic had to fight two battles permanently: one against the Communist party and the other against General de Gaulle's revisionism. But it should nevertheless be recognized that they accepted reconciliation with Germany, finally agreed to Germany's rearmament, and conducted an Atlantic

Treaty policy that I found positive and still approve. They began the economic reconstruction of the country. And it was they who launched the idea of a united Europe. They signed, first, the coal and steel treaty and, then, the Treaty of Rome. So, retrospectively, the balance sheet was not so negative, except for the colonial wars and one other thing that, unfortunately or fortunately, was very grave. For foreigners and for the French themselves, the regime seemed a bit ludicrous. The French did not respect the Fourth Republic. And when a people does not respect its institutions, the harm is profound. Now, since the advent of the Fifth Republic, at least up to the present, the French consider they are not less well governed than the other democracies. They didn't say that at the time of the Fourth Republic.

D.W. – The principal weaknesses of the Fourth Republic were attributable to what, in your opinion: the internal situation, the institutions, the quality of the politicians, the events of the period?

R.A. – A little of all that. What it managed to do was not easy. When all is said and done, though, its accomplishments lacked style, with governments that changed once or twice a year, but always redistributing portfolios among the same people. It was not decorous; even today, I feel it was not decorous. Still, those men were patriots like the rest of us, as much as the politicians of the Fifth Republic, but the circumstances in which they lived were different. I think it was a stroke of luck that General de Gaulle returned to power in 1958, bruising democratic legalities a bit, it is true.

b) De Gaulle and Decolonization

D.W. – Exactly, didn't the conditions of General de Gaulle's return grate on your democratic sensitivities?

R.A. – Yes. I was indignant, at the time. But I thought that the fundamental problem was to end the war in Algeria. And from what I knew of General de Gaulle's opinions, I thought there was a chance that he could bring the Algerian hostilities to an end.

D.W. – But did you show your discontent? Did you write on the subject? Not much, it seems to me.

R.A. – I think I wrote in the introduction to one of my brochures: "It was seduction after sedition." And it was rather that way. Formally, de Gaulle returned in a legal manner.

J.–L.M. – But there really was an act of sedition, even a coup d'etat.

R.A. – It wasn't he, it was the others who brought off the coup d'etat.

D.W. – You're being formalistic.

R.A. – He was, in fact, in contact with those revolutionaries. But he received the National Assembly's vote, just as Marshal Pétain had. The two men were different. But it was the second capitulation of the deputies before the savior. Pétain passed for being the savior in 1940. In 1958, de Gaulle was the savior, or, as I wrote at the time, he was the dictator in the Roman sense, that is, the legal dictator. When it has an impossible situation to unravel, democracy gives one man, whose virtue is recognized and admired, absolute power of a temporary nature, both to resolve the most urgent problems and to revitalize the country's institutions. For a period of six months, de Gaulle really was a Roman dictator and lawmaker. From that moment on, one had to accept the situation and hope for the best.

J.–L.M. – Did this capitulation of parliamentary democracy surprise you?

R.A. – Not very much.

J.–L.M. – However, in 1961, you wrote, and I cite: "I have always had a tendency to underestimate the chances of those who foment coups d'etat. Even in 1958, I believed, probably in error, that the Fourth Republic was still able to defend itself."

R.A. – You are really perverse. Well, if I wrote that, I must have thought it at the time. But, in 1961, I was correct in not fearing the OAS coup d'etat. I like a phrase of the elder François-Poncet, who said, "The French are always surprised by events they have foreseen." Well, I was probably surprised by the event I had foreseen in 1958.

J.–L.M. – For you, in fact, the essential thing was that de Gaulle was the only one capable of making peace. How did you judge his Algerian policy from 1958 to 1962?

R.A. – You've read the articles I wrote in *Preuves* on the subject. One day, I would admire de Gaulle, and, the next, I

would find myself irritated by the General's slowness of progress and his style. He had been pitiless toward the Fourth Republic. I tended to remember what he said against those in
power when he was in the opposition. But, basically, each
time there was a crisis, I wrote supportive articles. At the
same time it is true, I had difficulty understanding why—
since he believed the war could end only through negotiations with the FLN—he gave the FLN in advance everything it
demanded and that could have been the subject of negotiations. He wound up by negotiating at a time when he had
hardly any more trump cards, when he had practically
granted independence to the FLN.

To which one could retort that when, in his statements, he
let his intentions—that is, Algerian independence—even be
perceived, there immediately occurred revolts like the affair
of the "handful of generals" in April 1961, and earlier, in
1960, that of the barricades.

So, perhaps the course he followed, which I found rather
slow and zigzagging, was the only possible one. In any case,
he arrived at the desired result without civil war. To say today
that "it could have been better handled" would be insufferably pretentious. But, to have had some reservations at the
time, well, it was almost inevitable for a commentator. I nevertheless regret some of the critical articles I wrote at the time
and would not want to have them republished today.

D.W. – There was one in particular, *"Adieu au Gaullisme,"*
in the October 1961 issue of *Preuves*, which was a violent attack on de Gaulle's style and even on his inability to establish
peace in Algeria—six months before the Evian agreements.
Were you a prescient observer that time?

R.A. – Another perverse attack that you prepared very
well. All right, it's true. Of all the articles I have written in the
course of my life, that is the one I probably regret most. It was
written in a mood of resentment, suggested to me or inspired
in me by what appeared to be endless protraction of the negotiations, when the nature of the conclusion had become
quite evident. But I don't think you accurately summed up
the article. I commented on the Bizerte slaughter which had
horrified me. I didn't doubt that the outcome would be Algerian independence, but worried that it would occur with a catastrophe. I was also exasperated by events that were

vindicating my 1957 predictions: Following years of war, we were going to abandon everything and explain that, after all, Algeria really didn't interest us. After French Algeria, disengagement. I felt that de Gaulle didn't have many more trumps and that the important thing was to make peace. But such reflections are too facile when one is on the outside. Well, it was a nasty article.

J.–L.M. – And how did de Gaulle react to *"Adieu au Gaullisme"*?

R.A. – It was then that he said to André Malraux, as I told you before, "He was never a Gaullist." It was a perceptive remark. From time to time, he alluded to unkind articles in the media. That article was unkind and I regret it.

D.W. – Your relations with de Gaulle give the impression that with him, too, you didn't succeed in being the prince's counselor.

R.A. – But he didn't have any desire to have a prince's counselor beside him. In the RPF period, if he had arrived in power quickly, it was his intention to give me a position. From what I was told, he wanted to make me responsible for the Plan—a curious idea, I thought.

D.W. – But Malraux was nevertheless among his associates. You could have had the same kind of relationship, in a different tone.

R.A. – I don't think André Malraux had the slightest influence on General de Gaulle. As for me, during the 1958 to 1962 period, after having written *La Tragédie Algérienne*, I could not echo de Gaulle in everything he said. And that was an obligation for everyone in the Gaullist movement. In 1961, I went to the United States. Shortly before, there had been elections in Algeria. I gave a lecture on the situation, arousing the anger of the French consul in Boston. After my lecture, he declared, "The representatives of Algeria are those who have just been chosen in free elections controlled by the French army." Finally, I told him that I felt General de Gaulle thought more nearly my way than his. But as an official, he was obliged to use language compatible with the General's position. The French ambassador in Washington followed me around trying to persuade me not to say things contradictory to General de Gaulle's policy at the time. To accept such obedience, you have to be a political person who focuses exclusively on the goal to be achieved.

D.W. – You think de Gaulle foresaw Algerian independence as early as 1958?

R.A. – I can't say. I am inclined to believe, however, that he hoped for quite a while to achieve Algerian independence without going through the FLN and without an overall collapse. It is difficult to have a categoric opinion on the matter. For example, he chose Michel Debré as prime minister. Now, Debré had declared several times when he as in the opposition: "Any French government that questioned French sovereignty in Algeria would legitimize revolt." And it was he who ultimately granted independence to Algeria. There was a kind of sadism in the choice of Debré. To select the person who had spoken with the greatest emotion in favor of a French Algeria, and make of him the very official responsible for Algerian independence really was extraordinary and merited perplexity. My one belief was that when the chips were down, de Gaulle would accept independence. My reasoning went approximately as follows: As a philosopher of history, de Gaulle know that Algeria will be independent. As a politician, he would like to avoid simply surrendering to the revolution organized by the FLN or to the provisional government. As a matter of fact, he often said, inside government circles or to his associates, "I will never give Algeria to the FLN." But, finally, he did give it to the FLN—an act, by the way, that is at the origin of the relentless hatred of some Frenchmen who accuse de Gaulle of having deceived the men who fought the war on the battlefield.

Today, I'm inclined to say, "Well, I was right in claiming that Algeria would be independent; but I was occasionally wrong in criticizing what General de Gaulle was doing. I tried to do my best and leave to others the right to judge me."

c) The Intellectuals and Anticolonialism

D.W. – With the publication of *La Tragédie Algérienne*, did your relations improve with the Left and with the intellectuals?

R.A. – Yes, certainly with the Left, and also with some intellectuals. I met Jean-Paul Sartre on the street one day in 1960. He came toward me and we shook hands. "Hello, my friend," he said, and I responded in kind. "We should have lunch together one of these days," he said; and I answered, "Yes, of course." I even added, "What a lot of rubbish we have both said!" But it never went any further than that. There was no lunch. Probably, too much time had elapsed. We had become too distant from each other. Our friendship had been essentially an intellectual one and was centered on a philosophical controversy that no longer interested him. We could have resumed a passable relationship, since we were agreed on the Algerian question. But he wrote a preface to Fanon's book that was so characterized by hatred and extraordinary violence that it shocked me. So, it was better for each of us to remain in his own corner.

D.W. – You didn't sign the "Manifesto of the 121," that of Sartre and of the leftist intellectuals most committed against the war in Algeria. Why?

R.A. – First, I was in the United States. Second, I would certainly not have signed it any more than Merleau-Ponty, who refused. The manifesto encouraged young Frenchmen to refuse to answer the draft call, that is, to desert.

I find it objectionable for intellectuals with nothing to lose to motivate young people to become deserters, thereby incurring risks. You don't tell other people to desert; you desert, yourself.

Furthermore, as long as a society is governed democratically, that is, with those in power chosen by universal suffrage, and as long as the right to protest exists, I am against acts tantamount to civil war, to the violent rejection of the existing government.

Now, The 121, in encouraging desertion, at least indirectly, stepped beyond the legal norms of democracy. In any case, I found it premature. When this declaration of The 121 was published, I was at Harvard University. A number of American professors wanted to sign it or at least sign a message congratulating The 121. "Suppose you were fighting a war, as we are in Algeria," I said to them, "and some French intellectuals drafted a message telling young Americans not to report for military duty—to desert. What would you think of it?" The argument impressed them. A few, very few, nonetheless signed something in favor of The 121. Most of the others recognized such an initiative was in very poor taste.

D.W. – What was perhaps lacking in your political position on Algerian independence was a break. . . .

R.A. – I should have left France? That's laughable. Just because we had chosen leaders with whom some of the French were not in agreement? What would a break have meant?

D.W. – A symbolic act to demonstrate your disagreement with the government's Algerian policy.

R.A. – A writer manifests his disagreement by writing. I think I've already told you once that I don't seek popularity. The moment I wrote what I thought about Algeria—and at a time when no one else was doing it—I had done what I could. After writing the pamphlet, I was in touch with people in political circles and I tried to bring them around to my point of view.

Later, the Gaullist revolution took place, and I wrote a book repeating in more elaborate form what I had sketched out earlier. I insist that I did everything that was in my power to do.

J.–L.M. – You did sign Merleau-Ponty's manifesto that was much more moderate than that of The 121.

R.A. – As a matter of fact, I believe I did. In any case, I have come across a letter in which he congratulated me for an article I had written, called "*De la Trahison.*" Briefly, what I said was: "The time has not come to resort to treason. We are still living in a democratic community."

J.–L.M. – It appears that you hold against the intellectuals of the Left their moral commitment, while you claim for yourself the right to a political commitment.

R.A. – No, I don't reproach them for their moral positions. But when they tell young people not to report for military duty, they are asking them to commit a political act. A number of intellectuals did more than that, it is true. They aligned themselves, in a sense, with the FLN in France. They worked with the Algerians who were pursuing the war in France.

J.–L.M. – That was the case of Jeanson, who created the Jeanson network.

R.A. – That was courageous. But I did not agree with the initiative. It's one thing to criticize government policy, but it's something else again to go over to the enemy's side. The Algerians were the enemy, since French soldiers were fighting Algerians. Well, it could be called a civil war in the sense that Algeria was part of France, but everyone realized that it was Algeria's independence that was at stake. The French situation being as it was, I didn't think people should be fighting for the other side.

J.–L.M. – But there was torture, there were lies. Didn't you agree with the moral revolt of the intellectuals, with their effort to reawaken the moral conscience of the country?

R.A. – I fully agree. But torture and lies are attributes of war. What was necessary was to stop the war. However, let me reiterate that I was in favor of the moral protests.

D.W. – Nonetheless, while remaining within the boundaries of legality, why not denounce the French army's use of torture? Some people took the risk of denouncing torture. . . .

R.A. – I don't think there was any particular risk. Everyone spoke about it. Essentially, you are reproving me, after I had taken a position in favor of Algerian independence, for not having written any literary pieces on the horrors of torture.

D.W. – No, for not having made a political commitment against torture.

R.A. – But I wouldn't have taught anyone a thing by proclaiming that I was against torture. I've never met anyone who was in favor of torture.

J.–L.M. – One section of your article *"De La Trahison"* seems to me an accurate reflection of your position. You write, "Pacification, it is true, is not feasible without torture, but a war of liberation is not feasible without terrorism: torture to preserve French Algeria versus terrorism to achieve Algerian independence—it's the purpose (not the means used) that leads to the choice of one or the other." One might say that your pragmatic position is evidenced in that quotation.

R.A. – It is, precisely, not a pragmatic position, but a moral one. The methods used by the Algerians were often just as horrible as those used by the French army. The village of Melusa was decimated, almost exterminated, by the FLN. But I wrote no articles against the FLN's terrorism, just as I wrote nothing on torture, although I detest both torture and terrorism. The atrocities on both sides did not cancel each other— they were cumulative. The terrorism of the Algerian revolutionaries was almost inevitable. The torture practiced by the French army was perhaps not inevitable, but experience seems to indicate that in this kind of war, even a civilized army almost always ends up committing absolutely inhuman acts. To put an end to them, it was necessary to put an end to the war.

D.W. – Isn't this moderate position a cause for reproach in that it leaves to others the burden of daily political action?

R.A. – But it wasn't a moderate position; it was a categoric, extremist position of a political nature. I favored the extreme solution of Algerian independence. As far as moral positions were concerned, I left that mission to the self-righteous moralists, because, once and for all, let me make it clear that I am not one of them—"*die schöne Seele*," as Hegel calls them. I favored Algerian independence; I did not favor civil war in France. Since I wanted to stay within the French community, I took my stands orally and in writing; I did not become an FLN militant. I make no moral condemnation of those who did become FLN militants. I am explaining my position; I am not justifying myself. I am saying that I considered myself a French citizen in a democratic France, where people had the right to tell the government: "You are mistaken; you should come to a settlement." As long as one had the right to say that and to write it, I had no desire to become a militant of the FLN.

J.–L.M. – But didn't the radical position of some intellectuals favor the evolution of public opinion?

R.A. – I am not sure who contributed most. It's not my habit to give out grades.

J.–L.M. – For leftist intellectuals during this period, anticolonialism was another way of bringing revolution about. I don't imagine your reconciliation with them went as far as that?

R.A. – If that's your analysis of the leftist intellectuals, I certainly would not be with them on that point. But I don't associate them with such a concept, which seems to me rather puerile and stupid.

D.W. – On the contrary. The struggle against colonialism was sometimes experienced as a continuation of the 1950s fight for the proletariat and revolution

R.A. – The result was that they were disappointed again. I thought the struggle for decolonization by the peoples concerned was just and normal, so I approved decolonization. But it wasn't a revelation of the future; it was not the light at the end of the tunnel. As far as the search for a Mecca other than Moscow, it wasn't to be found in any of the decolonized countries. True, there was Belgrade, Havana, Algiers....

J.–L.M. – Like others, you went to Cuba. You were not converted?

R.A. – That's it, I was not converted. I went there as a tourist and I wasn't received by Fidel Castro, as Sartre was. But, I listened to Castro's speeches with the help of an interpreter. I did have a talk with Rodriguez who had a sociology background and who knew something of me. He was the head of the Communist party, and spoke Spanish and Marxism—his was the only Spanish I was nearly able to understand in Cuba, so much was it permeated with Marxism. He tried to explain to me why a proletarian revolution had been carried out by the petty borgeoisie. He made a very persuasive case. For this kind of dialectics, it was very well done. It didn't make any sense, but made good dialectics.

Sartre wrote a report that I am sure pleased you both. I don't think it is a fundamental contribution to his collected works. It's a report on Cuba. As usual, my trip didn't provide the occasion for the kind of reporting you prefer. It was at the start of the regime, in 1961, sometime before the anti-Castro landing at the Bay of Pigs. I wrote some rather moderate articles in *Le Figaro* on what I had seen in Cuba. It was the end of one society and the birth of another. It was too early to make a definitive judgment. That Castro was building a Soviet-style regime was well known. But it wasn't yet possible to know the exact form that the regime would have.

D.W. – What did you think of the Third World that emerged from decolonization?

R.A. – I don't like the expression. Thrown together in the Third World are China, the world's oldest empire, and Guinea and other African countries that have a civilization, but an unwritten one. Latin America, which is something entirely different, is also considered a part of it. The Third World is a confused mixture created by words and diplomacy. My opinions differ, depending on which Third World country is being discussed.

J.–L.M. – In that, we have another glimpse of what separated you from a number of leftist intellectuals at the time. They lived the Third World—Algeria, in particular—like a revolution.

R.A. – There, I must say that I find mine is the sensible side. The Algerians had every right to create an independent state. But the idea that a revolution in the Western sense, that is, the transformation of society, the creation of a better society, etc., could be effected through the Third World seems completely idiotic to me. The Algerians created their country in tragic circumstances. They had lost in the war a part of their cadres formed by the French—this was, by the way, one of the most disastrous aspects of the war. However, Algeria managed rather well, but France really had nothing to learn either from Algerian politics or from the Algerian economy.

We must have the best possible relations with Algeria. But the idea that the Third World is the world's hope seems to me wholly unreasonable. It makes no sense. One must naturally retain hope, but one must not place one's hopes here or there, without reflecting about what is at stake.

You tell me that for awhile the leftists thought the Third World would provide enlightenment. They were wrong. It is no service to countries trying to survive with great difficulty to make them believe they have such a mission.

III
PEACE AND WAR AMONG NATIONS

a) Thinking About Nuclear War

J.–L. Missika. – Between 1959 and 1967, you were a professor at the Sorbonne and you published a large number of books:

—First, an analysis of the transformation of industrial societies, with one of your best-known books, *18 Leçons sur la Société Industrielle,* and the follow-up books, *Lutte de Classes* and *Démocratie et Totalitarisme;*

—Thereafter, a more theoretical work, *Les Etapes de la Pensée Sociologique;*

—Finally, you treated the problems of strategy and geopolitics in 1962, with, especially, *Peace and War among Nations.*

Let's begin with this last title. Your goal was to create a conceptual system of the most difficult phenomena to analyze: war and relations among states.

Why did you want to create a theory of war?

Raymond Aron. – It is not a theory of war. Through a series of circumstances, I found myself commenting on diplomatic events at *Le Figaro.* And since I had retained a few recollections of philosophy and my taste for abstraction, I began to place these daily articles in a framework of global analysis with my *Grand Schisme* and *Les Guerres en Chaîne.*

At the time, I realized that my analysis was historic or sociologic, but it was not organized, and the concepts were inadequate. So, I wanted for a long time to write a book that would be an introduction to the theory of international relations. I took a year of vacation, if you can call it that, away from the Sorbonne. I spent a semester at Harvard, where I began to write *Peace and War among Nations.*

I should add, by the way, that I had given courses on the same subject. In fact, the first two parts of the book were taken from my Sorbonne courses. Its size always impresses people, mistakenly. But, to my great surprise, even the *Annales*, which generally didn't much like me, dedicated two series of articles to a discussion of the book. This was a way for me to become totally integrated again into the university world. *Peace and War among Nations* has, by the way, a number of defects characteristic of university people.

J.–L.M. – You wanted to build a system of global analysis, although you say and repeat that history is sound and fury. Isn't that a contradiction?

R.A. – Not at all.

D. Wolton. – Though you always rejected the great systems, you wanted to build one?

R.A. – In *Peace and War*, I did not, unfortunately, fashion a great design, a great theory. I tried to show how one could analyze global situations, what I called systems, in which I introduced a number of ideas, such as homogeneous and heterogeneous systems. I tried to illustrate the innovations implied by nuclear arms.

J.–L.M. – To focus on this subject: In what ways did the thermonuclear bomb radically change the elements of strategy and diplomacy in comparison to all the wars that humanity had previously known?

R.A. – That is a question difficult to answer in a categoric way. The dominant idea of modern strategy since, let's say, Napoleon's time, was that the objective was victory through destruction of the enemy; this meant taking from the enemy his ability to defend himself, disarming him.

Now, between the two nuclear powers, a disarming in this sense seemed almost impossible, at the very least, when I wrote that book. It has become less inconceivable in that today's missiles are so precise that each nuclear power can, theoretically, destroy the adversary's missiles. That remains extraordinarily difficult because, even if one of the two powers can destroy the land missiles of the other, there remain submarine missiles, airborne missiles, etc.

But, one of the ideas immediately perceived is that—from the moment that the escalation to the extremes (Clausewitz's expression) becomes the escalation of nuclear arms and, at the same time, carries the risk of mutual suicide—something has changed.

So, has the essential changed or not? The Soviets say that the essential has not changed; the West says that it has.

D.W. – What is the essential?

R.A. – Well, the West uses the concept of dissuasion as a kind of absolute. Nuclear arms are essentially destined to prevent the enemy from doing this or that, but are not destined to achieve a victory over him. Even today, the Americans say, officially, that there can be no victorious side in a nuclear war.

On the contrary, the Soviets do not use the notion of dissuasion, or they hardly, use it. They employ Clausewitz's phrase, "War is the extension of the pursuit of politics by other means." Thus, they consider that if there is a war, there can be a winner and a loser, even if nuclear arms are used. In any case, whichever is right, the fact remains that escalation to the extremes, when the escalation in question concerns nuclear arms, is something different from Austerlitz. Austerlitz was total military victory. Jena was total military victory. Thus, Prussia's disarmament was possible. Austerlitz did not suffice to disarm Russia, but it was a victory of annihilation. Today, to conceive of a victory of annihilation by the Soviet Union over the United States, or by the United States over the USSR, is almost impossible. That doesn't mean that there will never be a nuclear war; it means that one must now think of something new, that is, to determine not only what resources to commit in a war, but to know what level of commitment to make, with which armaments, to know how to avoid excessive escalation, and so forth.

J.–L.M. – How do you manage to speak of nuclear war with such realism?

R.A. – Once again, you're going to say that I am cold, that I lack sensitivity. You're enough to make me angry. Anyone who thinks about war, considers it to be a detestable thing. And I find it detestable.

J.–L.M. – You didn't let me finish. I wanted to ask you if this obsession with war doesn't have a link to your pacifism of the 1930s? Pacifism was a refusal to think of war, while your books *Guerres en chaîne, Peace and War, Penser la Guerre, Clausewitz*—all focus on the theme of war.

R.A. – But, tell me, are you aware that we have been living in the twentieth century? Do you realize that one of the great events of this history was the First World War; and that an even more important event was World War II? From World

War II emerged the power of the Soviet Union. Even today, the dominating element of the present situation is the Soviet Union's power.

Before 1940, because I detested war, I never studied it. During the war, I was forced to think about the subject; I even read, at that time, a classic text, Delbrueck's *L'Histoire de l'Art de la Guerre*. He treated war in the political framework. Since then, having given myself the task, when I was twenty-five, of being a committed observer of history, it was necessary for me to understand economics, that's why I studied economics. I also had to learn as much as possible about international relations, an effort that I began during the war, in 1940, and that I have continued to pursue, though detesting war.

But I must admit that diplomatic events and, in particular, war, are rather fascinating objects of reflection because they include both drama and planning. Military affairs should be studied, like all the other subjects studied, at the universities. This is what Liddell Hart wrote and it is the Liddell Hart phrase that I used as an epigraph at the beginning of *Peace and War among Nations*. But when I undertook these studies in an academic way, I was virtually the only one in France. Today, most universities have departments of defense studies, good or bad. If one wishes to be a sociologist and to understand one's epoch, to be haunted by past wars and by the risk of future wars is not too surprising. But if you prefer a psychoanalytic interpretation, why don't we say that writing books again and again on something that repels me is a way of punishing myself for my earlier pacifism. That is possible. But, one could also say quite simply that I was struck by the character at once mysterious and intelligible of great wars that are part of what I call, in one of my articles, "history as usual." This history is made up of nations, wars, heroes, and victims. Is it a senseless tumult or is it possible, through the tumult, to perceive something that might have been desired or thought in advance as rational? Is it all sound and fury or can one find a kind of rationality in these calamities that populations must bear?

J.–L.M. – Isn't what fascinates you today in war—in the nuclear age—the fact that it more and more resembles an intellectual game, a chess game, even a poker game?

R.A. – Yes, that's one aspect of nuclear strategy, but it is also a frustrating one. I don't know how many books have been written on nuclear strategy, not so many in France, but many, certainly, in the United States. But they are merely speculation. The speculation is focused on the psychological relationships between two states, or more exactly, between two heads of state, because up until now, fortunately, there has been no experience in the use of nuclear weapons.

Even their use in 1945 against Japan does not belong to the nuclear age. It was comparable to the bombing of cities to hasten capitulation, the surrender of besieged islands. It was the use of the first two bombs against a power that had none. Even the Cuban crisis of 1962 was not truly a nuclear emergency. The crisis concerned the installation of nuclear missiles in Cuba. But even if the USSR had tried to establish a non-nuclear base in Cuba, the United States would probably have demanded, perhaps more politely, that the Soviets dismantle the base.

D.W. – *Peace and War among Nations* appeared, precisely, in 1962, when peaceful coexistence raised certain hopes. Was that important for you? Did it open a new era in international relations?

R.A. – Peaceful coexistence is banal. Lenin used the expression to designate what would happen for a certain time between the Communist government and other regimes. After Stalin's death, the Soviet Union simply resumed, in a number of areas, relationships that had been interrupted. Once again, there are normal diplomatic relations, sports, and intellectual exchanges, etc. Peaceful coexistence is nothing very new. It simply means that the Soviet Union and the West are not at war in the usual sense of the term; they are not employing the classic tools of war. It does not mean that the rivalry between the Soviet world and the noncommunist world has ceased.

J.–L.M. – Was it only the death of Stalin that changed the direction of events?

R.A. – Today, most scholars believe that toward the end of life, Stalin had envisaged ending the extreme form of the cold war. It is likely that he would have altered his diplomacy in 1953, as his successors did. But his successors did it more rapidly because they were very worried, at the beginning, about the repercussions of Stalin's death, both domestically and abroad. However, the cold war continued—I would be ready to say to this day, but, at least until the end of 1962. After all, there was Khrushchev and the Berlin ultimatum. I think that was in the fall of 1958; it was the gravest crisis. Khrushchev demanded that West Berlin's status be changed. And West Berlin could not be defended locally. It is clear that the West did not have the ability to mobilize sufficient conventional forces against Soviet conventional forces. But it refused to accept the ultimatum and a kind of tug of war prevailed for a few years, with one side threatening and the other refusing to cede. The Berlin crisis was not resolved until after the Cuba crisis, in the fall of 1962. It was this adventurist policy of Khrushchev that was held against him by his successors.

J.-L.M. – Even for the Soviet Union, do you believe deeply in the importance of personalities in history?

R.A. – As far as the 1917 Revolution is concerned, it can be said without exaggeration that it could never have taken place without Lenin and Trotsky. I think Trotsky himself wrote that. Of course, it can always be claimed that there would have been a revolution in any case, because the Czarist regime could not have brought about the transformation of the Czarist empire. There is some truth to that. But it is a fact that men like Trotsky and Lenin played a significant role in history; I don't see why, in the name of what philosophy, one could take away from the heroes of history the responsibility and the greatness for having either founded a socialist empire, or for having forced their people into a totalitarian regime.

J.-L.M. – Wasn't the high point of peaceful coexistence the signature of the July 1963 Moscow treaty banning nuclear tests in space . . . ?

R.A. – . . . and limiting the power of the tests? Yes, it was the first agreement on arms control. It was an American initiative whose development I had observed while I was at Harvard. There was a seminar there at which the future counselors of Kennedy discussed arms control. The first agreement was signed between the Soviets and the Americans at the time when the Chinese and Russians were making their conflict public. The letters revealed to the world a conflict of which the experts were only partially aware.

J.-L.M. – Was that agreement on the limitation of strategic arms explainable by an awareness on the part of the two superpowers of the need to limit the nuclear race or by the schism between the Soviet Union and China?

R.A. – No, it was an American initiative. The Americans

started with the concept that no one could win a nuclear war and that while the rivalry between the two great powers was inevitable, it was necessary as far as possible to pursue this competition on a lower level of violence. They were quite properly obsessed by the desire to reduce to a minimum the risk of a nuclear war. Thus, they never ceased to ponder arms control. But consequences were not very significant. The Soviets continued to increase their armaments in such a way that, today, the military superiority of the Soviet Union is hardly in doubt. As far as the risk of nuclear war is concerned, it is virtually the same with or without arms control. I grant, however, that my affirmation is a bit categoric and that, although it expresses my judgment, I cannot demonstrate its validity. What is important and certain is that arms control was born at the Rand Corporation and at Harvard and was applied for the first time by Kennedy. It is the same doctrine that inspired the SALT accords, still under discussion because SALT II has not been ratified.

D.W. – People had faith in these agreements. Have they really served no purpose?

R.A. – To repeat, I do not think that they changed anything. But the Americans say that, first, they made it possible to limit expenditures somewhat. For example, it was agreed that no defense system against missiles, that is, no antiballistic missiles (or ABMs) would be developed. Fine. Was it a good or bad decision? It's debatable.

Second, they believe that, despite everything, the negotiations have permitted each party to better know what the other is doing. It's not a very persuasive argument because it is essentially the satellites that permit verification that the agreements are being respected.

For a long time, American doctrine was that of Mutual Assured Destruction, that is, the ability of each to destroy the other. To some extent, it is the same thing that existed earlier, without an explicit agreement. That leaves many elements in doubt, especially the effectiveness of dissuasion. If the use of nuclear weapons means mutual suicide, dissuasion through the nuclear threat is at the very least weakened.

I've always thought that the Americans wanted simultaneously two things that are largely contradictory. First, dissuasion through the threat of nuclear weapons; second, the creation of a situation in which nuclear weapons' use would entail mutual suicide. But it is not easy to threaten to kill the other if you are going to die with him.

So, the effectiveness of nuclear dissuasion is certainly weakened by the doctrine of MAD (Mutual Assured Destruction). Brennan, one of the American critics of this policy, didn't fail to observe that MAD in English means crazy.

J.–L.M. – You said that the Soviets didn't believe in dissuasion. Does that mean that they consider nuclear arms as traditional weapons?

R.A. – They say they are weapons just like others, except that they have a higher destructive power. They, of course, add that, to the extent possible, their use should be avoided. But if they were to use them, they believe Clausewitz's phrase would remain valid: There would always be a winner and a loser.

I asked a Soviet diplomat about this. "Why do your books on military strategy always claim that nuclear weapons are arms like the others and that they are usable?" I asked him. He reflected for a moment because he was embarrassed by the question, and then he found a clever answer, whether it is the right one or not. "You know," he said, "military people always need a doctrine. So, the civilians had to give them one. The doctrine is that these weapons are like others, which doesn't mean the Soviet leaders really accept such nonsense." So, you have the choice: You can believe him—or you can believe the official texts.

D.W. – But then, why did they sign those arms control agreements?

R.A. – They are not against them. As a matter of fact, the agreements were rather favorable to the Soviet Union. They permitted them, as I've already said, to catch up with and perhaps surpass the United States in nuclear weaponry. And, then, once they knew the American armaments ceiling, they could limit their expenditures for nuclear weapons, thus freeing resources for other weapons systems.

D.W. – So the West made an error?

R.A. – I wouldn't be that categoric. I think the agreements were rather advantageous to the Soviet Union, but I don't much like treating an extremely complicated question in a sentence or two.

D.W. – During this period of peaceful coexistence, marked by a number of crises—in Berlin and Cuba, for example—the United States involved itself (between 1960 and 1970) ever more deeply in the Vietnam War. Did you denounce the Vietnam War? Or did you simply explain it?

R.A. – I explained it. I judged it to be an error. I felt that the Americans' way of conducting the war was foolish. However, remember that there were plenty of Frenchmen ready to criticize vociferously American intervention in Vietnam. Personally, I found the American effort to defend South Vietnam less reprehensible than the 1946 to 1954 French Vietnam War. The French wanted to preserve their empire in Vietnam; the Americans had no intention of staying there. Rightly or wrongly—probably, wrongly—they wanted to save the South Vietnamese government.

D.W. – Yes, but the Americans didn't respect the 1954 Geneva agreements. They failed to organize elections.

R.A. – That's true. But have there ever been free elections under a communist government? If there had been elections in 1958, do you really think that the prime minister of South Vietnam, Diem, would have been able to make an electoral speech in Hanoi? It would be ludicrous to claim that. Those governing in the North didn't want free elections any more than those in the South.

That was not the question. Were the South Vietnamese patriotic enough to resist North Vietnam? That was the real question. In the Korean War, the West favored American intervention in South Korea. It tried to save South Korea and it succeeded. The Americans tried to do the same thing in Vietnam. But they didn't know the country and they didn't know how to conduct the war there. They plunged into it in headlong fashion. Materially and, even more, morally, it cost them dearly, and they haven't finished paying the price yet.

It is this situation that I tried to analyze at the time. When Nixon and Kissinger took office, they announced that they would not accept a government coalition, which was practically a demand for capitulation. I wrote then that in all probability the war would last for several years.

In addition, the war could not be other than unpopular. The Americans didn't know how to conduct it except by aerial bombings. They dropped hundreds of thousands of tons of bombs on North Vietnam and, especially, on the road used by the North Vietnamese soldiers. These measures caused people to forget that the objective—to save South Vietnam—was justifiable and it remains so today as one observes that countless thousands of South Vietnamese are trying to escape the country "liberated" by the North.

D.W. – Why do you say that Western democracies cannot win a war like that in Vietnam?

R.A. – That's easy to understand. First, in order to conduct a war, democracies must be convinced that they are right, that they are defending a cause that is, if not sacred, at least morally pure. Now, for both the French and the Americans, the Vietnam War was an equivocal combat. It was very equivocal for the French; it was equally so for the Americans.

Moreover, the Vietnam War was the first one in modern history experienced and seen by civilians in the home country on television, and that factor played a large role.

Also, the American army at the time was made up of draftees. Ordinary citizens were fighting the war, while in the nineteenth century, the Europeans fought their colonial wars with professionals. Too, as the war lengthened, the moral and political protests within the United States grew larger and more violent.

The United States sparked the worldwide inflation because it fought that war without imposing the taxes necessary to finance it. In 1975, the president could not obtain from Congress any funds to save the government of the South on whose behalf a war had ben fought for years. Finally, the Americans left Vietnam in 1975 under conditions that were less than honorable, that were even deplorable. The Vietnam War was a tragedy for the United States and one which they have not yet put fully behind them.

D.W. – Was it lost principally for military, moral, or political reasons?

R.A. – It was not won militarily, because it could not be so won.

D.W. – Was it the same situation as in Algeria?

R.A. – No, it was different. On the other side, there was a powerful Vietnamese army. It did not invade South Vietnam until the end of the war and the American army obviously was capable of resisting it. But what the American army could not do was to eliminate the guerrillas, partly because the latter were supplied in a permanent way by North Vietnam which, itself, received all the weapons it needed from the Soviet Union. So, the way that war was conceived and directed, it could not be won. It must be said that the civilians who directed it had not really analyzed the specificity of that war. They launched into it with an inexperience and a clumsiness that were incredible, eventually giving the impression that they were responsible for the war, that they were guilty and, in the bargain, that they had lost, which was the most disastrous image.

So, you see, sometimes it is useful to study the dynamics of a war.

b) Economic Growth and Ideological Rivalry

D.W. – In 1963, you published a book that had its origins in one of your 1955-1956 courses at the Sorbonne: *18 Leçons sur la Société Industrielle*. This book was followed by *La Lutte de Classes* and *Démocratie et Totalitarisme*. They were great successes.

R.A. – I didn't start with a success. When I began my course at the Sorbonne, in the Descartes amphitheater, I had between thirty and forty students. I had told them the course wasn't necessary for their examination. Later, when the courses were developed into books, I had, indeed, an ample number of readers. But that was seven years later.

J.–L.M. – How do you explain the success, because, in the final analysis, it was very much a success?

R.A. – Yes, the success of *18 Leçons,* particularly, can be explained, as always for a book of this kind, by the symbiosis between the nature of the book and what the public was interested in at the moment. It was rather a popularized book. It went back to the idea of industrial society that was traditional in the first half of the nineteenth century, before the triumph of Marxism. And the concept of industrial society gave me the opportunity to outline a comparison between capitalist societies on one side, and so-called socialist societies on the other, linking them through a concept that was the industrial society.

Now, at about that time, a number of intellectuals had more or less broken away from orthodox Marxism because of the impact of Khrushchev's speeches and the repression of the Hungarian revolution. They found in these three small books an interpretation—partially Marxist, but not at all communist-oriented—of the confrontation between the models of industrial societies existing in the two parts of Europe.

J.–L.M. – There is another important theme in the *18 Leçons:* the theme of economic growth.

R.A. – Yes, but the term "growth" already existed in the literature. I think the first important book on the subject was Colin Clark's *Economic Progress*. There were also Fourastié's books. But mine were perhaps different because they connected growth calculated in a purely mathematical way with social relations and with all possible types of growth. In this sense, one went from Colin Clark and Fourastié to a new kind of nondogmatic Marxism.

J.–L.M. – You say that your *18 Leçons* was one of the first books to analyze the structural transformations of societies. Were the leaders of the period aware of these transformations?

R.A. – They were aware of them, but they hadn't yet considered that growth of production and productivity constituted the essential structural characteristic of modern societies. When this fact was recognized, the French image of a society balanced between agriculture and industry, fashionable before 1939, disappeared. The French became conscious of their wish to adapt to the times, as General de Gaulle said later. I encouraged this awareness by providing an overall vision of the society in which we live and cannot get away from.

This didn't happen without resistance. In 1956, when the Suez crisis caused an oil shortage, some agricultural leaders took up the old theme, "You see, industrial society is all very well, but when oil is scarce, the whole country is threatened." There subsisted some nostalgia for agricultural-industrial balance, but it disappeared rather rapidly.

Since then, in 1973-1974, the theory of growth was again placed under scrutiny. But, at the time, everyone accepted the growth theory as a sort of introduction to the understanding of both capitalist and socialist societies.

J.–L.M. – On the whole, you were a modernist?

R.A. – Yes, of course, as I was before the war and as everyone of my generation was after the war. As I have said many times before: We remembered the decadence of the 1930s and the humiliation of 1940. To wipe out this past, it was necessary to modernize. In that sense, the *18 Leçons* was accepted to my great surprise, as a kind of standard text that was taught in the lycées and given also to business leaders.

D.W. – But in showing that industrialization and growth take place in the East as well as in the West, didn't you make people believe that there was a convergence between capitalism and socialism?

R.A. – Yes, I contributed to this error of interpretation. It was an error, for it was never my belief that the two types of societies would converge into a single form that would be a liberal socialism, as Duverger, I think, called it. I tried to analyze in the second book, *La Lutte de Classes,* the structure of groups, elites, classes in the two models of society, and I demonstrated as clearly as possible that there had been no convergence toward a social structure that would be the same on both sides.

As far as politics goes, I again illustrated, but with a stronger accent, that the Soviet leaders had no intention, nor had they the possibility, of liberalizing their system and becoming a pluralistic democracy. The Soviet Union is not Russia; it is a single party system governing in the name of an ideology. This ideology encompasses a global vision of history and a task to accomplish. With this situation in mind, I analyzed as precisely as possible, toward the end of my third book, *Démocratie et Totalitarisme,* the kinds of liberalization that are conceivable in the communist regimes, and also their limits. And the limits I fixed were very narrow. I was probably rather overly optimistic about the possibilities of the transformation of the Soviet regime. But what I said remains essentially true today.

J.–L.M. – So the two systems that are comparable in their industrial structures, diverge on the ideological level. But you yourself announced the end of ideology. Isn't that contradictory?

R.A. – The expression "the end of ideology" originated, I think, with Daniel Bell, in the United States. As for me, it is true that in the conclusion to *The Opium of the Intellectuals* I used as a heading, *"Fin de l'Âge Idéologique?"*. . . with a question mark. I think this heading was dangerous. The word ideology has several meanings. In a way, it is foolish to envisage the end of ideologies. I based my reasoning on a definition of ideology as a global representation of universal history that indicates both the future and what has to be done. Now, I tried to suggest that Marxism represented ideology *par excellence,* that there was no substitute ideology, and that if Marxism lost its authority over people, there would remain, of course, values in the name of which people would fight; there would be transformations in the name of some ideas, but there would not be a system as complete or as imperative as Marxism-Leninism.

In the United States, an intellectual debate on this subject went on for a period of several years. It was even made the subject of a book: *The End of Ideology Debate.* It is no longer very topical, but one question remains: Is there a global ideology comparable to Marxism, and that could replace it? Up to the present, there are leftists, ecologists, a great number of people who protest against one aspect or another of contemporary society, but I don't believe any of them has succeeded in conceiving the equivalent of Marxism. In this sense, there was some truth to the phrase "end of the ideologic age." Since then, I have written at least a half-dozen articles to refine my point of view. But I will spare you my refinements. . . .

D.W. – Do you think a class struggle still exists in the developed countries?

R.A. – Of course. We have already spoken of it. But the sense you give to the term "class struggle" is important. If you're speaking of the rivalry among different social groups in the distribution of the national product and in political and economic organization, then there clearly remains a class struggle in most Western countries.

But the question arises as to whether we are talking about an implacable struggle, the consequence of a total representation by the proletariat or the parties opposing the ideal society. In that case, the battle among the classes is not merely a rivalry that can be resolved through compromise. It becomes an inexpiable struggle that can be resolved only by total victory, that is, a revolutionary victory of the party that refuses the existent society.

I would say that there is no class struggle in the second meaning of the term in the United States, because none of the unions, none of the big parties favors a basic revolt against American structures.

In France, it is possible to say that there subsists an element of the traditional class struggle to the extent that a fraction of the proletariat is, or appears to be, faithful to a kind of Marxist revolutionary spirit. But in most Western countries, while there might be a class struggle in the first sense—and sometimes a very bitter one, as in Great Britain—the parties and the classes most hostile to the existing regime remain respectful of the law. In Great Britain, the unions and the Labor party continue to be law-abiding in their opposition of the policies of Mrs. Thatcher, whom they abhor.

D.W. – Despite certain commonalities from the viewpoint of social structure between the socialist countries and the developed capitalist countries, you believe there is no affinity on the level of political organization. So you believe that the political system is determinant in comparison with economic structures?

R.A. – That is what I think. The Soviet regime is defined by the single party system, that is, total power concentrated in the party. And even within the party, it's a small minority that really governs and manages the country.

J.–L.M. – Then, ownership of the means of production is a secondary question?

R.A. – It is not secondary, but it is possible to conceive of an economic system where the public ownership of the means of production would be very widespread without being total and where there would be no messianic party—an ideological party that imposes a discipline of word and thought upon the whole of the population. That's the essence of the matter: the dominant role of the party.

Let's take an example. When the unions in a Communist country claim the right to speak for the workers, the government replies, ideologically: but that is contrary to the principle of the party's dominant role, that is, that unions must not have any autonomous power *vis-a-vis* the party. As long as a

Communist regime doesn't renounce the party's dominance or monopoly—and, above all, doesn't renounce the slogan: The party's power is socialism and liberty—as long as these characteristics of the Eastern European regimes are unchanging, whatever liberalization there might exist is not to be scorned, but it will remain very limited.

One can consider it a kind of liberalization when the Soviet leaders renounced the claim of an ideological truth in genetics. In Stalin's time, they sent the geneticists to concentration camps because they considered that genetics was in contradiction with Marxism. Exaggerations or stupidities of that kind have largely disappeared. Scientists, especially those useful in the development of military power, enjoy relative liberty of thought.

However, on important occasions, they must continue to parrot the official line, the mechanical language, that represents the distance separating East and West. As long as that continues, there will be no convergence between the two types of regimes.

J.–L.M. – Is that why you call the Soviet regime an ideocracy?

R.A. – During the war, I spoke, rather, of a "secular religion." The expression applied at least partially to Nazism. It applies also to the Soviet Union. It refers to an ideology that is presented as a kind of religious truth, or perhaps as a counter-religious truth, a negation of religion. But it always concerns a supreme truth of which the party members are the high priests. Stalin, clearly, was the high priest of the Marxist-Leninist religion and his work was fiat throughout the Soviet world. Today, there are fissures in this impressive unity of Soviet thought or words, but its essence remains.

J.–L.M. – Paradoxically, the theme of the end of ideologies was accomplished, during the mid-1960s, by a renewal of Marxism, this time in its structural version. How can the resurgence of Marxism be explained when we were in a growth society, moving away from situations of pauperization or revolution?

R.A. – You are alluding to Althusser's Marxism. Althusser was a member of the Communist party, a philosopher, one who excelled in preparing Ecole Normale students for the examination called the *agrégation*. As a member of the Party, reflecting upon Marxism, he searched for themes that would revitalize the interpretation of the theory. Everyone said there was structuralism in Althusser's books; I am not sure I found any. Let's say he had a certain way of reading *Das Kapital* that was, to a point, different from earlier readings.

One day, he decided to brush up on economics, in order to refute me better. He went to one of his friends from lycée days, a banker, to ask him what he should read in order to understand economics. The banker replied, "The best thing for you to do is to read Raymond Aron's books." Naturally, Althusser turned elsewhere....

J.–L.M. – You took up your polemic with Althusser and the structuralists almost ten years after the one you had with the existentialists. Was it really necessary to clash swords like that again?

R.A. – I'm not sure. But I found a title, *D'une Sainte Famille á l'Autre,* that motivated me a bit to write the book. When Levi-Strauss read it, he thanked me, saying, "Now, I realize I was right not to read Althusser." The relationship between the structuralism of Levi-Strauss and that of Althusser existed only in the imagination of Parisians. Well, let's say that I wasted a few months writing that little book which, while it amused me, was probably useless.

J.–L.M. – Did economic growth and the consumer society accentuate the divorce between French society and its intellectuals?

R.A. – Which ones? Those of the *Nouvel Observateur?* Those of *Les Temps Modernes,* of *Espirit?* If you include among the intellectuals the ENA[24] students, they are rather indifferent to the acrobatics of Parisian *agrégés* in philosophy. Those so-called intellectual movements are very limited. They can be explained by the traditional role of the lycée philosophy professors a few years ago and by their need to find every now and then a clever interpretation that permitted one to present a vision of the world more or less favorable to the Soviet Union, in a form tolerable from a philosophic point of view.

J.–L.M. – To qualify ENA students, a different word was invented: they are not intellectuals, but technocrats....

R.A. – Someone told me that one day Sartre met an ENA student. The student told him that Raymond Aron had a certain amount of influence on the ENA students. Sartre was surprised and irritated. But I think I had more chance to influence the ENA students than Sartre—not because of his literature, but because his politics would be of limited use to high government officials.

D.W. – You suggest that those debates among intellectuals—or among "some" intellectuals, if you prefer—don't have much importance. However, as far as the Left is concerned, there exists a direct relationship between intellectual and political debates. Because it isn't your own clan, but the one with which you quarrel, you say, "basically, that didn't have much importance." But if you look back over the political problems of the period that were discussed in publications like *Le Monde, L'Observateur,* or even *L'Express* or *Le Figaro,* you find, at the origin, debates among intellectuals.

R.A. – Tell me how Althusser's philosophy had an impact on real political debates?

D.W. – It was on the basis of Althusser's work that a Left to the left of the Communist party was constituted for the first time. The leftist movements created in the mid-1960s, and that came to public attention in May 1968, nonetheless had some influence on society, at least until 1974. A decade of French political life thus had its roots in the intellectual debates of the mid-1960s.

R.A. – I don't find in the works of Althusser the origin of leftism. It's rather the contrary. There is more leftism in Sartre's *Critique de la Raison Dialectique.* What is true is that among Althusser's disciples, a number became leftists, others became Maoists, others remained in the Communist party. I'm willing to agree that Althusser had some effect in leftist movements, beyond the Communist party. But I don't think his influence was very great. First, his writings are very difficult for anyone who doesn't have an advanced degree in philosophy, and then, the consequences he draws from his reading of *Das Kapital* remain obscure for me.

J.–L.M. – During this period, you often went to the United States, particularly to teach. What importance do you attach to your experience in the United States?

R.A. – I've always had a taste for foreign countries. And I've always had a taste for being "at home," outside of France as well as in France. In 1953 or 1954, I taught at Tübingen, in Germany, where I gave a sort of summary, in German, for a student audience, of what was to become *Les 18 Leçons*. It was a very enriching experience. I was able to compare the German students I had known in the 1930s with the students who had come out of the war.

As for the United States, it had practically a monopoly on international relations studies. There was no department of international relations in France, not many in Great Britain, almost none in Germany. So, it was normal enough for me to want to go there and take a look. Moreover, a large number of Harvard professors were friends of mine. The president wanted me to become a professor at Harvard, something I naturally did not want to do. But I spent a semester there as research professor.

J.–L.M. – Beyond the matter of friendships, wasn't it also your political and cultural affinity with the United States that drew you there?

R.A. – It wasn't that. What seems to me essential is that I am not and never have been anti-American. It's a singularity of a great number of the French to be readily hostile to Americans, to their culture, and to American organization. The so-called mercantile society *par excellence,* that of the United States, is often the subject of heated debate. I don't know the United States well, but I know American universities. So far, they are the best universities in the world. If you go to the University of California, at Berkeley, as I did, or to Harvard, you will meet a substantial number of scientists who are Nobel Prize winners. So, whatever one's agreement or disagreement on political problems, one finds an enriching environment in American universities.

D.W. – Yes, but also, you favor the U.S. political regime. At the time, your image was that of a pro-American, of an "Atlanticist." Is that correct?

R.A. – Yes, but that is not insulting, to the best of my knowledge. I don't see why the French would be hostile to the United States, a country that ensured them the 1918 victory, that contributed to their liberation in 1944-1945, and to reconstruction after the war, unless they resent those who have assisted them. At worst, the United States could be scored for having been antagonistic to the French empire. But, now, the French regret not having abandoned it earlier. In retrospect, one is tempted to say that their advice was better than our convictions.

J.–L.M. – What many Frenchmen fear about American influence is the disappearance of French culture, a weakening of the role of the French language.

R.A. – I am not so pessimistic. I don't think that the power of American culture is such that French culture is in danger. It is a fact that in the twentieth century, a number of the most representative institutions of our society originated in the United States. It is an unfortunate truth that English has become the universal language. Whether one is happy about it or not, it is an incontestable fact in most scientific congresses. Of course, the French language should be defended as much as possible, but I find it petty to bear ill-feeling toward the United States for having been, during a short period, the dominant world power. After all, it didn't last long and already people are beginning to speculate about the decline of the United States. That should tone down the resentments of the French.

J.–L.M. – But economic imperialism, the multinational corporations, aren't those real dangers?

R.A. – In what, except by definition, are the multinational corporations imperialist?

J.–L.M. – One has the impression that you use a double standard. All the evil is on the Russian side, while the Americans are treated with indulgence.

R.A. – That is foolish. I have never said that any society is perfect. As for multinational corporations, let's take, for example, IBM. It had almost a monopoly in computers. It is still far in the lead. There is a subsidiary of IBM in France. Since you have studied these questions, do you feel that the existence of an IBM subsidiary in France is contrary to French national interests?

J.–L.M. – In any case, General de Gaulle thought so, since he went about the creation of a French computer industry in a very authoritarian way.

R.A. – You respond with a sophism. He didn't say that the IBM subsidiary was contrary to French interests. He judged it desirable that France also have an important computer company. And we have one now. But it was preferable at the time to have IBM, rather than nothing at all.

J.–L.M. – So then, the policy of independence seems a bit ridiculous to you?

R.A. – That depends upon your definition of a policy of independence. In a free trade economy, no country is independent. For example, we depend today on the oil producers much more than we depend on the United States. What might legitimately be called independence today is to depend, not on a single country (for vital imports or exports), but to have, rather, a multiplicity of dependences. It also means having on our side a certain number of trumps so that others are dependent upon us. In today's economic society, which is in fact an international society of free trade, to refer to multinational corporations as instruments of economic warfare seems to me a very superficial analysis.

The multinationals have become a kind of monster. When one speaks of the multinationals the way you did, it sounds as if it were indecent not to be against them. It seems to me that in each case one should study as calmly as possible the advantages and the disadvantages, what price one pays for multinationals and what one gains by having their subsidiaries.

As far as American society as a whole is concerned, I have no intention of claiming that it is perfect. That would be frivolous. First, its structures are not comparable to those of the Soviet Union; it has an extraordinarily heterogeneous population, with the best and the worst to be found everywhere, depending upon what you're looking for. . . .

J.–L.M. – Then, the only multinational that worries you is the Third International?

R.A. – No, it is the Red Army. The Communist party multinationals don't worry me. What does worry me is that we have on the other side of Europe a force that is, on the whole, an economic failure, but an important military power at the same time. IBM has a lot of power, but not the same kind of power.

If Russia were still Russia (while today, instead, it is the Soviet Union), if Czarist Russia had its troops stationed 120 miles from the Rhine River, everyone would agree that the real danger, and the only one, would be the military superiority of the Russian empire.

But, since this Russian empire is, additionally, a Soviet or ideological empire, it seems to me there is every reason to take the Eastern menace seriously and to make a distinction between the Western multinationals and Soviet missiles.

D.W. – One always thinks of Raymond Aron, the liberal. What characterizes your liberalism?

R.A. – First, I believe that what one must fear most in modern societies is the one-party system, totalitarianism. Today, there is a great measure of agreement between the moderate Left and a "liberal" like myself. Alain Touraine, for example, recognizes as I do that the essential menace to our societies is precisely the totalitarianism that is expressed, not by the nationalization of the means of production, but by a subjugating ideology, specifically Marxism-Leninism.

By defining myself in the refusal of the single party, I quite naturally come to the idea of pluralism, and from the idea of pluralism to a certain image of liberalism. In contrast to the liberalism of the nineteenth century, my liberalistic concepts are not based on abstract principles. It is through the analysis of modern societies that I try to explain political and intellectual liberalism. Montesquieu earlier explained liberalism through sociologic analysis, and so did Alexis de Tocqueville and Max Weber. Since I claim kinship with all three—based on a study of modern economic societies—I see the dangers that result from the concentration of all power in a single party. So I seek to determine the economic and social conditions that permit pluralism to survive, that is, both political and intellectual liberalism.

D.W. – You could also be a Socialist. Why aren't you one? Socialism, particularly social democracy, defends pluralism.

R.A. – The reason I am not one is that I think most Socialists, particularly in France, are not as firmly liberal as they should be. For economic reasons that I don't have time to develop, I think it is important today to maintain free market forces, while a number of French Socialists continue to be antagonistic to these market forces. They are obsessed by the multinationals. In spite of everything, their way of thinking is not radically different from my own.

c) De Gaulle, Israel and the Jews

J.–L.M. – In 1967, after the Six-Day War, de Gaulle, during the course of a press conference that has remained famous, spoke of the "Jewish people, sure of itself and dominating." You. . . .

R.A. – "An elitist people. . . ."

J.–L.M. – You reacted with a book. . . .

R.A. – Oh! An article, a rather long article. . . .

J.–L.M. – It's nonetheless a book, whose title is *De Gaulle, Israël et les Juifs*. It was your first book on Judaism. You hadn't written anything in 1933, when Hitler and the first evidence of anti-Semitism appeared. Neither did you write anything in 1945 at the Liberation, after the Holocaust. In 1948, on Israel and Zionism—silence. But finally, a press conference by the chief of state caused you to take up your pen on Judaism?

R.A. – You are always surprised when I choose to speak at a moment that, in your opinion, is not the right one. So, with a certain cleverness, you're trying to reconstruct a biography that suits you, a better one, you think, than the real biography. I think that one should respect the personality of the person one is interviewing.

I have told you of my reactions to the discovery of anti-Semitism in Nazi Germany, and of the reasons why I had nothing particular to say on the subject. In 1945, also, I had nothing precise to write. I wrote incidentally in periodicals that asked me for articles on the Jews.

And then there was General de Gaulle's press conference that offended me. It hurt me because it was easy to recognize the origin of the formula "elitist people, sure of itself and dominating," for those who remember anti-Semitism. "Dominating" was the word used during the war by Xavier Vallat to describe the Jewish people. And I felt that, twenty-two years later, in 1967, to describe in this manner the Jewish people— both the Israelis and the French Jews—threatened to rekindle the debate on the Jews, even anti-Semitism. De Gaulle was not an anti-Semite, I am convinced of that.

D.W. – Are you sure of it?

R.A. – In all honesty, I don't think he was. He was shocked by the reaction of French Jews in 1967, that is, by their enthusiasm for the Israeli victory. He had advised the Israelis not to go to war. So, he said to himself, "These French Jews are Jews, they are not Frenchmen like the others." That was, I think, the origin of this press conference. But he himself was so convinced that it was dangerous that, a few weeks later, he turned to the Chief Rabbi to put an end to certain interpretations of his words.

D.W. – Just the same, your book is more than a simple reaction. It is an act. It was your only book on the subject of Judaism.

R.A. – Yes. The reason was that not one among those—Jewish and non-Jewish—to whom we looked in France as defenders of moral principles, had reacted to General de Gaulle's press conference. I realize that different people interpreted his words differently. Father Riquet, for example, who is anything but an anti-Semite, was convinced that General de Gaulle's words in no way suggested anti-Semitism. But a number of Jews said, "It's beginning again." As I told Father Riquet, the era of suspicion had returned. Whenever there is a situation implicating the Jews, people ask "Do the French Jews act as Frenchmen or as Jews?" The fact is that the situation of Jews is ambiguous, paradoxical. I have already told you that. Each Jew must determine his own destiny.

J.–L.M. – But in 1967, with the Six-Day War, you had a feeling of solidarity with the Jews.

R.A. – As a matter of fact, I wrote an emotional article at the time, the kind of article that pleases you, I suppose, since you scold me for not showing indignation in my articles, for always being insensible. This once, it was an impassioned article. For a moment, mistakenly as it turned out, I was afraid that Israel was in danger. But Israel was not really threatened; its military superiority was incontestable. What I had written earlier should have spared me this emotion.

D.W. – Do you regret having written that article?

R.A. – No, no. I regret an article like *"Adieu au Gaullisme,"* for which you have rebuked me, because I consider it to have been excessive and unjust. But when it is a question of an article that constitutes an emotional outburst, I am obliged to respect it, even if, upon reflection, I ask myself, "Why was I moved to such an extent?"

D.W. – Your excitement, or your passion, was, however, very relative. You wrote in your book, "I have more in common with a French anti-Semite than with a Jew from southern Morocco." So, as passion goes, that was really restrained!

R.A. – In keeping with your usual polemical attitude, you have taken a phrase out of context. Even when I write an emotional article, analysis is never lacking. This phrase that might seem shocking, but is strictly the truth, I can justify with the following references. Do you know *La France Juive* by Drumont?

D.W. – A sinister person.

R.A. – Good. Do you know who Drumont's disciple was? Bernanos, who wrote a book glorifying Drumont. So, if I tell you there is more in common between Bernanos, even in his anti-Semitic moments, and me, than between me and a Jew from southern Morocco, is it false or paradoxical?

We could carp about my phrase indefinitely. But it signifies simply the following: A Frenchman of Jewish origin who does not believe in God and who, as a result of considered reflection, or affection, decides upon a certain solidarity with the Jews in general, can at the same time say: The fact is that I have more traits, more ideas and experiences in common with, let us say, a Bernanos or a tolerable anti-Semite—there are some who are not tolerable—than with a southern Moroccan with whom I have in common neither language, nor experience, nor religion.

My book, or my long article, has been analyzed, notably by my friend, Father Fessart. The latter left among his papers a work recently published, after his death: *La Philosophie Historique de Raymond Aron*. Gaston Fessart's interpretation makes me out as essentially Semitic. That was his right. But I must say that, despite my friendship for him, which was very warm, I do not find his interpretation persuasive.

Section Three

Liberty and Reason

I
THE LEFT, STEADFAST AND CHANGING

a) May '68

J.–L. Missika. – You left the Sorbonne in January 1968. Did you feel the storm coming?

Raymond Aron. – Actually, I was a bit disgusted by what the Sorbonne had become. I left the Sorbonne the first time in 1928, after having passed the *agrégation*. I returned in 1955. Basically, it was about the same. But between 1955 and 1965, things changed. The setting was the same, but everything else was different: the number of students was enormous. I had the feeling I could no longer do my teaching as I conceived it, that is, through courses that could become books, which was a way to work on problems that I considered interesting for me and for the students.

So, I decided to shift from the Sorbonne to the *Ecole Pratique des Hautes Etudes*. There was also the perspective, for a year or two later, of the *Collège de France*. So, I returned to the *Ecole Pratique* before being elected in 1969 to the *Collège de France,* where I carried out my final years of teaching from 1970 until 1978.

D. Wolton. – Did you enjoy your experience at the *Ecole Pratique des Hautes Etudes?*

R.A. – Yes, but I preferred the *Collège de France,* because I had to work harder there. Teaching was for me always a way of protecting myself from journalism, of forcing me to work seriously. So, in that sense, the *Collège de France* was excellent. The *Ecole Pratique* was less demanding.

J.–L.M. – You had no regrets on leaving the Sorbonne?

R.A. – None. On the contrary. I found it was necessary to make sweeping reforms and I couldn't obtain any concessions. In meetings of the teaching staff, my observations and ideas met with no success. To begin with, there were too many professors. No, it had really become impossible.

I had written an article in *Le Figaro* some years before 1968 called *"La Grande Misère de la Sorbonne."* At the beginning of the 1967-1968 academic year, a curriculum reform took effect that contained cardinal errors. The students who had entered the university under the old system risked losing a year in the changeover to the new program. You can't do that in France. That was one of the minor tensions at the origin of the explosion.

D.W. – In May 1968, you appeared to be the spokesman for the silent majority. What did you do to find yourself—still again—in that situation?

R.A. – Well, I wrote some articles in *Le Figaro* toward the end of May or at the beginning of June. And then I wrote, or rather, I "spoke," in an interview with Alain Duhamel, a small book, *La Révolution Introuvable.* I immediately acquired the reputation for being most resolutely in opposition to the May 1968 events.

J.–L.M. – You were a conservative?

R.A. – To make you happy. . . . In fact, on university questions, I had always been rather revolutionary. I was very much opposed to university organization as it existed. But I was not in favor of destroying the university as your friends (because you were both students at the time) wanted to do.

J.–L.M. – By the way, in 1960, eight years before the May 1968 events, you wrote:

> I do not propose to abolish the *agrégation*. Such a revolution is inconceivable in a country known for its taste for revolutionary ideology. I do not even insist on the fusion of the *capès*[25]*–agregation* examinations. I just hope that the professors will in fact cease to confer upon an academic and anachronistic competition an importance that it really does not have.

But the students were saying the same thing!

R.A. – I don't think the students were saying the same thing; in any case, they didn't say it in the same spirit.

D.W. – Oh!

R.A. – After those *Figaro* articles, I received a lot of letters, some from *agrégés* insulting me. Not knowing that I was an *agrégé* myself, many were convinced that I had written out of resentment because of my academic failures. In any case, the *agrégation* was only one question among the many that were discussed in May 1968. What was May 1968? It was a week of student brawls. Then, two weeks of strikes that progressively spread to the whole of France and paralyzed the country's economic life. There was one week of political crisis when it seemed almost possible that the regime might collapse under the blows of Cohn-Bendit. On that day during the final week, I was a Gaullist.

D.W. – So! Finally!

R.A. – And when I heard General de Gaulle's short talk on the radio (on May 30, I think), I was convinced the episode was over. I listened to it with some friends and cried, "Vive de Gaulle!"

D.W. – For once!

R.A. – I found it absolutely outrageous that groups of young people could overturn the government, the regime, and political France.

D.W. – But what were you afraid of?

R.A. – I wasn't afraid of anything. I simply believed that the students were wrecking the old University without building another. At the same time, they were trying to make a mess of the French economy which, after all, had been reconstructed for a generation. The events of May 1968 brought back memories of the revolutionary days of the nineteenth century. Once again, one had the impression that the French were incapable of making reforms, but quite capable, from time to time, of making a revolution.

Before the events of May 1968, Pompidou said, "We are especially proud of what we have done for the University." Indeed, he had increased the number of students and teachers more than any other prime minister. But it wasn't a reform. He had simply squeezed into the old structures an enormous number of students and teachers.

There was at the same time a movement of revolt of a part of the youth against the establishment all over the world; it was a revolt that assumed the form of a student revolution. Since France didn't have universities in the plural, but a single University, one for the whole of France, revolts in the University branches all over the country broke out almost at the same time, rather than successively at the various universities, as in the United States.

And then, there was a more mysterious phenomenon, the general strikes.

D.W. – What shocked you most? The student revolts? The professors' attitudes? The strikes and the social crisis? Or the disequilibrium and caving in of the state?

R.A. – The weakening of the state bothered me most. Excessively, perhaps. The idea that a state with a decent, respectable form gave the impression of falling apart under such feeble blows, that was rather discouraging. France was so centralized and, under the Gaullist regime, everything was so concentrated in the person of General de Gaulle that when his authority was impaired even incidentally, it seemed that the whole structure was challenged. It was ridiculous for de Gaulle to have brought up the student brawls at the Council of Ministers during the first week.

D.W. – But who was responsible for the situation? The institutions or the men? Someone must have been responsible. What about the Minister of Education? Who was he?

R.A. – You know who he was since you were a student at the time: Alain Peyrefitte. But responsibilities were so diffused that it is absolutely impossible to determine whether he was more or less responsible than the other ministers.

D.W. – How can a historian like you say that in such an event there was no one especially responsible—that there were only diffused responsibilities?

R.A. – You think that historians determine causes with certainty. De Gaulle several times said something both disappointing and profound about the disturbances: "They were unfathomable." In a way, they were indeed unfathomable, because, before those events, France seemed quite normal. Viansson-Ponté had written an article in *Le Monde* that, in the light of events, became famous: *"La France s'Ennuie."* But, except for this, there was no sign of any profound discontent in the country. Waldeck-Rochet,[26] who was to publish this book on the Communist party after the vacation period, said, "There is no need to publish this book before the summer; nothing is going to happen in the meantime." The Communist party was as surprised as everyone else.

D.W. – It was not, after all, the first time in history that politicians had failed to foresee events, but you, an observer of current events, a historian, and a sociologist, how did you fail to see coming. . .?

R.A. – Listen. I am not a seer. Trouble was expected in the universities, but it was impossible to foresee that, at the climax, after the student demonstrations, there would be nine or ten million strikers. The workers, at least the CGT,[27] had no empathy for the student movements—above all, none for Cohn-Bendit. There were wildcat strikes organized by the leftists without CGT approval. Then, in order to recover its control over the masses, the Communist party put practically everyone on strike. It was difficult to realize in advance that the leftists had the ability to upset the Communist party's customary relationship with the Gaullist government.

During the whole period, there were secret meetings between the Communist party and the government. There never was, I believe, a truly insurrrectionary situation, except during the last week when, after the Grenelle agreements,[28] the base refused to accept what was offered the strikers. Thus, during that week, phenomena were observed quite comparable to those of 1848: there was no one in the ministries; the civil servants had disappeared. In the Ministry of National Education, Secretary-General Paul Laurent was almost lonely. Others awaited new masters. It was as if a revolutionary wave were swelling; as if the regime had remained as unstable, as precarious, as fragile as in the past. That was what upset me most.

J.–L.M. – You took action because of that?

R.A. – No, no. It was the carnival aspect that finally exasperated me.

D.W. – Just a moment, I don't understand: Was it an institutional crisis or a carnival? They are not the same thing.

R.A. – It was both. It was necessary to try to put an end to the student carnival that was really not an authentic expression of discontent. In France, relations between professors and students were generally neither very intimate nor very good. The professors had too many students, too many theses. They couldn't meet with the students individually, as American professors do. And then, all of a sudden, in some universities students and professors fraternized and addressed each other familiarly, using their first names. It was absolutely ridiculous because they weren't genuine relationships. I thought my rapport with the students was authentic. . . :

D.W. – You?

R.A. – Yes, I. And I never had any urge to play carnival.

Then, there was the debating marathon. During a two-week period, the French made up for their usual silence.

They talked, talked, talked. . . .

J.–L.M. – It was a readiness to speak up. There's nothing wrong with that.

R.A. – Yes. The readiness to speak up. Do you have a pleasant memory of yours?

J.–L.M. – A very pleasant memory.

R.A. – What did you get out of it? The conviction that you knew how to speak? Fine. Excellent!

D.W. – So you denounce everything that happened? You were not in accord either with the weakening of the state or with the students' carnival. But this time, you fail to analyze the causes. You are satisfied to say, "They are diffused." You are very critical of the events and very lax in analyzing the causes. However, there were nonetheless institutions, a state, a government, political parties. . . .

R.A. – No, I am not denouncing anything, and I am nevertheless making an analysis. Well, I did that in my book. Must I repeat myself? The French are a very surprising people. Toward the end, a day before General de Gaulle's radio talk, I had a long, forty-five-minute chat with Kojève. When there were problems in the country, Kojève always gave me a telephone call. He said to me:

> It's not a revolution; it can't be a revolution. No one is being killed. To have a revolution, there must be killing. Here, students are in the streets. They call the police the "SS," but these "SS" don't kill anyone—it's nonsensical, it's not a revolution.

At the end of the conversation, we decided to get together early in June. He was leaving for Brussels where he had to give a lecture on June 2nd. He died suddenly in the middle of his talk. That telephone conversation was our last one, and I was not able to discuss with him the significance of the May 1968 events.

D.W. – You say, "I feared the collapse of the institutions." But at the same time, you speak of a psychodrama or a student carnival.

R.A. – Yes, that's right. I said, "psychodrama." It was on Radio Luxembourg, on June 1st; I aroused some sharp, almost indignant reaction among the trade unionists.

D.W. – Yes, but you can't have it both ways, as Raymond Aron would say: Either it was a question of the collapse of the institutions, or it was a psychodrama.

R.A. – As always, when one says "either-or," there is a third possibility: something can begin as a carnival or student brawling and, little by little, as strikes stretch out indefinitely, it can become a political crisis. The fact is, starting with a psychodrama, there existed for forty-eight hours a perception of impending political crisis, or at least of the possibility of political crisis.

Today, when it is all over, I tell myself that I, too, was a bit crazy, but only for forty-eight hours. During those hours, I asked myself: What if it should become serious? Don't forget: the day de Gaulle left without telling Pompidou where he was going, Pompidou had visits from, I think, six deputies; some of them asked for de Gaulle's resignation; the others, that of Pompidou.

And during the month of May 1968, there were sessions of the National Assembly in which the government was violently attacked. Giscard d'Estaing held a press conference that was not very friendly toward Pompidou. And Pisani, who was supposed to speak for the Gaullists, gave an anti-government speech. It was a kind of political upheaval very typical of the French.

I was reading Flaubert at the time and found details in *L'Education Sentimentale* that resemble very closely what was said during the May 1968 debates. For example, Frédéric goes to a meeting during the Revolution of 1848. Someone cries, "Comrade, diplomas should be abolished!" "No," replies another, "we shouldn't abolish diplomas, comrade, but it is the people who should give them out." In 1968, the intellectual level of the student discussions was not very different.

J.–L.M. – But there, you took action. You launched an appeal at the beginning of June to create an "Action Committee Against the Conspiracy of Cowardice and Terrorism"!

R.A. – Yes, to give a little confidence and courage to those poor professors who were feeling very dejected. I received three or four thousand letters. For a few weeks, professors visited me after school hours still frightened by everything that had happened during the day. And I tried to reassure them, telling them it was not so terrible. However, I dropped the project after a few weeks.

D.W. – But why did you decide to act on the occasion? It is really rather astonishing.

R.A. – As usual, when I have done something, you ask me, "Why did you do it?" I don't know! At that moment, I had the impression that it was necessary to do something and I did it. Well, I had some friends at my apartment and we were discussing the situation. Leroy-Ladurie came a few times, as did Alain Besançon. We told ourselves that we were resistants. There were also Papaioannou, Baechler, and others.

J.–L.M. – And with Jean-Paul Sartre? Polemics again?

R.A. – A unilateral polemic. First, he wrote a hateful article against General de Gaulle in which he said, "The king is naked." And then (it was flattering for me), he put me almost on the same level: I was as monstrous as de Gaulle.

D.W. – I found the interview in the *Nouvel Observateur* of June 19, 1968. Sartre makes three very precise statements. First: "I'd bet my right arm that Raymond Aron has never questioned himself. And that's why I think he is unworthy to be a professor."

R.A. – Oh, yes!

D.W. – The second one does in fact concern the nudity of General de Gaulle: "Now that all of France has seen General de Gaulle naked, all the students, all of them, should be able to see Raymond Aron naked, too!"

R.A. – Yes, that was it.

D.W. – "His clothes will not be returned until he agrees to make an examination of conscience."

You did not reply?

R.A. – Listen. The memory of that incident makes me laugh. But, I must say I found the quality and tone of the attack so contemptible that it was beneath my dignity to respond. To the best of my knowledge, most people who have sketched an intellectual portrait of me have stressed the fact that I put everything in doubt and that it is rare that, after having made an affirmation, I fail to add, "But, after all. . . ." So, to present me as a person so self-assured that he never questions himself, I find mildly idiotic. Furthermore, despite his genius, Sartre had a strong propensity for monologues. There came a time when he ceased to exchange ideas with other people, except, perhaps, with Simone de Beauvoir, and when he rejected dialogue and controversy. He spoke for himself.

J.–L.M. – But how was it that you became, in a way, the symbol of the old university system?

R.A. – As always happens with me, it was a misunderstanding. A misunderstanding, because I had never been a defender of the old system. The articles I wrote in *Le Figaro* in 1960 created a great stir and were challenged by all the conservatives. Whenever I discussed the future or questions of reform at university meetings, I was always on the side of the reformers. But as soon as I saw that honorable and decent teachers were being treated in a shabby manner, I defended them. I didn't agree with them, but I defended them and I don't regret it at all.

D.W. – You became an opinion leader at the time. Did that please you?

R.A. – Do you see any commanding reason why that should have displeased me? You know, one writes in order to be read; when one wants to persuade people, one hopes to succeed. That for a few days I had become the "hero" of the resistance to the events of May seemed rather bizarre to me, even ridiculous, although, after all, why not? But it couldn't last and indeed it did not!

My book, *La Révolution Introuvable*, that I dictated over a period of four mornings, and then touched up a bit, purified me of any irritation I still harbored about the events of May 1968. After having written it, I was, if you will, cleansed.

As for Sartre's attacks, they didn't bother me at all. When a reader writes to me, "Your style is poor; you repeat the same word too often"—that does bother me. But when Sartre told me I was unworthy of teaching, I was amused. Amused, because I could have taught at practically any university in France, the United States, England, or Germany. It was very unlikely that I was unworthy of teaching."

J.–L.M. – On the whole, might it be said that in May '68 you preferred the state to society?

R.A. – There wasn't any more society.

D.W. – On the contrary, it was in full effervescence.

R.A. – What you call a society in effervescence was workers without jobs, students obsessed with talk, civil servants on vacation, all that.

D.W. – No, on strike.

R.A. – It was very pleasant, perhaps, but it wasn't a society. It was a society that had ceased to function. When General de Gaulle gave his final talk, on May 30th, he said, "It is time for the professors to teach, for the students to learn, for the workers to work," and so on. In other words, it was necessary for society to become itself once again. So, it wasn't that I preferred the state to society: I said that the deterioration of society had reached a point where it was reasonable to call a halt to it.

J.–L.M. – Was it really deterioration? In an interview in the *Nouvel Observateur* in March 1967, you said, "At heart, I am a sociologist with limited interest in the social side of things. I think I have an interest in economic and political problems, but I have to force myself to take an interest in social affairs as such." Well, wasn't May 1968 precisely the eruption of social affairs as such? And didn't you miss the point because, essentially, that didn't interest you greatly?

R.A. – I'd like to see the whole text. I'm suspicious of your citations. However, I see your point well enough. I find it pertinent. However, you mustn't take a remark of self-criticism or self-analysis too literally. I don't ignore society or the social dimension. Quite clearly, there was a student social movement. Nonetheless, students constitute a particular kind of group. You don't remain a student all your life. So, we weren't dealing with one of society's permanent groups. As for the strikes, most of them were organized by the Communists to weaken the influence of the leftists.

J.–L.M. – Yes, but if the workers went on strike in May 1968, it was also perhaps because they had reasons, even very deep-seated reasons, for going on strike.

D.W. – Ten million workers don't go on strike, just like that, on a cue from the Party.

R.A. – All right. Since it did happen, there were obviously reasons for it beyond the rivalry between the leftists and the Communists. But the extended strikes of millions and millions of workers remain even today rather mysterious, because there were no warning signals.

D.W. – What about the inequalities? The enormous difference in incomes? The stagnation of the minimum wage?

R.A. – It is true that in 1968, a number of intolerable situations surfaced that simply had to be modified. But I am convinced that it was really those earning the minimum wage who constituted the active element of the strike movements. From what we have been able to learn, the first strikes were started by Maoists or leftists. And those were wildcat strikes not called by the unions. It became evident then that millions of workers were disposed to go on strike, while the Communist party itself hadn't been aware of it. What more is there to say except that the frame of mind of the French in 1968 was inadequately understood and that I didn't foresee what happened any more than others did?

J.–L.M. – You didn't foresee it, but above all you were not sensitive to it. Some were touched, moved, convinced, or simply sensitized by the May events, while your own reaction was one of rejection.

R.A. – Listen. It wasn't the strikes that aroused the enthusiasm of the young bourgeois. And the cult of May 1968 is not a workers' cult, it is a cult of intellectuals who, on that occasion, discovered that economic progress does not resolve all problems, that living conditions in industrial society are often difficult, and that to be obsessed by the rate of growth is basically a mistake. These are all ideological conceits characteristic of intellectuals. Workers' strikes don't have much to do with all that.

J.–L.M. – May 1968 also marked the birth of a number of social movements: Ecology, regionalism, more sexual freedom. . . . social conflicts, indeed, that are far removed from the class struggle.

R.A. – Yes, all that is Alain Touraine. Bertrand de Jouvenel had explained it a long time ago. All those ideological themes already existed in the literature. May 1968 popularized several that were suddenly perceived by public opinion and particularly by the young bourgeois. But that was only one aspect of the phenomena of 1968. I wonder if the student discontent did not stem more from the fact that some of those young people were the first in their families to arrive at university-level education. It was a situation they didn't know how to handle very well. And they felt a sort of anxiety about their careers and future.

There is a humanistic explanation that goes as follows: "These admirable young people have discovered something their elders had not understood: that economic progress is not synonymous with human progress. They shook up the old people, and how right they were."

And then one can look at the problem from a sociologist's point of view and wonder if those students were not also concerned about their future, their career opportunities—such concerns being just as legitimate, if less poetic, perhaps, than the other aspects of the problem.

D.W. – Yes, let's return to the student crisis. What I don't understand about you is your tendency. . . .

R.A. – You never understand what I've done. I just don't have any luck with you. And to think I have a reputation for clarity! Well, continue. . . .

D.W. – It really is a problem of understanding, that is obvious. I don't understand why, instead of seeking responsibilities in the government's action, you say, "Responsibilities were so diffused that it's impossible to determine who was specifically accountable."

Second point: Then, there followed a social crisis, with ten million strikers. But, there again, you say, "It is diffuse; it is mysterious." But what is apparently certain is that for you there was no momentous significance in having ten million workers on strike.

Third point: There was a crisis of the state. Once again, you condemn those young people who might have destabilized the state. But, there, too, you were not interested in determining who was accountable. Finally, you didn't like what was happening, but you didn't try to analyze it.

R.A. – Are you really serious? Is this your impression after having listened to me now or after having read *La Révolution Introuvable*?

D.W. – I must say that in *La Révolution Introuvable*, you were more nuanced than now.

R.A. – "Nuanced." You make me laugh.

Listen. By pushing me like this, you are forcing me to be vehement, which I am not normally. And when you tell me that I condemn without analyzing, then I can only laugh. Let's return to the student crisis, since that is what you wish. I am not saying at all that I cannot see the causes. They are very clear. The number of students was increased unreasonably—as I've told you—without providing the necessary resources for the functioning universities. Moreover, many of the students were distressed about the uncertainties of their future.

On top of everything else, the phenomenon was so widespread in its extent that one must wonder why countries so different had student revolutions at almost the same moment.

A second phenomenon is the eight or nine million strikers. Now that is peculiarly French, and I must again say that it is difficult to find a satisfactory answer.

There have always been strikes, everywhere, and there are no more of them in France than elsewhere. But where the French have a special knack is in the almost revolutionary transformation of general strikes. Why? Again, I have no categoric answer. But it is not easy for anyone to know why in May 1968—when none of the trade unions had foreseen it—there was unleashed one of the most extraordinary movements of social protest in the history of France.

So, when I say I am not sure of the explanation, I am questioning myself, as Sartre would put it. I do not know the exact answer to a difficult question. My personal contention is that the critical phenomenon was the relationship between the leftists and the Communist party. Why didn't the electrical workers strike? Because the company *Electricité de France* was entirely controlled by the Communist party, and the latter realized that to cut off the electrical supply was tantamount to embarking upon a revolutionary phase.

J.–L.M. – And the state? This collapse?

R.A. – In my opinion, it can be explained only historically. De Gaulle was furious. He said, more or less, "Why don't they start shooting?" But the ministers, especially Pompidou, were convinced that it was necessary to let things develop, to wait for public opinion to change. At the beginning, it was favorable to the students. . . .

J.–L.M. – Do you mean that de Gaulle wanted to fire on the crowd?

R.A. – He envisaged resorting to extreme measures, while Pompidou, as he wrote me, made the avoidance of bloodshed his major objective. In the letter that I received after one of my articles, he said, "The reason why I capitulated on Saturday, 11 May, while the order was out for a general strike and protest march on Monday, was that if the Sorbonne were still closed, the events projected for Monday would end in bloodshed." Before Pompidou's return, de Gaulle did not want to make this capitulation to the students. He was exasperated. When he returned from his trip to Romania, where he had praised everything that we were not doing in the French University, he spoke of the masquerade and all the rest of it. But Pompidou had put his portfolio on the line. He had accepted, so to speak, the paralysis of the country for several days until public opinion reversed itself and was, at month's end, behind the government.

D.W. – But May 1968 was nevertheless the most striking example of the fragility of Gaullist France!

R.A. – Look, we are returning to the starting point of our conversation. What kind of fragility was it? Perhaps it was an impression of fragility. In *La Révolution Introuvable*, there is a chapter called *"Effondrement et Renaissance du Gaullisme."* The whole thing ended after a five-minute talk by General de Gaulle declaring the dissolution of the National Assembly. The French people have retained an exceptional talent for making something out of nothing and creating dramatic events that are thereafter discussed endlessly.

b) The Squared Circle

D.W. – In 1973, when the Left alliance[29] was at its zenith, when one really had the impression that the alternation of power would finally become possible, you took a position resolutely opposed to the Common Program[30] in a *Figaro* article called *"Le Cercle Carré."* What do you have against the Left and the Common Program?

R.A. – The article did, in fact, have a certain impact. It was probably my greatest journalistic success. First, a paper that is not systematically on the Right, as you would put it, *L'Express*, reproduced *"Le Cercle Carré"* in its entirety. Then, Giscard d'Estaing, Minister of Finance at the time, telephoned me after having read it. He told me he had found more arguments in my article than in all the reports his counselors had submitted to him.

So, in a way, it was a modest event of a political nature. But I didn't write the article because I am systematically against the Left, as you are determined to demonstrate to me. It is simply that the Left's economic program was completely absurd: the goal it gave itself, that is, an increase in the rate of growth and a new distribution of income, was in contradiction with the means the Left intended to employ, as outlined in the Common Program. I wrote a critique, based on economic arguments, of the contradictions intrinsic to the Common Program. And I recalled what happened in 1936, when the Left lost because the economic program it had launched could not succeed.

D.W. – Were you in disagreement with the goals or with the means?

R.A. – With the contradictions between the goals and the means. I am not at all against an increase in the rate of growth. If growth can be accelerated, I am all for it. If the distribution of income can be made more equitable, I have absolutely no objection. My objections were that the nationalization of industries, the nationalization of the whole system of credit, the reduction of business profits—accompanied by the desire to increase investments—all that, inevitably meant disaster. At that moment, the Left would have taken over an economy that was developing at a very good pace: an annual growth rate of 5 to 6 percent. If the Left had been able to apply the 1973 Common Program, it would have again provoked a profound economic crisis. I know I can't convince you of that. But my article was not rightist; it was simply based on common sense.

J.–L.M. – But it was an article that provided the Right with a lot of ammunition.

R.A. – Doubtless. The unfortunate thing is that the Left had no common sense. If it had had some, it would not have drafted the program.

J.–L.M. – So you think the Left has learned nothing about economic affairs since 1936?

R.A. – Some men of the Left have learned. The Communist party has learned very little because it isn't interested in learning. As for the Socialist party, about half have learned something and a good 25 percent don't want to learn. Within the party, there are men capable of understanding current problems, but it would be necessary to increase their power. The Socialist party is still torn between various tendencies, between a left wing close to Marxism, even Marxism-Leninism, and, in the other direction, a Michel Rocard. Rocard must have accepted the Common Program with a heavy heart, and today he will support the Socialist program of 1981, I think, with honesty, sincerity, and hesitation.

J.–L.M. – In 1973 and 1974, you took a stand at the time of the elections. So why do you tell us you are nonpartisan?

R.A. – I never told you I was nonpartisan in that sense. I am partisan, in the sense that I take part. The article *"Le Cercle Carré"* began with a paragraph in which I said that for the first time in my political life, I was intervening in an election, and I intervened because the stakes were large. When the stakes were not large, when it was simply a matter of knowing the relative strength of the Socialist party, the MRP, or others, I wasn't very interested. But there, the stakes were important. They were equally serious in 1974 in the choice between Giscard d'Estaing and Mitterand for president of the Republic. And when the stakes are important, a journalist who has some influence must take sides.

J.–L.M. – You are one of those who believe that if the Left came to power, chaos would result?

R.A. – No, not the Left as such. Rather, a Left alliance composed of the Communist and Socialist parties, and armed, in the bargain, with a senseless program. But one could imagine these two parties presenting themselves at the polls under a single banner in order to win the election, without launching at the same time a program guaranteed in advance to fail. Concerning my article, *"Le Cercle Carré,"* Jacques Attali, a Socialist with whom I enjoyed good relations at the time, wrote me to say—not that I was right—but that it was the best critique of the Common Program that had been written. You're an economist, do you find the program rational?

J.–L.M. – No, I don't.

R.A. – Then why do you reproach me for thinking the same as you?

J.–L.M. – But I'm asking myself a different question. Why do you present something as an analysis, when it is only an opinion?

R.A. – It is an opinion, to be sure, but one founded upon analysis. It's not an opinion tossed up in the air, just like that. It stems from an analysis that hews as closely to economic knowledge as possible in a newspaper article. And as a teacher of political economy, you really find that my *"Cercle Carré"* is largely on target.

D.W. – But, there are two questions that are different, though linked: the political economy of the Left and a leftist political commitment. Some people who have never been particularly enthusiastic about the Left's Common Program did not vote for the majority in the elections of 1973 and 1974.

R.A. – I don't doubt for a moment that the myth of the Left retains its power of attraction. I executed it once and for all, but I am sure that the execution, while definitive from an intellectual point of view, will be ineffective in real life.

J.–L.M. – One gets the impression that you bear a grudge against the Left.

R.A. – You don't give up, do you? Once again, in all honesty, let me say that I would hope for the possibility of an alternation of power in the country. But, in order for there to be an alternation, the Left must be able to show first that it is capable of governing—that the Socialists and the Communists can govern together. On the other hand, its program must be comparable to that of Socialist parties in the other countries of Europe.

Among those countries, only France and Italy have a large Communist party. But in Italy, I can talk with the Communists. The Italian Communists talk sense. I was in Milan one day for the publication of one of my books in translation. A Communist deputy made a speech. He sent me a little note saying, "M. Raymond Barre would surely have been happy with what I said." "Certainly," I told him, adding, "In France, no Communist deputy would give that kind of speech."

D.W. – You criticize readily the illusions and the failures of the Left. But you censure less frequently the social injustices or the attacks on liberty by the regime in power.

R.A. – That is possible. But even those who try to be honest observers are led, as a result of their preferences and friendships, to be more sensitive to the faults of adversaries than to those of their own friends. However, I have never presented the several governments as faultless.

Pompidou had occasion to confirm that once, and it gave me great pleasure. I visited him one time, at my request. A few days later, I wrote a very severe article about him on a question that escapes me at the moment. One of his counselors said to him, "That really was not very nice of Raymond Aron; you agreed to see him and now he writes that article!" "You can never count on Raymond Aron," was Pompidou's reply. It was a way of saying that Raymond Aron always criticizes what he wants to criticize, that he thinks and writes as his conscience dictates. In this sense, although I have taken very categoric positions on given questions, I've never been at the service of any man in power. With perhaps one exception, I've managed to be on bad terms with every president.

D.W. – Who was the exception?

R.A. – The former president, Giscard d'Estaing. He probably accepted with some difficulty certain articles of mine, but he never got angry with me.

J.–L.M. – You nevertheless wrote a line about him that became famous: "Giscard's problem is that he is not aware that history is tragic."

R.A. – That's true. I have often written that Giscard d'Estaing, who is very intelligent and cultivated, is also a man of conciliation, a man of peace. When you listen to his speeches, you have the feeling that everything can be resolved through negotiation, compromise, and by being reasonable. He almost never gives the impression that there are in this world some conflicts that are probably irreconcilable, that there exists the risk and the danger of tragedies. In the kind of world we live in, he is a paradox. He talks about decreasing tensions. He even tries to have relaxed tensions with the Communist party. Now, the twentieth century, in which we still live, is a world of violence, passions, and hatreds. Even today, between the Soviet Union and ourselves, there is something very fundamental in what divides us. But, listening to Giscard d'Estaing during his presidency, one never had the impression that he sensed the tragic aspect of relations between countries or between ideas. For him, the Soviets are men whose way of thinking is not fundamentally different from our own. I don't think he can understand the true Bolsheviks or Soviets in depth, because their way of thinking is foreign to his rational mind. He has to do violence to his own personality to imagine the Soviets as they really are. This difficulty was at the origin of my disagreement with the former president, particularly on his foreign policy.

I must add that, before him, General de Gaulle, when he was president, always spoke of the Russians, instead of the Soviets. He was inclined to think he was dealing with eternal Russia, rather than with the Soviet Union. I often wonder whether, for Giscard d'Estaing, as for de Gaulle, the Soviets were not simply another incarnation of the eternal Russians. But the Russian reality, for a long period to come, perhaps, is not the traditional Russians, but the Soviets; Marxist-Leninists.

THE CLASH OF EMPIRES

a) Illusions of Detente

D. Wolton. – How can the misinterpretation of the Soviet reality be explained? Isn't it the nature of the totalitarian phenomenon that escapes them, whether it be a question of Nazi Germany or the Soviet Union?

Raymond Aron. – Yes, and it was a very serious problem, as early as the 1930s. Most statesmen in France and Great Britain failed to understand Hitler's monstrous intentions. With the Soviet Union, it is more difficult to be completely mistaken. First, it has endured for sixty years and seems to have an exceptional capacity to remain true to itself. Also, even if one doesn't understand the Soviet Union well, one recognizes its military power. One is therefore forced to pay attention, even if in one's imagination the Soviet Union is just another incarnation of Russia. I think certain decisions taken by the former president of the Republic can be explained only by a lack of understanding of the true nature of the Soviet regime. For example, I think he wrote a preface to a book on the pacifying value of trade, *Armes de la Paix,* a theory I consider to be radically erroneous.

D.W. – However, the West believed that for fifteen years.

R.A. – It is a way for Western countries to reassure themselves, but nothing has so far confirmed the theory. It has been contradicted by the fact that our trade with the Soviet Union has resulted in promoting the economic and military development of that country, while the Soviet Union has shown no sign of transforming itself in the direction we seek. We sell to them on credit, at favorable rates, our instruments, our machine tools,. and so forth; they buy and we sell, but they remain what they are. Everyone knows that the people who go to the Soviet Union to assemble factories have practically no contact with the Soviet population. So the idea that trade contributes to peace between East and West has, I think, yet to be demonstrated. And I am trying to be moderate; the truth is that I think it is an error.

D.W. – But what should be done?

R.A. – We should have no illusions. As for the question of whether it is good or bad for France to have commercial relations with the Soviet Union, that is another question which I am not ready to discuss in a few words. I say simply that the claim that we are going to change the Soviet Union and the other eastern European countries in depth by maintaining or intensifying commercial relations is not tenable. Just think of what is happening in Poland. The billions of dollars that Western countries have lent to Poland have not been sufficient to transform the economic system. The regime's inefficiency continues. As for the people's revolt, it did not originate in Poland's trade with the West.

D.W. – Under what conditions might the system in eastern Europe and the USSR change?

R.A. – As far as the countries of eastern Europe are concerned, the conditions are very simple: it would suffice for the Soviet Union to give the satellite countries the liberty to modify the system—and it would change immediately. In eastern Europe, the Soviet empire has not been accepted: There is military domination by the Soviet army. Revolts have been many. There was one in Hungary, another in Czechoslovakia, two in Poland. All of these movements were stopped the day the Soviet Union decided that the changes had breached a line that must not be breached; that is, when they touched upon an essential aspect of the Soviet regime—for example, the Party's leadership role. Autonomous trade unions, not subordinate to the Party, contradict the very nature of the regime as it has defined itself.

J.–L.Missika. – Do you mean that if revolution toward detente, toward a transformation of the Soviet regime, doesn't work, confrontation would be inevitable?

R.A. – No, no. Let me go back to the expression I used in 1948: Peace is impossible; war is improbable.

I continue to believe that as long as the Soviet Union thinks as it does, as long as it is governed by men who are prisoners of the same ideology and the same ambitions, there will be a confrontation between the Communist world and the West;

this confrontation will not necessarily take the form of a war in the traditional sense of the term because of the existence of nuclear weapons, and because the Soviet Union is not Nazi Germany. Communism is an important historical movement. It thinks of itself as the wave of the future and sees no purpose in rushing into dangerous military adventures.

What I very often find foolish in Western thought is the idea that there must be either detente or war. Whether there is a cold war or detente does not at all mean that in one case there is a danger of war and in the other, none. Detente and cold war constitute different aspects of the same confrontation. During the Cold War, violence went a little too far in terms of the desirable; in times of detente, relations are less tense, but that doesn't prevent the Soviet Union from taking over one country or another in Africa or elsewhere. It is not at all desirable to return to the cold war, but if new tensions should develop between East and West, and even if journalists began again to say: It's terrible, there is a return to the cold war—there would in fact be no additional danger of war.

D.W. – Essentially, you are saying: the situation could change if the Communists ceased to consider the countries of eastern Europe as their possessions. . . .

R.A. – But that's not it at all! It would be sufficient for the Soviet leadership to demand of the countries of eastern Europe only that they remain loyal to the alliance with the Soviet Union and, in exchange, to give the men who govern those countries a certain liberty of interpretation of socialist doctrines. If, for example, the Kremlin were to accept the freedom of the trade unions, or a certain degree of autonomy for them. . . . But to guarantee its political and military domination, the Kremlin wants to be sure of the faithfulness to the Soviet Union of the men who govern those countries. It is there that one perceives the true nature of the Soviet leaders. They are convinced that they can have confidence in the leaders of the eastern European countries only if the latter are good Marxist-Leninists according to the definition accepted by Moscow. When Dubcek, who had always been a faithful Marxist-Leninist, began to employ some dangerous expressions, and began to tolerate the freedom of the press—at that moment, the Soviets decided they could no longer count on

Czechoslovakia. And for the Soviet Union, Czechoclovakia was the frontier.

D.W. – We Europeans, Westerners, what are we doing for the countries of Eastern Europe?

R.A. – We trade with them and, as the occasion arises, we give them our blessing, immediately adding, "If you have any problems, don't count on us."

D.W. – You have told us that Yalta did not constitute a partition of either Europe or the world. But then. . . .

R.A. – I never said there was no dividing up of Europe; I simply said that this partition was determined by the movement of victorious armies against Nazi Germany, not by the Yalta conversations or accords.

J.–L.M. – But in these conditions, if it is true that Soviet armaments largely surpass—and will surpass to a still greater extent—American armaments, won't this "partition by weapons" shift westward?

R.A. – As far as Europe is concerned, any shift of the demarcation line would require military force. What could happen—and that would present a very grave danger—would be a drifting of the Federal Republic of Germany into neutralism. There are today a number of disquieting signs of this.

D.W. – What is the significance of a neutral Germany?

R.A. - West Germany is within the Atlantic Alliance and, until recent years, it based its security and its future on American protection. But the Germans have less confidence today in the United States. Also, they look toward the Soviet Union because they have been able to obtain, thanks to treaties, more humane treatment for the Germans on the other side of the demarcation line. For example, several tens of thousands of Germans have come from the East to the West.

Chancellor Schmidt would like to hold onto these advantages. So, he tries to carry on what we might call a double-barrelled policy: have both the protection of the United States and good relations with the Soviet Union. Thus, the Germans intend to grant significant credits, billions of marks, for the construction of a pipeline through which natural gas would arrive from Siberia. A good part of Western Europe would then depend on the Soviet Union for its energy supply, thus clearly reducing West Germany's freedom of action.

I am not at all saying that the Germans would split away from the Atlantic Alliance, because, in order to carry through successfully this policy of rapprochement with the Soviet Union, they would need protection or support for the other side. But the temptation would become very great. We would see the drift toward neutrality the day West Germany could reasonably hope to obtain some kind of unity with the other Germany, with the blessing of the Soviet Union. For the moment, that day is relatively far off.

D.W. – Thus, the condition for reunification would be Germany's neutralization?

R.A. – At least. But, in my opinion, the Soviet Union for the time being in no way wants the unification of the two Germanies. It wants only that the Federal Republic be the least "Atlantic" possible.

D.W. – What are the principal sources of weakness of the Soviet empire presently and for the future?

R.A. – In Europe, the Soviet Union's weakness is that the peoples it dominates are only imperfectly committed, and not at all converted. At the other extreme, in Afghanistan, Soviet troops are finding it difficult to pacify the country. In the short term, these sources of weakness are not very dangerous. But the fact is that the Soviet empire is not very attractive to its vassals; this factor risks undermining it in the long run.

In another regard, the Soviet economy has in many ways revealed itself to be inefficient. The rate of growth is diminishing. The Soviet Union today is essentially a military power with an economy that, on paper, produces a great deal of hardware, but provides very few goods to the population. So, the standard of living is very low. The population is used to it and accepts it. In our time, in a civilization that terms itself economic, this is paradoxical. We confront a kind of historical monster: the regime that was created in the name of prosperity and Marxism has become in effect a military empire where the people's well-being has no priority.

D.W. – Doesn't the disparity between an excessive military buildup and low living standards constitute a war risk?

R.A. – No matter how low the living standards are, they are superior to those of twenty or twenty-five years ago. Nonetheless, the Soviet Union's living standards of 1928, that is, before collectivization, were not again approached until sometime between 1950 and 1960, at best.

J.–L.M. – Yes, but if the whole economy is geared to armaments, that is, to militarization, doesn't that pose a threat of war?

R.A. – It is indeed reasonable to observe that armaments are not manufactured just as a hobby. But the Soviet Union is a very singular historical phenomenon. It permanently maintains forces facing Western Europe that are superior to those of NATO. Why? Not necessarily to wage war. Most likely, perhaps, to intimidate, to exercise pressure so that West Europeans will remember that they are continually menaced by a superior military power. That doesn't mean that they intend to launch an attack against Paris. If, in fact, the tanks were to change, there is no telling what would happen. There is also a great deal of weaponry in the West, and heavy nuclear armaments on both sides. So, the Soviet Union uses its military power toward diplomatic ends.

Will the Soviets take greater risks precisely because they have now acquired a measure of superiority? It is quite possible. They took such a risk, for example, in Afghanistan, at a time when they were certainly convinced that the balance of forces had tipped to their advantage. The Soviets constantly employ the term "balance of forces." Do you know how they explain detente to the Soviet people? They say, "Detente between East and West exists because of the improvement of the balance of forces in favor of the East." It is a conception of detent different from that obtaining in the West, and a very special one. But all you have to do is to read Soviet documents to be aware of it.

D.W. – In view of this balance of forces, what is Europe's principal weakness? Political or military?

R.A. – You know, it is very difficult to be strong politically when you are weak militarily. I well realize that there is today in the United States, among the theoreticians of international relations, a school of thought which holds that military forces now play only a secondary role. The decisive factors are alleged to be politics, ideology, economics. Unfortunately, that doesn't seem to me to be true. The weakness of Western Europe is fear, and because it is afraid, it doesn't have much political will. Moreover, there is no real unity in Western Europe for the good reason that the only nuclear arms available here, constituted by the French nuclear force, are not formally at the service of European security—they are exclusively at the service of French security.

D.W. – From 1983 to 1988, it is practically certain that the Soviets will have increased military superiority. Will this supplementary gap increase risks?

R.A. – You are speaking of what is called "the window of vulnerability." The one in question, when we speak of the balance of forces between 1983 and 1988, refers essentially to the fact that during these four or five years, the Soviet missiles—in particular, the 308 SS 18s—will, on paper, be capable of destroying the U.S. ground-based missiles, that is, the Minutemen 1, 2, and 3. Well, it is a theoretical possibility, but in such an extreme and pessimistic hypothesis, the United States would still be able to respond with airborne and submarine missiles.

The fact remains that during this time when there would be, on paper, a situation of USSR nuclear superiority, the Americans would tend, in any confrontation, to show less firmness than during the periods when they had the advantage. That's all that can be said. So, when we speak of opportunities that the Soviets might seize upon between 1983 and 1988, it's anyone's guess.

b) Decline of the American Empire

D.W. – Over a period of fifty years you witnessed the rise and decline of such European powers as France and Great Britain, the madness of Hitler's Reich, the gradual rise of the Soviet Union, and also the dazzling surge of the American empire. But, as early as 1973, in your *Imperial Republic*[31], you predicted the collapse of this American empire.

R.A. – No, I did not predict the collapse; what I did say was that the unique stature of the United States between 1947 and 1972 was anomalous and could not endure. Today, people talk a great deal about America's decline. Personally, I prefer to speak about a relative decline, one that was inevitable. In 1950, the American GNP represented 60 percent of the total of all the OECD countries; in the meantime, the figure has fallen to 34 percent. The earlier dominance was not normal. Productivity in the United States was double or triple that of the European countries—it was simply not a normal situation. So there has been a relative decline of United States wealth compared to that of the Europeans and Japanese, and also a relative decline of American productivity. The Europeans and the Japanese have caught up with the United States and, in certain areas, surpassed it. The United States has returned to the ranks in a number of ways.

J.–L.M. – So there has been no decline?

R.A. – The decline possibly lies in the fact that Americans no longer have the same confidence in themselves. They are no longer pioneers to the same degree; they accept the obsolescence of certain industrial sectors, and lack the courage to modernize them. Nonetheless, they remain pacemakers in a number of advanced technology industries.

Let's not eliminate the United States too quickly from the list of the most powerful nations; the United States is, after all, the only Western country to combine a vast geographical area, a large population, and an industrial productivity among the two or three highest in the world, perhaps still the highest. The United States remains a towering reality, the leader in science, the most important country of the West, and the guarantor of liberty for Western Europe. It is simply that in a number of areas, one does perceive a kind of fatigue, a lack of confidence, of initiative. . . .

J.–L.M. – You're using a lot of psychological terms. Do you mean that it is essentially a spiritual crisis?

R.A. – There is, in fact, a certain loss of confidence, a loss of confidence in the country's institutions, a loss of confidence in the ruling elite, itself deeply divided. It is also true that the United States no longer enjoys military superiority. The army is mediocre and unworthy of one of the world's two great powers; it is a volunteer army recruited from among the least-educated groups in the society. Even when it comes to missiles, one can say that the two superpowers are now about equal, but—to the extent that the concept of superiority or of inferiority has any meaning—the Soviet side will in two or three years possess a relative advantage in intercontinental missiles.

J.–L.M. – You have spoken of "the suicide of an elite," referring to the American liberals' commitment against the Vietnam War.

R.A. – They were at first in favor of the war. The East Coast establishment, the liberal elite, my friends in the United States—everyone around Kennedy: McGeorge Bundy, for example—were at least partially responsible for the Vietnam War. For them it was the same thing as defending South Korea: it was a matter of defending a country threatened by communism, a probably excessive and dangerous interpretation of the containment doctrine. Then, when it began to turn sour, and with Nixon's election, they opposed American involvement and pressed polemics and propaganda attacks against the Nixon-Kissinger administration. They, and many others, helped tear the American people apart over this war in Vietnam that was such a disaster for the United States and remains a heavy burden even today.

D.W. – Was it a military or a moral disaster?

R.A. – It wasn't a military disaster because America did not lose the war on the battlefield. But after the war, it renounced the draft in favor of a volunteer army. This army, whose quality is very questionable, is a consequence of the Vietnam War.

In terms of the economy, the Vietnam War was at the origin of the galloping inflation that started in 1965 and that led to the present generalized monetary crisis. Since 1965, the United States has helped throw the whole world into an inflationary economy, further aggravated by the oil price increases. And then there was the moral crisis of Watergate with consequences that endure to this day. The American citizen no longer has the same confidence in his system of government and in his leaders.

D.W. – Even after Reagan's election?

R.A. – It is too early to judge.

J.–L.M. – Do you think the United States can emerge from this moral crisis?

R.A. – Of course. The United States is a young nation, quite capable of bouncing back. At one moment, it appears crushed, even desperate, and a few years later it becomes excessively optimistic. Americans are a historically youthful people who forget as time passes. During a visit to the United States to receive a doctorate *honoris causa,* I spoke of the

Vietnam War and had the feeling that my student audience wondered why I brought up this old story again. It was striking.

D.W. – What are the principal strengths of the American system?

R.A. – The force of the American government lies in the fact that it is the only political system, with perhaps that of Great Britain, that enjoys the fundamental respect of its people, because the political system is the founding principle of the United States.

The United States is not a historic nation like France or Great Britain—the United States is a contract between men or between groups. This contract gave life to a political community. On this foundation, the one thing that cannot be called into question is the political system; those Americans who are different in color, in national origins, in religion, are, together, the citizens of the American Republic.

D.W. – For you, then, that is its principal strength?

R.A. – In any case, it is the basic principle of its existence. Moreover, in terms of production Americans remain the leaders, along with the Japanese. And then they have something that the Japanese lack: their universities and their scholars continue to produce the greatest portion of scientific discoveries. It could be that one of the reasons why the United States is less brilliant from a production standpoint is that its universities have become, like those of Great Britain, "universities of excellence," producing Nobel Prize winners, but less interested in transforming scientific discoveries into production techniques.

c) China and the Third World

J.–L.M. – In this confrontation between the Soviet Union and the United States, the emergence of China modifies the balance of forces. In a recent article in the periodical *Commentaire,* comparing the present situation with World War II, you asked the question, "Must the democracies always ally themselves to one totalitarian power in order to do battle with another?"

R.A. – It was a nice sentence to conclude an article. However, it really was meant quite seriously. For the moment, we in the West have an objective alliance with China. I say "objective" in the sense that the Soviet Union is forced to maintain some fifty divisions and a third of its air force in the Far East—all of which is consequently not in the West. Hence, we have some shared interests with Communist China. However, we wouldn't go to China's assistance if it were attacked by the Soviet Union, and the former would not help us if we were attacked by the Soviet Union. Thus, as Soviet terminology would go: an objective, but not a subjective, alliance.

At present, China is not yet a great power because its economic and technical development is insufficient, and its army, as far as armament is concerned, is twenty years behind the times. Nonetheless, if, in the years to come, Japan should decide to arm China, it would signify in the eyes of the Soviet Union an unfavorable modification of the balance of forces.

But there is also the opposite risk: If the Chinese feel they can hope for nothing from the West, particularly from the Americans, it is possible they would make some arrangement with the Soviet Union to escape danger.

D.W. – You mean that Western countries should provide more help to China?

R.A. – They should consider the fact that in the world balance of forces, some progress by China is in their interest. And the only reason we give practically no aid to China is because we are afraid of the USSR. The Europeans are certainly afraid. The Americans think that it is too dangerous a game to help the Chinese openly. They have, however, told the Europeans, rather curiously, that they would "have no objection if the Europeans armed China." Each one suggests to the other that he do it. Interpret that in whatever way you wish.

D.W. – You said earlier that to help the Soviet Union—to trade with it—has not served detente but has, rather, increased the military potential of the USSR. Now, you say that China should be helped. Isn't there a contradiction between the two positions?

R.A. – No. Unfortunately, foreign policy is a game for thieves and gangsters. When one has a proximate enemy, one tends to help a distant, future enemy against the proximate one.

J.–L.M. – You mean we should close our eyes to the Chinese dictatorship?

R.A. – If they were to have as allies only those who respect human rights, I think the Western democracies would have none beyond their own ranks.

D.W. – Aren't there problems graver than the East-West confrontation? Hunger and population questions will confront us in the coming years.

R.A. – They are not of the same order. The matter is indeed discussed widely, but I have no answer. In a way, the rivalry between the Soviet bloc and Western countries is stupid, given the fact that both are developed areas. If it were not for ideological considerations, relations between them would be normal. But the Soviet bloc being what it is, the great conflict of our time, since 1945, has been that between East and West.

In this same period, all of the colonial peoples have been liberated. This was a historic movement as significant as that of communism. Today we are told, and it is true, that millions suffer from hunger. So people ask, "Is that more or less important than the rivalry between the Soviet Union and the United States?" What is the sense of the question?

D.W. – Wait. We are asking it in terms of the risks of war.

R.A. – From that point of view, the answer is easy: Hunger is not a cause of war. There is excess population in Southeast Asia, there is a danger of famine in one spot or another, perhaps in Indonesia, but no longer in India. All of that is true. It is an affront to human conscience, but it does not constitute a danger of war.

D.W. – And spontaneous wars?

R.A. – The war between Iraq and Iran has nothing to do with either population or economic factors. It is a war between two countries harboring grievances against each other and having a taste for fighting things out.

D.W. – Hold on. I really must come back to that question. Do you think that from 1945 to the 1970s most sources of tension lay in East-West relations?

R.A. – Oh, not always. Decolonizations; the French Vietnam war of eight years; another eight years of war in Algeria. Those were not East-West conflicts. The Algerians don't represent the East, nor are they with the West. There was the decolonization factor and the Soviets always took the side of the countries in revolt. The Americans also favored those peoples, but because they were allies of the French, they couldn't say so.

D.W. – But the Americans in South Vietnam? That really was an East-West conflict?

R.A. – To a great degree. But the conflicts that took place in the world during that period were, let me repeat, not exclusively East-West quarrels.

D.W. – What I mean is this: If we compare conflicts linked to the East-West tension with wars that are either spontaneous or tied to population or hunger problems, which ones carry the more important risks?

R.A. – I would put things differently. From 1946-1947 to 1970, there was a certain equilibrium in the world that sprang from American superiority and the rules of conduct between the United States and the Soviet Union. Today, no great power—whether it be the United States or the Soviet Union—controls the overall international system, thus the possibility of wars that you call "spontaneous."

As far as population, or hunger, is concerned, the problem has existed for a long time; more is said about it now, largely because countries that possessed raw materials and energy supplies needed by the West rebelled.

So, on the one side, you have the moralists who protest the waste of Western resources in armaments and who would prefer to assist the development of the poor countries. And then you have the others who reason in ways much less idealistic, much less sublime: they know that Europe can live only through its processing industries. Europe needs raw materials and energy supplies, especially oil, which must come from outside the continent, and often from so-called Third World countries. It must obtain them or cease to exist. This is a new aspect of Europe's situation.

However, I repeat that as far as Western Europe is concerned, and France in particular, the question is whether we can remain France or whether we must become a Poland. It seems to me that, for the French, that is a more important question than Bangladesh's excess population. But, certainly, excess population is a more important question for Bangladesh.

J.–L.M. – Can you make a guess about the chances of France remaining France or becoming a Poland?

R.A. – Listen: when you fight for something, you don't calculate the probabilities of winning or losing.

D.W. - Oh, but nevertheless, that is all a part of strategic calculations.

R.A. – No. When you have the choice between survival or death, you don't calculate, you fight.

D.W. – We haven't reached that extreme yet!

R.A. – No. But you've asked me the question: Will France remain France or will it become a Poland? My response is that if the question is ever presented in such terms, one does not make calculations, one fights. As long as the possibility exists, I would continue to fight.

You could then ask: Do you think your grandchildren will live in France or in the United States? The question is a serious one. Will they live in France, or will France have become so much like the Soviet Union that they will go to the other side of the Atlantic where, even if a conflict breaks out, there will still be a possibility of a liberal society? My answer is that I think they will remain in France; I hope this will be so, I am not sure of it.

d) Human Rights Do Not Make a Policy

J.–L.M. – The great event of 1974 was the expulsion of Solzhenitsyn from the USSR and the publication in France, among other countries, of his *Gulag Archipelago*. One has the impression that public opinion was shaken up by this event: the Left discovered, officially, let us say, the reality of the Soviet regime and of the concentration camps. It already had a certain awareness of the facts. With the *Gulag Archipelago,* this awareness assumed another dimension.

R.A. – For me, what is striking, and perhaps wondrous, is the act of genius. Documentation on the question existed already. Books covering pretty much the same ground could be found in any library. But Solzhenitsyn made an appraisal of the camps—an appraisal conceived and written by a writer of genius. Suddenly, the shock, the impact, was something altogether different. Did it have an impact on the whole of the French population or essentially on the intellectuals? I don't know.

Among the intellectuals, I wonder if they were not waiting for a good excuse to change their attitude.

D.W. – As a matter of fact, it was right then that the human rights theme appeared and was to become the focus of attention.

R.A. – Yes. Basically, I think those intellectuals were already prepared to reject the sophism which held that the creation of an ideal society excused all possible crimes over the short term. That was the primary moral of the communist movements. In the French Revolution, also, there were such phenomena. . . . In the 1940s, when Sartre and Merleau-Ponty said, "There are tens of millions of concentration camp prisoners in the Soviet Union," it had virtually no impact—a rather astonishing fact. Only, it seems that after fifty-five or sixty years of revolution, the argument became less and less acceptable. Perhaps it is the genius of Solzhenitsyn that made the difference, but it is also possible that the leftists were tired of this trick they were playing on themselves, and that they had a deep-seated desire to return to their basic values and to recognize that some things are not acceptable, even when the goal is sublime.

D.W. – In your opinion, might the human rights movement explain this change in attitude?

R.A. – The human rights movement is more complex. In part, it was the result of an evolution in the thought and action of those who had participated in the events of May 1968.

D.W. – And of the women. . . .

R.A. – And of the women; I make no distinction in this matter. The "militants" of 1968, if you prefer, could have been coopted by the Communist party. Some of them were, in fact. Others could have been attracted, like their counterparts in Italy, to terrorism. What is striking is that the best of them, at a certain moment, felt that they risked becoming Fascists. They refrained from becoming so, however, and I think it was the concept of human rights that restrained them, while the Italians continued in that direction. And then, it seems to me, there was in them a quest for something that was not the acceptance of the government, or revolution, or terrorism. The human rights theory was a way for those men of 1968 to remain faithful to themselves, but at the same time to express something completely different.

It was not simply prosaic and boring Aronian liberalism. It was a matter of rediscovering the poetry of action in the name of something superior: the respect that is every man's due.

D.W. – Is it a phase of retreat while awaiting another utopia? Or do you think it connotes a deeper conversion to Western democracy?

R.A. – Forecasts are difficult. The cult of human rights among some members of the intelligentsia can also be interpreted as the absence of an ideology to replace communism. In its absence, one finds a whole series of attractive substitute ideologies: Women's liberation, and that of children, blacks, etc. They are attractive and altogether normal, but they are inadequate to fulfill the aspirations of young people who yearn to devote themselves to a transcendent cause. Communism was a universal cause. It signalled the end of one period of history and the beginning of another. The liberation of men and women—particularly women—is more fundamental than the transformation of society. But I don't think the young people who concern themselves with it experience the same enthusiasm as the young Communists of 1945 or the young leftists of 1968. It's a different kind of thing.

Those defending human rights didn't realize it, but their action was a way of returning to bourgeois society. It represented the possibility of being at once against the government in power and against the other side; it was a way of not choosing one side over the other, because it goes without saying that in all societies there are examples of failure to respect human rights, examples of failure in respecting rights. But one sometimes forgets that there are differences in degree that become, gradually, differences in nature.

D.W. – Do you believe that a policy can be based on human rights?

R.A. – One can live in the obsession of the need to defend human rights. But when it comes to shaping a foreign policy, no, it isn't possible to do that with the human rights issue as a base of departure. If the United States adopted as an absolute principle the recognition as allies of only those governments respecting human rights, I wonder how many countries outside of Western Europe could qualify.

D.W. – Assuming the United States itself always respects them, by the way. . . .

R.A. – I said just a moment ago that there is no country where human rights are always respected, especially *all* human rights. The definition and the enumeration of human rights is not easy to make and one doesn't know very well by what criterion one aspect is considered fundamental and another, secondary.

J.–L.M. – I have the impression that, basically, you almost think that human rights are, for intellectuals, a new way, a new dodge for refusing to think their politics through....

R.A. – That would be going too far. But I do think that it is a way to avoid engaging in equivocal battles—and all political battles are equivocal. Politics is never a conflict between good and evil, but always a choice between the preferable and the detestable. It is always so, especially in foreign policy. So, when a person has imbibed the atmosphere of 1968—you know, its dream and purity—when one has rebelled against adults, and against society, it is difficult to return to the equivocal issues in which we are all involved. Now, human rights, in a way, and in the best cases, but not in all, is a pure, not an equivocal, cause.

J.–L.M. – Although the accent is on human rights, isn't it the thinking of Raymond Aron that triumphs?

R.A. – At least something of what he has been saying for a long time. I have always been ready to think and act politically. I have never aspired to angelic purity, otherwise I would have renounced studying political matters. And I think that others, too, have taken a step in the same direction in recognizing the sophism or, if you prefer, in renouncing the intellectual comfort that comes with the acceptance of terrorism—the scorn for human rights in the name of a cause considered exalted—which is the first step toward frightening, horrible acts. Some people have indeed understood the sophism, not because of me—but because of the things that have happened.

D.W. – You say that the study of political affairs is the study of the reality of things, but you also say that it is the study of reality based on certain values. Why couldn't human rights be one of those themes forming the basis for the study of political affairs?

R.A. – They could be, on the condition of determining what kind of political organization, what kind of government, is most likely to respect human rights. To do so, reality must be observed, and governments compared, to know what led to the acceptance of a given system, despite its lack of purity, because it insured more opportunity for the exercise of human rights. Now, most of those who fight for human rights protest all over the world, everywhere defending to the best of their ability the victims of those who govern. It is a useful, respectable task, in which I participate to the extent possible. But it doesn't constitute a base for defining a foreign policy. It is not possible for a country like the United States; it is not even possible for a country like France. France cannot determine its friendships or make its decisions on the basis of the degree to which human rights are scorned or respected in the various countries. And I do not know of any country in history that founded its foreign policy solely on the virtues of its allies.

D.W. – In other words, morality never has a role in international relations?

R.A. – In international affairs, there are always elements of immorality because foreign policy is a conflict, to one degree or another. Also because there is no court in international relations. Within nations, there are rights, laws, and there are courts. But there is no international court. To that you will retort that after the last war, there was the Nuremberg court. But we know now—and I think I wrote it at the time—that any nation losing a war will be subjected to the decisions of a court like that of Nuremberg. But it is sure that the country subjected to a Nuremberg court will be the guilty country; it will certainly be the country that has been conquered. In the case at hand, the conquered nation was also the most guilty one, that is, Nazi Germany. But as soon as we begin condemning "crimes against peace," for example, I am sure the country that wins a war will demonstrate that the vanquished was responsible for it.

J.–L.M. – Wasn't your meeting in 1977 with Jean-Paul Sartre, after thirty years of quarrels and polemics, symbolic of the importance accorded to human rights? You and he made a joint approach to the president of the Republic in favor of the Vietnamese refugees.

R.A. – Yes, of course. . . . I have no intention of denigrating the significance of this meeting for Sartre and me. But I think its significance was greater for the journalists who took photos of us together. What were we there for? To ask the French government to accept a larger number of refugees, to save human lives. From the moment men are no longer prey to ideological emotions, asking the president to open our borders to people in a tragic situation is an act of simple human compassion. . . . I am happy that we were both at the Elysée, even though our effort was not very successful. In any case, it was not an event that signalled a conversion of the intelligentsia.

D.W. – Twenty years before, however, that approach would not have been conceivable. So there was a change just the same.

R.A. – Listen, Sartre is dead and I don't want the responsibility of speaking alone. Let me say that in similar circumstances, I would have accompanied anyone in order to make a plea for those wretched souls. Twenty years before, Sartre was politically committed. He accepted more easily than I the hard, even pitiless aspects of political activism. At that time, he would not have agreed to a joint approach with me, even though we did agree on Algerian independence. But in the last years of his life, he did change on certain points, under the influence of those around him. He thus agreed without hesitation that we go together to see the president. But this meeting was really just one incident in our personal relationship—not an episode of universal history.

To repeat, I find it altogether normal and good to make a gesture to try to alleviate misery, to try to save the unfortunate. When one can do it, one must. When I see distinguished men dedicate their lives to such work, I admire them. I have absolutely no reservations about what they do. Unfortunately, politics is not coterminous with the activities of good Samaritans. If politics were only that, how much better things would be!

e) Decadent Europe

D.W. – In this rivalry between empires, Europe seems to be both the spectator and the prize. You wrote at the end of *Penser la Guerre, Clausewitz*, "Europeans would like to walk away from history, great history, that written in letters of blood. Others, by the hundreds of millions, are beginning to make such history." In your opinion, can Europeans walk away from history?

R.A. – No, I don't think Europe can just leave history behind it. But Western Europe as a whole—still one of humanity's richest areas—is incapable of defending itself and believes it can be defended only by, or at least, with, the United States.

Look, I recall something. It was shortly after the Portuguese revolution, when we thought it was going to end up as a leftist or extreme leftist regime. A journalist was interviewing me on TV. He had just said to me, "Fundamentally, it is a setback for the United States." "That's a way of looking at things that I find absolutely extraordinary," I responded. "Lisbon is closer to Paris than to New York. If there should be a communist government in Lisbon, for you that isn't a setback for Western Europe, but for the United States. Well, that's idiotic. You still hold to the illusion that Europe is in the forefront of history. In fact, Europe just keeps the score." When something happens in Afghanistan and particularly in the Persian Gulf, the region on which the very existence of industrial Europe depends, everyone considers it to be the exclusive concern of the United States.

J.-L.M. – What is the source of this attitude? Doesn't collective resolution any longer exist in Europe?

R.A. – No longer. Europeans have fought too many wars; they have seen how stupid and sterile were those implacable wars. They prefer to seek a degree of security under American protection. They also have a vague nostalgia for neutrality. They would like to have American protection, on the one hand, and good relations with the Soviet Union, on the other. This is not a very heroic posture; but it is probably the only one Europeans deem possible today.

I hope this confidence in Soviet prudence is confirmed by events. And I hope that the United States, or good luck, will suffice to ensure Europe's oil supplies. That's making a lot of optimistic bets. . . .

I have never been a neutralist. No one is today, in theory: the Europeans belong to the Atlantic Alliance. Fine. Their ambitions are restrained; they know the limitations of their armaments; they know what armaments the other side has. . . .

J.-L.M. – However, in 1977, you wrote a plea for this Europe lacking in resolve. Your book has a bizarre title: *Plaidoyer pour l'Europe Décadente*.

R.A. – Yes. And it wasn't willingly accepted by the publishers, to such an extent that in some translations, *Défense de l'Europe Décadente* became *Défense de l'Europe Libérale*.

I wanted to say two things at the same time. The first was that if you compare Western Europe with Eastern Europe from the point of view of civilization, liberty, creativity, it is evident that no one would choose Eastern Europe over Western Europe.

However, if history "continues as usual," as the English say—if it continues to be harsh, if it continues to favor the villains over the virtuous, it is not at all evident that, in the state of present competition, the West Europeans are the most resolute, the best armed, the most likely to achieve agreement and defend themselves. If—to adopt a pessimistic philosophy of history—the earth belongs to the villains, then a brilliant Europe can become a doomed Europe.

J.-L.M. – You also analyze in that book what you call "the self-destruction of the liberal democracies." Do you believe that the democracies are suicidal? The expression is yours.

R.A. – Yes, I know. But when it is put that way, it becomes excessive. What I say is that Europeans lack confidence in themselves, that they are not aware of their human and economic superiority over Eastern Europe. I also think that the Western democracies tend to go beyond what is tolerable for the cohesion of nations. I think it was with this point of view in mind that I spoke of Western Europe's "suicidal tendency." In any case, this is what seems to me to be essential: If the verdicts of history are pronounced by a court of virtue, there is no question but that Western Europe would win. But if the court that pronounces the verdict is one that treats virtue in the Machiavellian sense, or that evaluates collective unity or the resolution of peoples, then I am not sure that the court would be indulgent toward West Europeans. Because they really don't have confidence in their strength, they prefer to rely on the prudence of the Soviets.

J.-L.M. – Doesn't this collective resolution contradict the morality of the individual and that of democracy?

R.A. – No. Civic morality puts survival, the security of the community, above everything else. But if Western morality has become the morality of pleasure, of individual happiness, rather than civic virtues, then survival is in doubt. If nothing more remains of the citizen's duties, if Europeans no longer have the feeling that they must be ready to fight in order to conserve the opportunity to enjoy their pleasures and their happiness, then, indeed, we are both brilliant and decadent.

That's what I tried to explain in the contradictory title of my book, a title that pleased me very much, but irritated everyone else. I kept it because I wanted to say those two things at once.

J.-L.M. – But isn't all of Western culture moving in the direction of the search for individual happiness?

R.A. – That is true. It is a hedonistic civilization. But this philosophy could be accompanied by civic traditions. One should also be aware of the conditions required to safeguard the chances for the pursuit of happiness so passionately desired by everyone. De Tocqueville remarked that one day Americans seem to have a deep desire for personal well-being and the next they appear to be overwhelmed by a sense of patriotism; that is, seized with the determination to preserve the general welfare. It is characteristic of a living democracy. When the second element no longer exists, you must beg history to be indulgent with those who have forgotten its lessons.

D.W. – The twentieth century is a time of conflict between totalitarian governments, in their fascist or communist guise, and democracies. Do you think that Western democracies still have a chance to be Europe's dominant system of government?

R.A. – I really don't know.

D.W. – You are not very optimistic.

R.A. – Neither optimistic nor pessimistic. It's a question of observation, of analysis. I think that, barring exterior pressures and diplomatic mishaps, Western Europe should remain an area of liberal civilization until the end of the century.

However, this expectation is contingent upon a certain number of events over which we have no control: in the Middle East, in the Persian Gulf, in Eastern Europe, and so forth.

Liberal Western Europe will not destroy itself, but it is hostage to a great number of forces over which it has no control. Also, if it is not to lose too much confidence in itself, it is obliged to take a number of risks. And it is always dangerous to take too many risks.

D.W. – Simultaneously.

R.A. – Or successively.

D.W. – But how can Europe strengthen its collective resolution, upon which you believe its survival depends?

R.A. – Europe must remember that individuals in a democracy are at once private persons and citizens. What bothers me most is that it seems to me almost impossible in France to have courses in citizenship in the schools and it is probably very difficult, even at the university level, to program a course on the citizen's duties and to recall that our civilization, to the extent that it is a liberal one, is a citizen's society and not simply one of consumers or producers.

Our societies, our democracies, are citizens' countries. Today, the citizens are essentially consumers and producers. That's fine, of course. But it is a corrupted Marxist image.

The paradox is that in the country that calls itself Marxist, individuals are always being reminded that they are first and foremost, not citizens, but servants of the Soviet state.

This comparison between the two extremes, between the two blocs or entities, provides no cause for enthusiasm and no assurance that the future is ours.

But if the future belongs to the liberty of men, we have won.

III
THE COMMITTED OBSERVER

a) The Unity of the Aronian Oeuvre

D. Wolton. – Everything considered, you have dealt with a considerable number of themes or subjects, and in very different genres. Where does the unity of your work lie?

Raymond Aron. – Assuming there is a unity, it is essentially that of an individual, but if you are determined to find it, I think it can be said that there was a philosophical reflection on history, accompanied by a reflection on the condition of historic existence: I refer to my prewar books.

And then I found myself involved in the historic tumults, principally as a journalist. In this period, between 1947 and 1955, I wrote two books that constituted an attempt to analyze the global situation: *Le Grand Schisme* and *Guerres en Chaînes.* And then, *The Opium of the Intellectuals,* a book that has its place among my writings in the ideological debate with the Left, the Marxists, Jean-Paul Sartre, Merleau-Ponty, etc.—part of the French Intellectuals' debate on the political situation in the light of a certain philosophy.

When I returned to the university, I wrote what I had been wanting to write for a long time—a tentative analysis, at least a succinct one, of the characteristics of Western societies, on the one hand, and of those of Soviet societies, on the other. That produced three small books, *Les 18 Leçons sur les Sociétés Industrielles* and the two others that followed. If I had not been a journalist, I would have written a single large volume. But I lacked the time to write *the* book. And then, I don't like to rework a subject that I have already handled in a certain way. At first, I refused to permit the publication of the Sorbonne courses, then I finally accepted, whence those three small books that are substitutes for a single book that would have been better.

At the same time, there was this innovation so enormously troubling for humanity: nuclear weapons. Being a kind of "diplomatic correspondent," as the English say, for *Le Figaro,* I had to analyze the worldwide situation and take account of the new factors in economics, armaments, etc. So, I began to write books on international relations. They were *Peace and War among Nations,* then, another that is more readable because it is shorter, *Le Grand Débat: Initiation à la Stratégie Nucléaire,* and, finally, a book for which I have perhaps a certain weak spot: *Penser la Guerre, Clausewitz.* I say "weak spot," because it is a book that I should not have written.

J.–L. Missika. – Why?

R.A. – In that book, I tried, not only to interpret in my way the greatest strategist of the past, but also to find in his work the sources of the contradictory interpretations given to his thought. It would have been more difficult, but more useful, to apply the same technique to Marx. With my usual laziness, I probably hesitated to do with Marx what I tried to do with Clausewitz. The number of people who followed in Clausewitz's footsteps is limited; Marx's followers are truly numberless. It would have been more interesting to understand why the work of Marx lent itself to do many different interpretations. Clausewitz was in a way too easy a case.

So, what do all those books have in common? They constitute a reflection upon the twentieth century, in the light of Marxism, and an attempt to understand better all the sectors of modern society: Economics, social relationships, class relationships, political systems, relations among nations, and ideological arguments.

After all, Nietzsche wrote that the twentieth century would be a century of great wars fought in the name of philosophic concepts. So, when I try to justify myself for having participated in the ideological debate through my books and articles, I say that I have simply been participating in the great twentieth century wars fought in the name of philosophic concepts. All of that doesn't make up a unity; it is all imperfect, just sketched out, but one who wants to cover everything cannot possibly treat exhaustively each of the subjects he has selected. Perhaps there is room for amateurs like me who, while being university professors, take liberties that the best university professors never accord themselves.

J.–L.M. – I think you judge your work severely.

R.A. – No. I do not myself know the value of my work. I am not sure whether, a decade from now, it will be considered simply one person's views, or whether people will still be reading the books to which I give importance. It is impossible to know.

J.–L.M. – You said in a 1970 interview, "I fear imagination in philosophy as much as in politics, which makes of me an analyst or critic."

R.A. – I think that's true. I have analyzed many political and economic situations pertinently. I think that on the whole, my judgment has been good. When there were fundamental debates touching the essence of modern civilization, I think I have always been on the right side. I had no illusions about Hitler, nor about Stalin. I did not believe that France could renew itself through a French Algeria. All of that is, if I may say so, in my favor. I am not being pretentious. I think it is true and I say it simply and with detachment.

On the other hand, if I am asked today what *Peace and War among Nations* is worth, I am less optimistic than fifteen years ago. Today, I see the weaknesses of the book, the journalistic aspects that I could have avoided. Being an attempt at theory, it could have been more abstract and more detachable from current affairs.

D.W. – There is something else. You prefer to explain reality, rather than dream about it or invent it. One has the impression that you have suppressed part of your personality.

R.A. – Bertrand de Jouvenel always says that to me. But when one analyzes present-day societies, one is so aware of the constraints that weigh as much on those who govern as on those governed that it is difficult to dream or invent as you suggest. When one studies the different types of political systems that exist today, it is very difficult to imagine one that would differ radically from the two we know—always understood, of course, that there are Soviet-type patterns and Western-type patterns, and that it would be absurd to say that the choice is between Washington and Moscow.

I am simply saying that politically, so far in this country, the big question has been: Is dialogue accepted? Do people accept discussion? Here, our societies accept dialogue. The essence of the Soviet regime is its refusal of dialogue. For thirty-five years, I have chosen the society that accepts dialogue. As far as possible, this dialogue must be reasonable, but it accepts unleashed emotions, it accepts irrationality: societies of dialogue are a wager on humanity. The other regime is founded on the refusal to have confidence in those governed; founded also on the pretention of a minority of oligarchs that they possess the definitive truth for themselves and for the future.

I detest that; I have fought it for thirty-five years and I will continue to do so. The pretention of those few oligarchs to possess the truth of history and of the future is intolerable. As they say today: it is unacceptable. . . .

D.W. – In any case, there is one constant in a number of your books: you like to compare your thinking with that of certain authors of the past: Montesquieu, Max Weber, Marx, Tocqueville, Auguste Comte.

R.A. – For several reasons. The first is that I continue to believe that the great social doctrines of the twentieth century were developed, in their essentials, in the nineteenth century. A culture requires memory. Precisely because there was a tendency at one time in American sociology, and even in French sociology, to start anew, as if there had not existed a pre-sociology, I was impelled to return to those great authors and read them in my own way. There is another reason: I find authentic intellectual satisfaction in confronting myself with great minds, harboring no illusions about the result of the confrontation. It is a way to protect oneself from mediocrity. One has to develop a dialogue with great minds. . . .

Concerning Tocqueville, I was instrumental in restoring him to the place he merits both in French culture generally and in sociological thought.

Auguste Comte is ignored today. The few chapters I devoted to him seem to me interesting, though little attention is any longer given him, which is unfortunate.

Max Weber is a different matter: before the war, he introduced into French thought a number of German sociological themes. I deal with them in my *Sociologie Allemande Contemporaine,* a little book I wrote when I was twenty-nine or thirty. It was translated into German after the war. The brother of Max Weber, Alfred, called it the best introduction of contemporary German sociology. Well. What is certain is that *La Sociologie Allemande Contemporaine* is still worth reading, even though it no longer concerns contemporary German sociology and though there are many books about certain authors that are far better than the very short chapter I devoted to each of them.

So, I enjoy the dialogue with great minds, a taste I try to communicate to my students. I find that students need someone to admire and since they cannot admire their professors because they are their examiners or because they are not admirable, it is important that they admire the great thinkers and it is important that the professors be the interpreters of these great minds for the students.

J.–L.M. – You think that ideas shape the world? For example, when you say that the social doctrines of the twentieth century were conceived in the nineteenth century.

R.A. – No, I don't think so. Neither do I think that world history is determined by the forces of production. I don't think that your question permits a precise response. I am convinced that Marxism, the Marxist idea, has very obviously played a considerable role, but the Marxist idea has transformed the world through the mediation of the Leninist translation that Karl Marx probably would have rejected. Let's say that, there, the misunderstandings about the meaning of a great author were at the origin of the success of Marxism and the world's transformation. This misunderstanding continues. Marxism, the Soviet Union, all that is still—for how long I don't know—our destiny; some will call it our "curse," others will call it a "blessing." In this last part of the twentieth century, we continue to live in the obsession of Marxism even if the high-level French, or Parisian, intelligentsia has recently discovered that Marx was wrong and, all of a sudden, proceeded to the curious idea that Marx was responsible for the gulag.

D.W. – Is there an Aronian school of thought?

R.A. – Certainly not.

D.W. – But your ideas have influenced many people and politicians. How would you characterize this influence?

R.A. – I can only say that in adopting certain positions, I have been a man very much alone in the face of history and in the face of intellectual styles. I have some friends who assert that they have been more or less influenced by me, but they are friends, not disciples.

J.–L.M. – An intellectual who proposes no ideology can have no influence?

R.A. – That is not true. The influence exists, but there is no Aronian school. There exists, for example, a periodical called *Commentaire*. It is edited by people who for the most part are friendly to Raymond Aron.

Everyone must accept his destiny; I was not destined to be the leader of a sect.

b) Journalist and University Professor

J.–L.M. – You have always been both a journalist and a university professor. Can the two professions be reconciled?

R.A. – I don't think that is really a problem. Naturally, if the professor is a specialist in Greek philosophy, he is not qualified to comment upon economic events; but if his university specialty is international relations or economics or sociology, he naturally has some desire to say what he thinks about events.

Moreover, I know several journalists who could easily be university professors. On the great newspapers, there are professors who write articles, and there are journalists who, sometimes, dream about becoming, or becoming once again, professors.

J.–L.M. – Neverthless, it's not the same kind of activity.

R.A. – I would say that journalists face a danger they do not always succeed in avoiding: an excessive preoccupation with day-to-day events. My scholarly books, I am sure, would have been different—perhaps better—if I had not been a journalist at the same time. I remember a phrase of, I think, Maurois, who remarked, "Raymond Aron would be our Montesquieu if only he could be more detached from reality." He was wrong on one point: In no way would I ever have been a Montesquieu. But he was right on the other: I was too obsessed by everyday realities to give my abstract books the breadth and dimension they probably would have had if I had not chosen the easy course, that is, journalism.

J.–L.M. – Why do you always insist upon calling journalism an easy profession?

R.A. – Because I respect journalists and journalism. But there is a danger: it's easier to write a more or less brilliant four-page article on a given event, than to write a book of substance on a fundamental problem. Journalists are just as intelligent as university professors, often more so. If one is only a journalist, over the long term one risks losing a feeling for the things that endure, for basic questions; also, one becomes too easily satisfied with commentaries imposed by events as they happen. That's where the danger lies. But to recognize it is not at all to signify contempt for journalism, quite the contrary.

D.W. – But if you practiced journalism at the same time that you were a university professor, journalistic activity must have brought you something. What did it bring you more than a traditional university activity?

R.A. – It's a question I occasionally ask myself, and which I cannot answer. Was my life a failure because I practiced journalism for thirty-five years? Or rather, in view of the role I played in French political debates, haven't I added to the influence of the books I might have written, a certain impact on events or on France—an impact that I would not have had with books such as those I wrote before the war?

D.W. – There is nonetheless a difference between writing occasional articles in newspapers, as indeed a number of university people do, and the discipline of editorial writer to which you subjected yourself for thirty-five years.

R.A. – That's true, but it is not an example to be recommended for others. When one has a teaching responsibility and a desire to produce books, one normally doesn't have time left over for journalism.

In my case, it was practically an accident. Because of personal bereavements, I sought refuge or flight in an obsessive dedication to work. Thus, I worked too much, did too many things. If I had reflected more, if destiny had been more indulgent with me, my work would have been different. I think my case is rather unusual. What I have done is probably acceptable, but neither professors nor editorial writers should emulate it. The result, moreover, was that in order to demonstrate to my colleagues that, despite everything, I had time to produce, I undoubtedly wrote more books than most of them, including one of seven to eight hundred pages that, as it happened, was respected for its size.

But another person of my generation was much more exceptional than I: Jean-Paul Sartre. We have already mentioned it. Sartre was at once philosopher, novelist, playwright, journalist, and politician. I didn't do as much, but I was nonetheless tempted to take upon myself too many activities that normally would be spread among several people. Today, in the new generation, my friend Touraine, a sociologist, obviously hopes to be the Left's commentator and he does it with his own style.

D.W. – You are, however, one of the first to combine scientific work with journalistic commentary. Won't this twofold activity be practiced more and more by intellectuals and university teachers?

R.A. – Both yes and no. I think the newspapers will carry more commentaries and editorials written, not only by journalists, but also by professors, civil servants and so forth. The newspapers will be open to others beyond the professionals.

However, it is rather much to carry on two full-time professions; that is why I say the practice should not be encouraged. As far as I am concerned, those of my books that I prefer are the ones that have absolutely nothing to do with journalism: *Introduction to the Philosophy of History, Histoire et Dialectique de la Violence, Clausewitz*. Those were not the books of a journalist and contained no references to journalism. I might add to that list a book for which I have a weakness: the *Essai sur les Libertés*, that I consider to be one of my most philosophic works.

D.W. – It is also very readable. . . .

R.A. – Yes, yes, by accident. But, beginning with the postwar period, I have paid for my clarity: my reputation has suffered from it.

J.–L.M. – You mean you were not obscure enough to be a real philosopher?

R.A. – After 1945, French thought had become very obscure and Germanic. In my case, I was a little Germanic, but certainly clear. There was an expression: "Aronian clarity." Depending upon who was using the expression, it was a sour or impertinent affirmation, or one nuanced with irony—but rarely complimentary.

D.W. – Weren't you a precursor in being one who takes a position on events while analyzing them?

R.A. – Yes. I think I've already told you that I had determined the intellectual path I would follow when I was a lecturer at the University of Cologne. I had decided to be a "committed observer." To be at one and the same time the observer of history as it was unfolding, to try to be as objective as possible regarding that history, and to be not totally detached from it—in other words, to be committed. I wanted to combine the dual role of actor and spectator. I wrote the *Introduction to the Philosophy of History* to show the limits within which one can be at once an objective spectator and an actor. They were "the limits of historic objectivity." That subtitle didn't mean that I scorned objectivity; on the contrary, it meant that the more one wants to be objective, the more important it is to be aware of the viewpoint from which one expresses oneself and from which one regards the world.

D.W. – In other words, objectivity is not at all incompatible with commitment?

R.A. – I hope not.

c) Political Choices

D.W. – In fact, you've spent your life going to the Left, while speaking the language of the Right, and going to the right, while speaking the language of the Left.

R.A. – It's the first time anyone has characterized me this way. The formula is astute. I think most of those who would characterize me would say, "He is a man of the Right." As for myself, I would say that sometimes my positions were closer to the Left than to the Right; on Algeria, for example. Concerning my opposition to Stalinism, people used to consider me rightist because I denounced Stalinism, but today leftists denounce Stalinism as much as I.

What is true, especially over the last fifteen years, is that there are two blocs in French politics: one is called the Right; the other, the Left. The fact is that when I vote, I vote for Giscard d'Estaing and not for Mitterand. So, if an intellectual's position is defined by his voting habits, I am an intellectual of the Right, but one of a rather peculiar breed, that is, undisciplined and rarely in agreement with the person he voted for. I

criticize the man I voted for as freely as I would the other candidate, had he been elected.

J.–L.M. – A rightist anarchist?

R.A. – No. An intellectual ambition or intention to have my
own viewpoint on every subject, whatever the opinions of
those in power. I consider that to be the only honorable posture for an editorialist. Today, at *L'Express*, I feel comfortable.
L'Express is rather more in favor of the majority than the opposition, but it is one of the papers that is most critical of the
government in power.[32] That is the journalist's role. But when
it comes to choosing, one can say that I am a man of the Right
because I chose Giscard d'Estaing.

J.–L.M. – A committed observer, at once actor and spectator, you have since 1940 taken a position on all the great controversies. So, why do you have the reputation for being
someone who analyzes, dissects—but fails to choose?

R.A. – This claim is both right and wrong. I have indeed
taken a position on all the great questions: The Soviet Union,
decolonization, Algeria, May 1968, General de Gaulle's press
conference on the Jews, etc. Those were questions that had
personal meaning for me as well as historic significance. But
since I used to write one or two articles a week on economic
affairs, I often analyzed a situation without saying in a sover-
eign manner, "Here is what the minister should do." I consider myself a fairly well-informed amateur, but not at all a
professional in economic matters. I know enough about political economy to understand economic problems and to explain and clarify them. But proposing a solution is another
matter. And this refusal to make categoric conclusions irritated a portion of the readership of *Le Figaro*. Readers generally expect a commentator to tell them what they should
think.

The reproach seems to me to be justified in certain respects. But my conviction is also very strong. I consider that a
well-informed journalist is not necessarily one who indoctri-
nates his readers. So, in the face of a difficult economic situation, I don't claim to know with certitude what should be
done, but I try to give readers at least the basic facts the minister should use in coming to a decision.

J.–L.M. – You say that while writing you always ask yourself, "What would I do if I were in the place of the government?" Do you write only for those who govern?

R.A. – No, no. To write for those who rule us is also a way to explain a problem to the governed who, for the most part, lack the information available to the government.

One day I was at the *Commission des Comptes de la Nation* and the minister of finance at the time, Giscard d'Estaing, courteously but firmly chided me for my most recent *Figaro* article. He faulted me for having criticized, without explaining what should be done. I responded as best I could, saying, "The duel is not an equal one. You are the minister and you have a whole series of offices providing you with the information necessary to understand a problem and make a decision. I am a journalist, working alone and without an information service. By the nature of my task, it happens that now and again I am led to criticize the ministry. The minister finds me unjust, irritating, insupportable, but that is more or less the normal relationship between a minister and a columnist." Michel Rocard recalls the argument. He told me recently that he had some difficulty in finding courteous terms to sum up the discussion, so sharp had been the minister's attack.

J.–L.M. – Another thing: your rejection of sentimentalism in the name of realism. Yet, there is no political action devoid of sentiment, unless one takes only the government's point of view.

R.A. – There you go again—always the same criticism. When I take a stand, people say the tone is icy, which means nothing at all. When I make an economic analysis, I try to be clear and factual. To add a sentimental angle to an economic analysis seems demagogic, almost ridiculous, to me. And the idea that my personality is defined solely by economic analysis and not by everything else that is peculiar to me and not to others, is equally ridiculous.

J.–L.M. – It is not only a question of your economic analysis. It's also a matter of the detachment you have shown toward such burning questions as Algeria, May 1968, etc.

R.A. – It is true that even when I spoke in favor of Algerian independence, François Mauriac criticized my icy manner. What can I do, everyone can't be François Mauriac. But I am not ashamed to write about political problems as a man who observes, reflects, and seeks the best solution for the welfare of people in general. And I find it a bit pretentious to mention constantly my love for humanity. Once and for all, it's up to you either to grant me that quality, or to decide that I lack it.

D.W. – In defining the role of the intellectual, you often say that he has the choice between "being the confidant of providence and the counselor to the prince."

R.A. – At the time, I used a different terminology: on the one hand, there was the politics of understanding—an expression that originated with Alain—and on the other, the politics of Reason, with a capital R. . . .

In the first instance, the politician doesn't claim to know the future; he knows only reality, and he tries to manage as best he can, remaining as close to the facts as possible. In the second, the politician—a Marxist, let's say—pretends to know the future. He makes political decisions on the basis of a historic evolution that he thinks he can foresee and master.

So, the counselor to the prince is the one who helps the prince to understand the circumstances in which he lives, what can be done on the basis of events, without having the pretension or the illusion of knowing the outcome of the drama or tragedy known as human history.

But there are also in our century people who believe themselves to be confidants of providence, that is to say, those who "know" that historic providence has reserved victory to the proletariat or to the Communist party. Their politics are based on a global prediction of history. They have the assurance—sometimes insufferable—that the outcome will be happy.

After having studied Marxism, it seemed to me impossible to claim that the struggles between classes and nations, the struggles that we were witnessing and enduring, would necessarily lead to a socialist society, such as it was imagined, rather vaguely, by those who claimed allegiance to Marx.

It is in this sense that politics for me are those of understanding. But I would add that one can be a counselor to the prince only on the condition that one has an overall image of the society in which one lives, and on the condition that one accepts that society. That is why all those who have been men of action have erred, as have commentators. It would be extremely easy, if one were to reread everything that I have written, to find mistakes here and there. You have found some, there are many others still, but it's the proportion that matters.

D.W. – So, have you found the prince whose counselor you could be?

R.A. – I haven't looked for him, so I haven't found him. Moreover, I'm not at all sure that I could have been a counselor even to a prince whose fundamental preferences I accepted. I wrote in *The Imperial Republic,* "I could never have been the counselor to the president of the United States, order the Vietnam bombings and then go to bed and sleep peacefully. . . ." I am intellectually capable of accepting, of understanding, such necessities, but my temperament is not wholly compatible with my opinions, if I may mention it. You see, I am not icy enough.

d) Values

J.–L.M. – What are the values to which you are most dedicated?

R.A. – The probable answer—and I believe this sincerely— would be: truth and liberty, the two concepts being indivisible for me. The love of truth and the horror of lies—I think that is what is most profound in my way of living and thinking. And to be able to express the truth one must necessarily be free. There must be no external power that restrains one.

However, I am also a citizen, a citizen of France. During World War I, of course, I was patriotic like all children, and thrilled by the greatness of France. I have remained a Lorraine-type patriot all my life. My father was born in Rambervillers. The Jews of Lorraine were passionately French. In this sense, I have remained faithful to my father.

J.–L.M. – And Judaism in your life?

R.A. – It is always difficult to explain. Reduced to the essential, I think that someone who finds himself, as I do, born in France, permeated by French culture, but who at the same time follows the Jewish tradition, has the right to choose the meaning he gives to his Judaism. A person who is a nonbeliever and who is not interested in the destiny of the Jews or Israel has the perfect right to say, "I am a French citizen of Jewish origin, but this origin does not bear upon my essential being."

My position, and I restate it as clearly as possible, is: I am a French citizen; I am French, of Jewish origin; and for reasons probably difficult even for me to puzzle out, I accept a certain solidarity with the Jews of the Diaspora and with the Israelis, but there is naturally a limit to that solidarity—when I write articles on foreign policy, I write them as a French citizen and not as a Jew.

Thus, I believe I have now come to peace with myself concerning both my French patriotism and the right I claim to have a special relationship with the Jews of the rest of the world and, in particular, those of Israel.

J.-L.M. – Was this peace with yourself long and difficult to find? Was it painful?

R.A. – Yes, it was long and difficult, but not traumatic, because my parents were already de-Judaized. I have told you earlier that I never went to the synagogue when I was a child, and I had little awareness of being Jewish. Jewish awareness was imposed upon me, you might say, by Hitler, by events of the period. Today, I justify my attachment to Judaism by a sort of fidelity to my roots. If, by some miracle, I should find myself face-to-face with my grandfather who lived in Rambervillers and who was faithful to the tradition, I would not want to be ashamed: I would want to give him the feeling that, even though I am not Jewish in the way he was, I have remained faithful in a certain way. As I've written many times: I don't like to be torn from my roots. It is not very philosophic, perhaps, but one tries to live with one's sentiments and ideas as well as possible.

D.W. – You don't have much confidence in the wisdom of men. You believe that history is controlled by emotions and yet, in the tumult and discordance of human beings, you attempt to make reason and lucidity triumph.

R.A. – My friend Eric Weil wrote in his thesis, "Man is a reasonable being, but it has not been demonstrated that men are reasonable." The period of history that I have lived through—that I have tried to understand—was indeed a senseless turmoil, full of sound and fury. Human history has always evolved amid sound and fury. The twentieth century has been in some ways still more horrible than others. But that is no reason for despair.

This century of frightful wars has also been one of extraordinary scientific and technological discoveries. Medicine has made more advances over the last thirty years than for centuries before. I recall what it was to have appendicitis when, while I was a child, my brother was operated upon. It was really like the seventeenth century. It must be accepted once and for all that humanity has to pay for whatever gains it makes; there is no progress that is without a negative side. During the few thousand years that the history of complex societies has existed, there has always been present this mixture of herosim and absurdity, of saints and monsters, of incomparable intellectual progress and persistent blind passions.

So humanity is; so history is.

D.W. – You don't have many illusions about human nature, about what societies can accomplish. You do not believe in the "sense of history," or in the great philosophies that affirm the existence of a beginning and an end. But you nevertheless have a certain degree of optimism. You think that man has a margin of maneuver.

R.A. – I am sure there is a margin of maneuver. On the other hand, when I say that I don't believe in the sense of history, I am not saying that human history does not move in a certain direction, and above all I am not saying that reflective man cannot provide himself with certain goals. I was a disciple of Kant and there is in Kant a concept to which I still subscribe: it is the idea of Reason, an image of a society that would be truly humanized. We can continue to think, or dream or hope—in the light of the idea of Reason—for a humanized society.

But what makes no sense is to imagine, let's say, that the collective ownership of the tools of production is the beginning of the realization of the idea of Reason. That is what angered me in reading, for example, Merleau-Ponty. Of course, the idea of Reason and of a society that would be humane is conceivable, but it is not the proletariat or collective ownership that defines a society conforming to the idea of Reason.

D.W. – Do men have a free destiny?

R.A. – That doesn't mean much. If you are asking whether men, considered collectively, determine their destiny, all right—if there is no God, then it is obviously men who determine it. But if the question is asked whether Mr. X has a free destiny, a free history, the response is obviously negative. We are all shaped by our surroundings, by our origins, by our chromosomes. We are surrounded by constraints. There is nevertheless a margin of liberty, an awareness of oneself that gives meaning to our decision to do this or that.

J.–L.M. – In the final analysis, you remain an advocate of progress despite all the criticism that it arouses today?

R.A. – If one is not, what is left? The biological philosophies make of man a carnivorous animal, destined always to remain so. They hold that each civilization passes through a number of phases and the outcome is always the same: the end of that civilization. It is all plausible. Everyone develops his philosophy within the context of history. As for me, despite my experiences, despite the twentieth century, I remain an advocate of progress. So, from time to time I become angry when I read articles by those known as the New Philosophers, who discovered rather tardily that the Communists are not tolerable and, from that point on, rushed every which way.

Humanity has no hope for survival outside of reason and science. Everything else is indispensable for living, too. But the essential condition, if man is to continue his extraordinary adventure—just think of the point of departure and of where we are today—the essential condition, if we want this adventure to be meaningful, is to have confidence in the process of thought that makes it possible to arrive at truth. It's a question of seeing the difference between illusions, emotions, hopes, and truths that are demonstrable. In political affairs, it is impossible to demonstrate truth, but one can try, on the basis of what one knows, to make sensible decisions.

D.W. – What is your outlook concerning the period from now until the end of the century?

R.A. – We have again entered a period of tumult, sound and fury. We must hope that the sound and the fury will not destroy everything. On the one hand, we find ourselves in a period of technological revolution that poses important consequences. Developments in the computer sciences, with which you are more familiar than I, will not transform society, to be sure, but they are going to change some of the ways of living and thinking in developed societies. And then, simultaneously, the world equilibrium that resulted from both American power and the semi-entente between the United States and the Soviet Union is, to say the least, menaced today. Stability is threatened by the relative decline of the United States, by the Soviet Union's military power, and by the increase in oil prices and raw materials. We thus continue to live in a state of East-West rivalry and confrontation. Added to all that are the dangers resulting from the power acquired by the oil producers, from a Western economy in total disorder, in which there are no longer any stable currencies, stable securities, or accepted doctrines. The developed world has lived in permanent inflation for years and it fears not only uncontrolled wars—as one might call them—but also, monetary, banking, and economic disasters.

The kind of stability the European countries enjoyed during the period of great expansion has disappeared. In my view, there is little hope that we will find real stability again for ten or perhaps fifteen years. Those who will have the good luck to live through those years will have no reason to be bored. For those with a sense of history, well, history there will be. And history is richer than the theory of growth. Obviously, the confrontation between developed and underdeveloped countries will be superimposed upon the East-West confrontation. All the problems that have been discussed with no great sense of urgency for thirty years are becoming critical, urgent, and in a way, unsolvable. But the essence of history is not the resolution of problems. When, through good luck, one is resolved, another is immediately created. Such are human societies. Such are men. Such are the consequences of their actions.

While awaiting this future, and in reviewing the past, it seems to me that the transformation of our living habits made possible by science and technology—a transformation that I have lived through over the past fifty years—has been, on the whole, positive. Positive, because I have the impression that, today, at least two thirds of the French people live in decent circumstances and that inequalities are not such as to make communication impossible.

When I was in India, what impressed me—rather, what shocked me—was the realization that there could be no communication between the intellectuals, or visitors, and the Indian masses. While today, in France, I can discuss things with artisans or with workers. Naturally, there can be a considerable difference between some men and others, but there are not, on one side, people possessing all the advantages, and, on the other, people so removed from that condition that they cannot even imagine the way of life of the privileged classes. In spite of the injustices in our societies—and it is a fact that all our societies are unjust; there is no fully satisfactory society—nonetheless, thanks to twenty-five or thirty years of economic growth, France has been transformed, and for the better. Today, some people criticize growth. The reason is simply that as soon as something good has been accomplished, one discovers there is a price to pay.

D.W. – Do you think that a society can be built on growth?

R.A. – Of course not. You don't live for a rate of growth. . . .

D.W. – But on the other hand, over the last thirty-five years you have condemned the ideologies or utopias that have cost millions of lives on a promise of a happier future. What is there, then, that can muster the collective resolve of our societies?

R.A. – It is necessary to awaken hopes, but, it seems to me, it is not inevitable to arouse these hopes through a dogmatic ideology that promises a future that is certain, and that confers upon a particular group the historic, or messianic, mission of saving humanity. Personally, I believe that I can awaken hopes among many men. But I certainly cannot play the role or carry out the mission of the Jewish or the Marxist prophets. I just don't have the talent, that's all.

D.W. – Do you think the values of Western democracy will have a better chance in these last years of the twentieth century?

R.A. – The Western democracies in which we live represent today a very small minority of humankind. But, in spite of the fact that Europeans or Westerners in general were conquerors and, on the whole, behaved as badly as other conquerors, they nonetheless left something that the peoples earlier conquered want to maintain: the means of production that were brought to them. They want to develop their capacity to produce. Moreover, despite the kinds of regimes that have been established, I believe many people who were mistreated or conquered by Westerners retain a certain nostalgia for liberal systems. The best proof is that many of those countries that do not wish to—or are unable to—preserve democratic institutions, nevertheless use the vocabulary of democracy in their rhetoric. They have also perhaps inherited our weaknesses. But in using our language, they imply that we Westerners are, perhaps, somewhat different than most other conquerors. We brought something that, despite all, retains its value and justifies the confidence I continue to have in Europe's future, even though this confidence is founded rather more on intuition than on incontestable facts.

J.–L.M. – You are the last liberal?

R.A. – No. Today, there are many who are joining me. I might even become fashionable. . . .

CONCLUSION

The interviews recorded in this book were not meant for publication and the style reflects it. Dominique Wolton and Jean-Louis Missika had carefully prepared the three television programs, read most of my books, a great number of my articles and jotted down some quotations and threw them at me at opportune moments. From these sometimes caustic discussions, almost nothing remains in the television programs. My friend Albert Palle, who was my student at the Le Havre lycée during the 1933-1934 scholastic year, took on the task of transposing into a semi-written style my remarks that had to be abridged for television.

My talk—sometimes stimulated, sometimes interrupted by the objections of my interviews—was thus doubly improvised because it was not destined to be heard or read. At my home, then in Liard Hall, finally at the Mazarine,[33] I said whatever passed through my head—not everything I think about my past or about the events I have experienced, but recollections that young people, who could be my grandchildren, and whom I did not know, brought to the surface. The initiative was theirs; they established the plan, conceived the dialogue, chose the themes. When I saw the three programs for the first time, I had the curious impression that my role in the finished work was, really, modest.

Inevitably, such is not true of this book, which is much more faithful to the interviews than the television programs were. Did these interviews deserve to be preserved and offered to readers? I hesitated to say *yes,* but my *no* wasn't strong enough to discourage either my friend Bernard de Fallois, or my young friends Dominique and Jean-Louis, who won me over by their kindness during the preparation and the two weeks of recordings.

More than six months have passed since our conversations. Dominique and Jean-Louis questioned me on the Common Program of March 1973. Today, they would query me on the victory won by the Left, and this, in a way, brings me back to the past, to the former administration, or, as was said in 1940, to the abolished regime. The victory of François Mitterand and the triumph of the Socialist party certainly open another phrase of the Fifth Republic and, in a larger sense, of French politics in general. I was a member of the one hundred personalities who constituted Valery Giscard d'Estaing's committee of supporters. I voted for the outgoing president and regretted his defeat. Thus, I am about to rediscover the austere pleasures of swimming against the current—pleasures to which I became thoroughly accustomed over the years. So, as a way of concluding this book, I imagined the dialogue that would have taken place if Dominique Wolton and Jean-Louis Missika had attacked me in their usual style on May 10, 1981. It goes without saying that I have drafted both the questions and answers that follow:

D. Wolton. – What did you do for Giscard d'Estaing, since you hoped for his election and feared the Socialists' accession to office, even if they had not been allied to the Communists?

Raymond Aron. – As usual, I did what you would term nothing or practically nothing. I explained why I was going to vote for Giscard d'Estaing and spelled out my arguments against François Mitterand's program. But I must confess that I was less inspired, less resolved, than in 1973 or 1978. In 1978, I wrote a pamphlet that I've never much liked. This time, the whole controversy bored me.

D.W. – Why this boredom?

R.A. – Basically, the debate hadn't changed much, but the Socialists had dropped the most outrageous inanities from the Common Program. In 1973, this program rejected the strategic nuclear force and at the same time announced "a military strategy making it possible to face any eventual aggressor." It also permitted employees to demand the nationalization of their enterprise—a demand that would be transmitted to the National Assembly. Under these conditions, to count on accelerated growth, or an increase in investments, would be absurd—a squaring of the circle. In 1981, François Mitterand

and the Socialist party did not repeat those blunders. There were three texts: The Socialist project edited by Jean-Pierre Chevenement, the Socialist Manifesto that committed the party, and Mitterand's own program.

In spite of its relative moderation, this program seemed unreasonable to me, but not of such a nature as to trouble those French men who wanted a change. Of what use could it be to nationalize eleven industrial groups, the most "multinational" in nature, when the government has so many means of exerting pressure on the big companies? To reduce unemployment by recruiting more than two hundred thousand civil servants in eighteen months seemed to me sordidly demagogic. But those who don't have the same opinion won't let themselves be convinced by an article.

D.W. – As usual, you see only the probable evil in the Left's policy and you say nothing about the mistakes the Right made while in power.

R.A. – As usual, you forget that I criticized Giscard d'Estaing's policies many times. Since you always have tactless quotations in reserve, do you remember the article *"Finlandisation Volontaire?"* The article on the visit to Warsaw? Unfortunately, Mitterand used arguments we developed in *L'Express*. What was reprehensible about the visit was not the content of the subjects discussed, but the very act of going to Warsaw when, as a response to the Soviet invasion of Afghanistan, the West had decided to suspend negotiations at the highest level with the Soviet Union.

J.–L. Missika. – You're evading the issue. You're anxious to focus on foreign policy questions because you consider yourself a professional, and with good reason, I admit. But what about unemployment, inequalities, restrictions on liberty?

R.A. – Until 1978-1979, I judged Raymond Barre's policy the least bad among several possibilities, and, in any case, courageous, in a difficult economic situation. In 1977-1978, it was possible to bank on a deceleration of inflation. The majority again won the 1978 legislative elections. The second oil shock jarred France as it did all the other European countries. Ever since the war, France has been more inflationary than West Germany. Do you think that the Left, with its program aimed at increasing social expenditures, will reduce inflation?

J.–L.M. – And unemployment? Do you accept it passively as if it were a calamity of nature? Instead of being a committed observer, you have become a resigned observer—resigned to the misfortunes of others.

R.A. – I've heard all that before. And the reply, also: "You're not the only one with a heart." Or another reply, this one being my own: "Does one have to talk nonsense to demonstrate that one has a kind heart?" I am as aware as you are that unemployment is, for most of those who are its victims, a cruel moral and material experience. But let's analyze the problem, just the same. Among the unemployed, there are some who will find other work in a few weeks or months. In a period of industrial redeployment, this first category of unemployed workers is inevitable. There is a second category of the unemployed, temporary victims of the failure of obsolescent industries, of technical progress. Finally, there is unemployment caused by the slowing of growth. The Left promises us stronger growth that would have an impact on one of the causes of unemployment; but on the other hand, it is going to make dismissals more difficult and, at the same time, reduce hirings. I hope I am mistaken. But I don't believe that seeking economic recovery through income enhancement will cure unemployment. This kind of recovery must in any case be slow, otherwise it risks aggravating further the inflation problem and the foreign trade deficits.

D.W. – As was true for May 1968, you don't perceive anyone as guilty; you see only diffused responsibilities.

R.A. – Well, then who are the guilty ones in your opinion?

D.W. – You're not going to tell me that the government couldn't have done better.

R.A. – Of course it could have done better. The law on capital gains was a failure, and I said so in one of my articles. Everyone agrees that the business tax is a disgrace, and without being certain, I am ready to believe it. Some people favor a wealth tax on the condition that it not be aggressively progressive and that it not provoke the collapse of real estate values. I am not a fiscal expert and I suppose that reforms are possible. We do not yet know what the Left's reforms will be. The marginal rates can be raised from 60-65 percent to 70-75 percent; why not 80-85 percent? Other countries, Great Britain for example, have had experience with such rates. You can't make the poor wealthy by impoverishing the rich. In any case, the most rigorous fiscal measures have never prevented inflation.

What Raymond Barre can most be reproached for—and what Michel Debré reproached him for, without awakening anyone's interest—is that he talked about austerity without imposing it. He undertook nothing against the bottlenecks that contribute to an increase in unemployment. The Rueff-Armand report remains topical. But I don't think the Left will seek such solutions as those. Apart from the fiscal reforms on which I will reserve judgment, the economic recovery program, an imitation of Léon Blum's of 1936, and of Allende's, risks the same destiny.

J.–L.M. – Are you hostile to the Socialists' goals or to the means they employ? This time you can't claim that they've made compromises with the Communists.

R.A. – There are, you know, three different programs: Jean-Pierre Chevènement's Socialist project, that François Mitterand prefaced, but did not make his own during the electoral campaign; the Socialist Manifesto, launched in January 1981, after the Congress of Créteil, when the candidate for the presidency of the Republic was designated; finally, the incumbent president's program that he elaborated during the electoral campaign.

To limit myself to this third version, I consider it demagogic; while it might provide some economic recovery, or slow down for a time the increase in unemployment, the cost will soon become unbearable. The recruitment of two hundred thousand civil servants will not cost too much immediately, but the state's costs will increase from year to year. The recruitment of civil servants finds its justification in meeting the needs of the state, but not as a means of countering unemployment. It is not possible to promise the French that they can simultaneously work less and earn more. In other words, over the next year to eighteen months, these economic recovery measures are likely to increase inflation, the balance of payments deficit, and probably employment, too.

The structural measures can be divided into two categories. The first concerns plans for decentralization that I do not condemn and that I might even approve; the second, nationalization (of the credit institutions and the eleven industrial groups) that, in the best of cases, will have no influence. There are nationalized businesses in France that function well, almost like private enterprises, and others that are permanently in the red (not always through their own fault). Generally speaking, I do not see the advantages of these nationalizations if the companies remain independent. The state already enjoys sufficient means of exerting pressure on all of French industry. Keeping a sector of private banking is justifiable for many reasons. I would add that our relatively liberal economy constitutes the last counterweight to a Socialist party that is today master of the Elysée,[34] Matignon,[35] the National Assembly and, partially, also the trade unions.

Beyond the policies of economic recovery and nationalizations, it is enough to read the Manifesto, or the Socialist party project, to be convinced that at least a portion of the Socialist party indeed intends to modify society in depth to such an extent that the term "change of society" seems appropriate. Just read the chapter on radio, television, and the press and tell me what would remain of freedom of the press or television, in the Western sense of the term, if the entire project were applied.

J.–L.M. – Why don't you admit it: basically, you are almost as ill-disposed to social democracy as to communism. Read, or listen to, Jean Daniel,[36] long converted to anti-communism—almost to *your* anticommunism. He is enthusiastic about the defeat of the Communist party and the triumph of the Socialists. On the contrary, you mourn the former regime; you deplore the defeat of those you supported, but rarely approved.

R.A. – There I am, finally classified where you want me. Let Jean Daniel enjoy his bliss; he will have ample opportunity to measure the awkwardness of heading a "pro-government" periodical. But, let's come to the question of social democracy. The expression is hardly more precise than that of socialism. As far as social legislation is concerned, France is already social democratic; it does not lag behind the other countries of Western Europe. Forty-two percent of national income passes through state or quasi-state agencies (social security). In the Manifesto, the Socialists promise not to increase this percentage. The only point of substantial

difference between France and the so-called social democratic countries, outside of the weakness of the Communist
party, is its fiscal system, the relatively weak percentage of direct taxes (income and inheritance taxes), and the manner of
financing social security (which reduces the direct salary).
Perhaps Pierre Uri[37] will succeed in modifying this structure
and I wish fiscal reformers good luck. This point aside—an
important one, to be sure—the French citizen, protected
from the cradle to the grave, is already well acquainted with
the social democratic paradise, though he is still a good distance from the Swedish version. Personally, I don't aspire to
the Swedish paradise for my country. I do not think the
French would tolerate it. Even in Sweden, the model citizens
there have discovered the charms of the black market. What
would the situation be in France!

As for me, I would reexamine thoroughly our whole body
of social legislation. The state would take care of those unable
to protect themselves against the accidents of life and would
leave to the others, who have the means, the responsibility of
taking care of themselves. There is no lack of mutual insur-
ance companies. But, of course, I am now lapsing into utopia
myself, though our rulers are soon likely to discover the
limits of financing social transfers via business enterprises. It
is not feasible to increase indirect salaries indefinitely at the
expense of direct salaries.

Am I an anti-social democrat? It all depends upon the kind
of social democracy. I could get along with Helmut Schmidt
better than François Mitterand will get along with him. On
the whole, I note that most social democratic governments
tend toward the tutelary state as Alexis de Tocqueville described it: steadily more responsibilities devolve upon the
state; steadily less responsibility is left to the individual for his
destiny. France probably needs fiscal reforms, but Sweden
should not be taken as an example. I would like to see France
associate itself with the liberal renewal. But I fear that is not
the road French Socialists will take.

We come to the former majority that has just been swept
out of office. I recall the phrase of Alain Peyrefitte, who visited me in 1958 and scandalized me with the slogan, "Cast out
the outcasts." Here he is, among others, the victim of the
French—a people "steadfast and changing." Did Valéry Gis-

card d'Estaing and the majority merit their destiny? To the ex-president's credit, I would note his rejection of demagogic promises during the electoral campaign. He kept Raymond Barre until the very end although he was, according to the polls, unpopular. He wanted to keep the country industrially competitive. He belongs to the post-war generation that, after having lived through or known the decadence of the 1930s, had as its overriding objective the restoration of France to its rightful status. It is possible that we of that generation have somewhat lost sight of the French who don't care whether we are in the "lead group" or not, and who are indignant about inequalities and unemployment. The former president made errors that had nothing to do with his aspirations for France. He wanted to—and, in any case, thought he did—incarnate liberalism, Orléanism, both against the Left and against the Gaullists who considered themselves the legitimate representatives of the Fifth Republic. But, in point of fact, he concentrated power in his own hands as much as Pompidou and more again than the General; he proclaimed the independence of television in a letter addressed to the three networks, yet his government's pressures, though perhaps more subtle, were no less frequent or insistent than those of his predecessor. Today, the new masters spend their time painting the former government as a despotic regime. They come close to comparing Mitterand's election to the 1944 Liberation; it would be closer to the facts to compare it to the arrival in power of General de Gaulle in 1958: the sweeping away of one political class and the arrival of another. I hope the new masters will not abuse their power more than did those of yesterday. As for a television free of state control, I am afraid it's necessary to cross the Atlantic to find it. In reading the Socialist project, I fear a worse dependence: on the parties and unions, exerting their influence under the guise of being "consumers," employees, etc.

Giscard counted too much on the Communists for his re-election and, as it turned out, the Chirac group was treated less well on television than the Communists, or even the Socialists. Chirac's campaign robbed the outgoing candidate of his last chance. But in victimizing Giscard d'Estaing, Chirac committed suicide. The former is also not without responsibility, even if the Paris mayor's violence remains inexcusable.

During the 1977 campaign for the mayoralty of Paris, I titled one of my last articles for *Le Figaro*, that of 21 February 1977: *"Le Suicide de la Majorité."*

Perhaps Giscard's defeat in 1981 was inevitable. According to the polls, he never enjoyed a popularity comparible to that of General de Gaulle or Georges Pompidou. The 1974 victory was paper-thin, and the win in the 1978 legislative elections coincided miraculously with a renewal of confidence in the president and with economic improvement. From 1977 to 1981, the president's score—the gap between favorable and unfavorable opinion—narrowed constantly. Mitterand's popularity was at a low ebb at the moment he thrust Rocard aside, but of the four political groupings, the Socialist party retained the most favorable image. In a few months, the popularity of Giscard d'Estaing melted away, and that of François Mitterand increased. The electoral campaign—mediocre on the part of the president, excellent on the part of his opposition—altered nothing in terms of the electorate's attitude. The French wanted a change, no longer having faith in the old majority. And it was the Communists who gave Mitterand what he lacked: proof that he alone, after General de Gaulle, had been able to steamroller the Communist electorate. He had marginalized the Communist party by allying himself openly with it—while the former majority tried, consciously or not, to avoid weakening the Communist party, its ally in a tactical sense. In earlier elections, the French had hesitated to elect a Socialist who seemed to depend on the goodwill of the Communists. When a quarter of the Communist electors voted in the initial ballotting for the first secretary of the Socialist party (Mitterand), they eliminated the last hopes of Giscard d'Estaing and of the former majority as a whole. The popularity of the Socialist party brought Mitterand to the Elysée and he, newly anointed by universal suffrage, assured his party's victory. So here I am, destined and resigned to living in a Socialist France. Here I am, by now definitely convinced that political writers should write books that last rather than articles that are ephemeral.

J.–L.M. – Here you are, an observer uncommitted and without hope after a change in the majority?

R.A. - The French wanted a change. These good lycée teachers, typically parochial, and, of course, Socialists, seemed to French voters perhaps more representative than the *énarques*,[38] or the distinguished gentlemen of the UDF[39] or of the RPR.[40] Alain would rejoice in the return of the teachers, protectors of the little people, and happily incompetent (competence is a characteristic of the polytechnicians). It is possible that Mitterand's Socialists, who have more time and knowledge than those of Léon Blum in 1936, will govern the country with enough wisdom not to waste their chances and those of France. I accept without bitterness the normal change of generations. These teachers are not, I fear, very sensitive to the questions of France's stature in the world. They will not miss the program of nuclear plants. I can't refrain from citing one of the last lines of Tocqueville's *l'Ancien Régime et la Révolution:* "The French rarely go to the very end of what they have undertaken." For the last thirty-five years, the Fourth and Fifth Republics, each in its own way—one too anarchic, the other too authoritarian—worked effectively so that France might become one of the most modern and prosperous of the medium-size powers. The effort was slowed by the two oil shocks; will the Socialists pursue the effort or will they be constrained to renounce it because of their illusions, their ideologies, their hierarchy of values? Reduce the workweek; increase salaries: I know the old refrain, that of Léon Blum, which the Left continues to hum because it was used to justify the first paid vacations. But I can't help remembering other things: where was the bread, the peace, the liberty three years after the lyrical illusion of the Popular Front? Obviously, the comparison doesn't hold up. We're not certain the worst will happen. Perhaps the fall of the Communist party will one day be celebrated as the great event of 1981, even if this cleansing of the electoral body costs a few years of economic disorder. Perhaps the Socialist party's Saint-Simonians—they are to be found on the Left as well as on the Right—will get the better of the ideologues.

I am never without hope and I am always committed. I leave to others the necessary task of renewing the opposition to socialism and, above all, of modernizing liberal thought. It's an ill wind that blows no good. Presidential candidates will not again, in their campaign rhetoric, spare the Communists in the hope that the latter will refrain from voting for the Socialists. In the 1981 elections, the ex-majority lost the halo effect of General de Gaulle, the tactical alliance with the Communist party, and even the scarecrow syndrome of the Communist party. The ex-majority—the new opposition—must now convince the French people not only that it will administer the country better than the Socialists, but that what it proposes is a preferable model of society.

D.W. and J.–L.M. – By now, do you have the feeling that you've wasted your time and your life in journalism? Or, rather, do you think *The Economist* was right in its article published when you left *Le Figaro?* It recognized your merit in having fashioned moderate politicians over the previous thirty years.

R.A. – If its true, I have been a poor teacher or I had mediocre pupils. Let's be sensible: anyone who has lived through the decadence of the 1930s cannot be contemptible of those who governed the two republics that returned to the French a country that they can respect and love. I will not say, as de Tocqueville did in his later years, that I feel more solitary than in a desert of the new world. I find myself once again isolated and an opponent, the usual destiny of an authentic liberal. And, to avoid ending this interview on an overly solemn note—in concluding, not a life, but a dialogue—let me say that I have gained two friends. I haven't convinced them, but I have communicated to them the fertile spirit of doubt.

—Raymond Aron

Identification of Persons Named in
THE COMMITTED OBSERVER

Emile-Auguste Chartier, known as Alain (1868-1951). French philosopher and essayist.

Raphael Alibert (1887-1963). French political and monarchist.

Louis-Pierre Althusser (1918-   ). Professor of philosophy, secretary and secretary-general of the Ecole Normale Supérieure.

Jean Baechler (1937-   ). French sociologist.

Jacques Bainville (1879-1936). French historian and royalist.

Raymond Barre (1924-   ). French economist and teacher, prime minister of Valery Giscard d'Estaing from 1976 to 1981.

Maurice Barres (1862-1923). French novelist and politician.

Simone de Beauvoir (1908-   ). French existentialist novelist.

Eduard Beneš (1884-1948). Czech statesman, president at the time of the Munich Pact.

Georges Bernanos (1888-1948). French novelist and essayist, disciple of Edouard Drumont, doctrinaire anti-Semite.

Alain Besancon (1932-   ). French sociologist, specializing in Russian studies.

Hubert Beuve-Méry (1902-   ). French journalist, writer under the pseudonym "Sirius."

Aneurin Bevan (1897-1960). British politician and member of the Labor Party.

Marc Bloch (1886-1944). French historian of the Middle Ages, shot by the Germans.

Léon Blum (1872-1950). French politician and writer. Joined the Socialist Party in 1902, later founder of the newspaper *Le Populaire.* He was president of the first popular front government from June 1936 to June 1937. Imprisoned in Buchenwald in 1943, he was freed in 1945.

Célestin Bouglé (1870-1940). French sociologist, director of the Ecole Normale Supérieure.

Pierre Bourdan, pseudonym of Pierre Maillaud (1909-1948). French journalist, one of the most eloquent broadcasters from London during the war.

Pierre Bourdieu (1930-   ). French sociologist and professor at the College de France.

Pierre Brisson (1896-1964). French journalist and writer.

Leon Brunschvicg (1869-1944). French philosopher.

Joseph Marie-Auguste Caillaux (1863-1944). French politician, Radical deputy, several times a cabinet member.

Roger Cambon (1881-1970). Minister at the French embassy in London during the war, (nephew of the famous ambassador Jules Cambon), he did not join the de Gaulle movement.

Albert Camus (1913-1960). French writer, journalist, member of the Resistance. He edited *Combat* from 1944 to 1946 and received the Nobel Prize in Literature in 1957.

Georges Canguilhem (1904-   ). French philosopher, physician, and professor at the Sorbonne.

René Cassin (1887-1976). French jurist, winner of the Nobel Peace Prize in 1968.

Albin Chalendon (1920-   ). French politician, deputy and a cabinet member several times.

André Chamson (1900-   ). French writer, member of the Academie Francaise.

Jacques Chastenet (1893-1978). French journalist and historian.

Jean-Pierre Chevénement (1939-   ). French politician, socialist.

Paul Claudel (1868-1955). French ambassador, poet and dramatist.

Karl von Clausewitz (1780-1831). Prussian general and military thinker.

Colin Clark (1905-   ). Australian economist.

Richard C. Cobb (1917-   ). British professor and historian of the French Revolution.

Daniel Cohn-Bendit (1945-   ). French student, of German extraction, spokesperson of the student movement in May 1968.

Auguste Comte (1798-1857). French philosopher.

Benjamin Constant (1767-1830). French diplomat and author; he wrote a classic pamphlet attacking dictatorship.

Edouard Daladier (1884-1970). French politician, Radical Socialist deputy; as premier, he signed the Munich Pact in September 1938.

Jean Daniel (1920-   ). French journalist, director of *Le Nouvel Observateur.*

Michel Debré (1912-   ). French politician, prime minister from 1958 to 1962.

Gaston Deferre (1910-   ). French lawyer and politician, militant Socialist.

Milovan Djilas (1911-   ). Yugoslav writer and politician; a longtime friend of Tito until he fell out of favor; he was accused of revisionism and spent several years in prison.

Pierre Drieu de la Rochelle (1893-1945). French writer who became an extreme rightist, collaborated with the Germans and was a suicide in 1945.

Edouard Drumont (1844-1917). French publicist and politician. A Catholic journalist, he attacked Jewish bankers.

Alexander Dubcek (1912-   ). Czechoslovakian politician, first secretary of the Communist party, who was replaced by Husak by the Russians.

Pierre Dupuy (1896-1969). Canadian politician, ambassador to Vichy France and Free France during the war.

Georges Duhamel (1884-1966). French writer and physician who published novels, poems, and plays.

Emile Durkheim (1858-1917). French sociologist.

Maurice Duverger (1917-   ). French teacher, writer, and journalist.

Alfred Fabre-Luce (1899-   ). French journalist and man of letters.

Frantz Fanon (1925-1961). Psychiatrist at a psychiatric hospital in Blida, Algeria, who supported the Algerian revolution.

Edgar Faure (1908-   ). French lawyer and politician.

Father Gaston Fessart (1897-1978). Jesuit, philosopher, and theologian.

Jean Fourastie (1907-   ). French economist and journalist.

André François-Poncet (1887-1978). French diplomat, ambassador in Berlin from 1933 to 1938 and again from 1953 to 1955, and in Rome from 1938 to 1940.

Louis Gabriel-Robinet (1909-1975). French jurist and journalist.

Robert Galley (1921-   ). French politician, a cabinet member several times.

Romain Gary (1914-1980). French novelist, born in Russia, the only novelist to win the Prix Goncourt twice—once under his own name and once under a pseudonym.

Etienne Gilson (1884-1978). French historian of medieval philosophy.

Henri Giraud (1879-1948). French general taken prisoner by the Germans. He escaped in 1942 and took command of French troops in North Africa, where he played an important role.

Valéry Giscard d'Estaing (1926-   ). French political figure, minister of finance and later president.

Joseph-Paul Goebbels (1897-1945). German politician, chief Nazi propagandist, who committed suicide after the suicide of Hitler.

François Pierre Guillaume Guizot (1787-1874). French statesman and historian.

Sebastian Haffner (1907-   ). German journalist and writer.

Elie Halévy (1870-1937). French political writer and historian.

Martin Heidegger (1889-1976). German philosopher and disciple of Husserl.

Heinrich Himmler (1900-1945). German politician and head of the Gestapo.

Edmund Husserl (1859-1938). German philosopher, founder of a philosophic school, phenomenology.

Francois Jacob (1920-   ). Biologist and winner of the Nobel Prize in Medicine.

Francis Jeanson (1922-   ). Writer and disciple of Jean-Paul Sartre; he organized secret networks to aid the Algerian F.L.N. Convicted by a French court, later pardoned.

Bertrand de Jouvenel (1903-   ). French economist and scholar.

Pierre Kaufman (1922-   ). Journalist, professor, member of the Resistance during the war.

Henri de Kerillis (1889-1958). French nationalistic journalist.

Victor Kravchenko (1905-   ). Soviet diplomatic functionary who defected to the West.

Arthur Koestler (1905-1983). Novelist born in Hungary who became a British subject. Originally a Communist, he later became strongly anti-Communist.

Alexandre Kojève (1902-1968). French philosopher and official.

Alexandre Koyré (1892-1963). French philospher.

André Labarthe (1902-1967). A physician, he devoted himself to journalism after 1940, when he founded and edited *La France Libre*.

Jacques Lacan (1901-1981). French psychiatrist and psychoanalyst.

Henri Lacordaire (1802-1861). French Dominican priest; he became one of the leaders of Catholic liberalism.

Daniel Lagache (1903-1972). French psychoanalyst and doctor, author of several studies on jealousy.

Pierre Laval (1883-1945). French politician, originally a Socialist, who collaborated with the Germans. He was tried and executed after the war.

Martha Lecoutre (-   ). Born in Warsaw, she became a militant Communist, especially active in Germany. Now a naturalized French citizen.

Alexis Léger (1887-1975). A French poet and writer known by the pseudonym of Saint-John Perse. He was awarded the Nobel Prize in Literature in 1960.

Emmanuel Leroy-Ladurie (1929-   ). French university professor.

Claude Lévi-Strauss (1908-   ). French ethnologist.

Georges Leygues (1857-1933). French politician who helped to strengthen the French fleet.

B. H. Liddell-Hart (1885-1970). British historian and journalist specializing in military affairs.

Gyorgy Lukacs (1855-1971). Hungarian philosopher, critic, and politician.

Niccolo Machiavelli (1469-1527). Italian statesman and writer whose cynical political philosophy has become known as "machiavellianism."

André Malraux (1901-1976). Writer and political figure whose poliltical career was linked to that of Charles de Gaulle.

Karl Mannheim (1893-1947). Hungarian, professor at Frankfurt; he belonged to the Hungarian school of Marxism.

Erich von Manstein (1887-1973). German field marshal and chief architect of the offensive against France in 1940.

Robert Marjolin (1911-   ). French economist and teacher.

Henri Irene Marrou (1904-1977). Respected French historian.

Thierry Maulnier (1909-   ). French journalist and writer.

François Mauriac (1885-1970). Celebrated French writer.

Andre Maurois, pseudonym of Emile Herzog (1885-1967), which became his legal name. French novelist and historian.

Charles Maurras (1868-1952). French writer and monarchist.

Marcel Mauss (1878-1950). French sociologist, nephew of Emile Durkheim; he became the leader of the French school of sociology upon the death of Durkheim.

Pierre Mendès-France (1907-1982). French lawyer and politician, member of the Resistance during the war.

Jacques Merleau-Ponty (1916-   ). Professor of philosophy at the University of Paris.

Maurice Merleau-Ponty (1908-1961). French philosopher.

Guy Mollet (1905-1975). French politician, member of the Resistance during the war.

Jean Monnet (1888-1979). Economist and international statesman.

Henri Moysset (-   ). French politician who contributed to the buildup of the French fleet in 1939.

Emile Muselier (-   ). French admiral who joined General de Gaulle in 1940 and broke with him in 1942.

Paul Nizan (1905-1940). French philosopher-essayist and novelist.

Albert Ollivier (1915-1964). French journalist.

Joseph Paganon (1880-1937). French chemical engineer who played a role in politics.

Gaston Palewski (1901-   ). French politician.

Albert Palle (1916-   ). French journalist and novelist.

Kostas Papaioannou (1925-1981). Greek philosopher and sociologist.

Jean Paulhan (1884-1968). French writer, director of the *Nouvelle Revue Française.*

Pertinax, pseudonym of Andre Geraud (1882-1974). French journalist.

Alain Peyrefitte (1925-   ). French politician and writer.

Pascal Pia (1902-1979). French journalist.

Antoine Pinay (1891-   ). French industrialist and politician.

René Pleven (1901-   ). French politician.

Léon Poliakov (1910-   ). French writer.

Georges Pompidou (1911-1974). French writer and politician;
president from 1969 to 1974.

Marcel Proust (1871-1922). Celebrated French writer.

Hermann Rauschnig (1889-1982). German politician who
broke with Hitler.

Paul Reynaud (1878-1966). French politician.

Father Michel Riquet (1898-   ). A Jesuit who played an important role in the Resistance.

Michel Rocard (1930-   ). French Socialist politician.

Colonel de la Rocque (1885-1946). Head of the Croix de Feu,
organization of war veterans with fascist leanings.

Carlos Rodriguez (-   ). Cuban politician and head of
the Cuban Communist Party.

David Rousset (1912-   ). French journalist and man of letters.

Jules Roy (1907-   ). French novelist and dramatist.

Bertrand Russell (1872-1970). British mathematician, philosopher, and sociologist.

Albert Sarraut (1872-1962). French politician, Radical Socialist
deputy and a cabinet member several times.

Jean-Paul Sartre (1905-1980). French philosopher and writer,
the chief representative of existentialism in France.

Alfred Sauvy (1898-   ). French sociologist, economist, and
demographer.

Maurice Schumann (-   ). French politician, spokesman for Free France in broadcasts from London during
the war.

Robert Schuman (1886-1963). French statesman. Deported to
Germany during the war, he succeeded in escaping. He
was the author of the Schuman Plan and one of the spon-
sors of the failed European Defense Community.

Jean-Jacques Servan-Schreiber (1924-   ). French journalist,
author, and politician.

Boris Souvarine (1895-   ). A Socialist in France during the
First World War, he became one of the founders of the
French Communist Party, later breaking with it.

Manès Sperber (1905-   ). French writer and psychologist, born in Germany.

Charles Spinasse (1893-1979). French politician.

Leo Spitzer (-   ). University professor and novelist; later taught at Johns Hopkins.

Alexis Charles Henri Maurice Clérel de Tocqueville (1805-1859). French historian and politician. As a junior magistrate, he was commissioned to study prisons in the United States; he enlarged the subject to write his classic, *De la Democratie en Amerique.*

Alain Touraine (1925-   ). French university professor.

Arnold Toynbee (1889-1975). British historian and author of the monumental ten-volume *A Study of History.*

Leon Trotsky (1879-1940). Russian revolutionary leader.

Pierre Uri (1911-   ). French economist and university professor.

Paul Valéry (1871-1945). French poet and philosophical essayist.

Pierre Viansson-Ponté (1920-1979). French journalist and writer, editor of *Le Monde.*

1. *Paix et Guerre entre les Nations.*
2. *L'Opium des Intellectuels.*
3. *L'Introduction à la Philosophie de l'Histoire.*
4. Billancourt is a workers' quarter in Paris.
5. Literally, "Higher Normal School." One of five such university-level institutions, all belonging to the prestigious group of "Grandes Ecoles," the ENS prepares students particularly for secondary school and university teaching positions. The school will hereafter be referred to in the text as the Ecole Normale.
6. Appellation given to the second year of special post-secondary school courses taken by students preparing for the competitive examinations for entry into an *Ecole Normale Supérieure.*
7. The French lycée has many variations. Broadly speaking, it includes students from eleven to eighteen years of age, and thus is roughly equivalent to the American junior high school, senior high school, and the first year of college or university. The term lycée will be used in this text.
8. -t-à la: to the (mass).
9. National oral and written competition of a very high level, requiring at least five years of university study. Those who pass are eligible for lycée and university teaching positions.
10. Original title: *l'Être et le Néant.*
11. Date of a riot at Place de la Concorde in Paris, costing 15 lives and 1,500 injured. The Daladier Radical party resigned the following day.
12. Institut Français d'Opinion Publique.
13. Anti-parliamentary, nationalistic organization of war veterans, founded in 1927 and dissolved in 1936.
14. An administrative and political division, of which there are 96 in metropolitan France.
15. An underground monthly newspaper published by the Resistance movement of the same name.
16. Known in the post-World War II period under his pseudonym, St.-John Perse. A diplomat and poet, he won the Nobel Prize in Literature in 1960.
17. Ultra-nationalist, monarchist, anti-democratic movement of Charles Maurras. The movement published a daily newspaper of the same name from 1908 to 1944.
18. Paris indoor sports stadium, now demolished. It was here that 13,000 Jews were brought, after being taken from their homes on July 16-17, 1942, and before being sent to French camps, then, to Poland and Germany.
19. On October 3, 1980, a synagogue on the rue Copernic in Paris was bombed, with a loss of four lives.
20. *Rassemblement du Peuple Français,* movement organized by de Gaulle in 1947.
21. *Mouvement Républicain Populaire.* Christian-Democratic party founded in 1944, with Georges Bidault as first president.
22. Socialist Party Congress held in December 1920. Léon Blum led the minority out of the Congress. The majority called itself the French Communist Party.
23. I have looked up the *Combat* article; it was very explicitly hostile to the war and reconquest. – R.A.

24. An iron and steel makers' trade association created in 1864 and long active as a conservative pressure group.
25. *Ecole Nationale d'Administration.*
26. *Certificat d'Aptitude Pedagogique à l'Enseignement Secondaire.* Lycée-level teaching certificate.
27. Secretary-general of the French Communist Party from 1964 to 1972.
28. *Confédération Générale du Travail.* France's leading trade union; closely tied to the Communist party.
29. So named, because the landmark labor-management negotiations, presided over by Prime Minister Georges Pompidou during the May 1968 social crisis, were conducted at the rue de Grenelle headquarters of the Labor Ministry.
30. *Union de la gauche.*
31. *Programme commun.* The electoral program of the Left alliance signed in June 1972 by François Mitterand, for the Socialist party, Georges Marchais, for the Communist party, and Robert Fabre, for the Left Radicals.
32. Original title: *La République Impériale.*
33. The interview took place before May 1981, when the presidential elections were held. Hence, the "government in power" refers to that of Giscard d'Estaing.
34. Library located in the left wing of the *Institut de France,* in Paris.
35. Residence and offices of the president of the Republic.
36. Offices of the prime minister.
37. Editor-in-chief of the leftist weekly, *Le Nouvel Observateur.*
38. Author of *Changer l'Impôt (pour Changer la France),* 1981.
39. Diminutive referring to graduates of the prestigious *Ecole Nationale d'Administration* (acronym: ENA).
40. *Union pour la Démocratie Française.* Coalition of the center parties: Republicans, Social Democrats, and Radicals.
41. *Rassemblement pour la République.* Political movement of Gaullist persuasion founded in 1976 by Jacques Chirac.

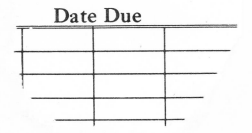

Date Due